SECOND WIND

SOMETIMES ALL YOU NEED TO DO IS BREATHE

THOMAS ALAN WHEELER

"Second Wind shares the experience of a man who once was a very successful Apple Computer employee focused on what he received, to a new man transformed by God's grace to someone focused more on what he gives - as a servant - to God's least. Rather than talking about helping the poor, Tom moved in with them. This is consistent with Christian Community Development Association's (CCDA) philosophy of relocation, reconciliation and redistribution. Second Wind is inspiring, uplifting and encouraging. I recommend Second Wind to anyone seeking to know the truth of God and the reality of loving our neighbor as ourselves."

~ John Perkins, Founder & Chairman, Emeritus, CCDA, President of the John Perkins Foundation

"Second Wind is a book that shows Tom Wheeler's pilgrimage from being a skeptic to a totally devoted follower of Jesus. He covers in depth topics from the unseen world and its reality, to Christian apologetics, to what Christian character should look like, to what faith in Jesus really means, to why Christians should give their lives away to the most destitute. He challenges skeptics. He also challenges Christians to embrace fully what it means to follow Jesus. It is my privilege to recommend this book to all who desire to understand authentic Christianity."

~David Chadwick, Sr. Pastor, Forest Hill Church, Charlotte, NC

"I must commend my fellow soldier, Tom Wheeler, for writing a candid and compelling book about serving the lost. In his book, Second Wind, he gives voice to the stark realities and dysfunctions that assault the inner city and hold captive, men and women who are literally dying to be free. In the end, there is an answer and Tom makes that abundantly clear throughout the book, and each of us who dare to read this book are a vital part of that answer!"

~ Colin Pinkney, Executive Director, The Urban Restoration Inc., 2012 Governors Gold Medallion Recipient for Mentoring Excellence and Chaplain, Charlotte Bobcats

"Second Wind has come from Tom's heart; the stories he tells come from his own life, and from among those people most of us cast out – or, at least, ignore. Tom is sold out to God and to God's love for those in need. As you read Second Wind, may you also be challenged to choose God's fast, to set the oppressed free and help the poor (Is. 58:6-7)."

~ Kelvin Smith, Lead Pastor, Steele Creek Church of Charlotte

"Second Wind is an inspiring book written by Tom Wheeler (no relation that we know of) who really has his priorities in the right places. Not only have I read his book, but I visited one of his facilities for men and was impressed most by the new hope the men have. Tom is selling hope at no cost and I know of no finer product on the market today. An amazing book by an amazing man."

~A.(Humpy) Wheeler, noted NASCAR promoter and member of 12 halls of fame

"Second Wind is a tremendous testimony to listening to God, getting the stones out of the path and counting on God to encourage and enrich and watch for transforming hearts to get the Second Wind."

~ Luke Witte, Director, Marketplace Chaplains, former NBA cavalier

"Second Wind is an honest and powerful look at the reality of life and where hope is found. Tom weaves together his own experiences with the truth of God's Word to stand in the gap when life comes unraveled. It is well worth the investment of your time to read and then give it to someone who needs hope."

~ Rev. Jim Kallam, Sr. Pastor, Church at Charlotte

"As a physician volunteer at the monthly medical clinic at Hoskins Park, I am privileged to witness first- hand the Second Wind life changing experience the ministry is having on these men. Tom Wheeler does not just "talk the talk" he also "walks the walk." Read Second Wind and then take your own step out in faith."

~ E Craig Evans MD, Surgical Oncologist, Surgical Specialist of Charlotte, Charlotte , NC

"What Tom Wheeler is doing at Hoskins Park Ministry is amazing. We are fortunate he is telling some of the stories that have evolved out of his ministry in his book Second Wind."

~ Cam Harris

"If you read Second Wind and still do not understand what it means to be a Christian, you may never understand. It's simple and direct. The funny, sometimes sad and awful stories, Tom writes about in Second Wind are the reality he faced moving into the "hood." If you really want to help the least and lost, I would encourage you to read Second Wind."

~ Steven Wile, Carpenter

"Just as Tom quotes his partner and friend Johnny Allen, he has pursued the ministry God has given him 'by sacrificing what I considered to be productivity for the sake of the person', and in the process of touching each Man individually, has built one of the most effective missions to the homeless, one that 'comes along side' of these men and, therefore, goes at their pace, and God's pace, not ours. However you read Second Wind, please be sure to read all the Biblical passages contained therein – they are solid truth and touch on all the foundational elements of faith in Jesus and the life and hope Tom tries to instill into the hearts of his participants."

~ Tom Emmrich, President and CEO, Entegreat Inc.

Second Wind: Sometimes All You Need To Do Is Breathe!

by Thomas Alan Wheeler

Previously released as *Bottom Fishing*

Published by HigherLife Development Services, Inc.

400 Fontana Circle

Building 1—Suite 105

Oviedo, Florida 32765

(407) 563-4806

www.ahigherlife.com

Unless otherwise indicated, Bible quotations are taken from THE HOLY BIBLE, NEW INTERNATIONAL VERSION®, NIV® Copyright © 1973, 1978, 1984, 2011 by Biblica, Inc.™ Used by permission. All rights reserved worldwide.

Bible quotations are also taken from the New International Version (s) of the Bible Copyright © 1984 by Tyndale House Publishers, The New Living Translation © 2004 by Tyndale House Publishers and The Message © 2002 by NavPress Publishing.

ISBN 13: 978-1-935245-56-8

ISBN 10: 1-935245-55-4

Cover Design: Rachel Lopez

First Edition

12 13 14 15 — 9 8 7 6 5 4 3 2 1

Printed in the United States of America.

This book is dedicated to all those whose lives
have not worked out as expected,
but are still seeking, still hoping, still listening.

"Go now to your countrymen in exile and speak to them. Say to them, 'This is what the Sovereign Lord says,' whether they listen or fail to listen" (Ezekiel 3:11).

ACKNOWLEDGMENTS

Special thanks to: My wife, Kate. I love you so much, and I will forever. You are a testimony to God's grace - I don't know what I would do without you.

To my mom, who has been an example of godly love all of my life. You are one-of-a-kind, mother — God blessed me first, through you. I will always love you. To my late dad, who never let obstacles stop him teaching me to always "creatively" persevere, by his example.

To Rev. David Chadwick and Rev. Luke Witte, two godly men who God used as my mentors. Thank you both for your encouragement, support, and example. Thanks to Bryan Davies, Knox Sherer, Steve Wile, Tom Kakadelis, Karen Flynn, Margarita Guzman, John Parker and David Vaught as well, eight other people whose support over countless years has been more important than they will ever know.

Thanks to my dear friend Johnny Allen and the staff of Hoskins Park Ministries for allowing me the time to write. You are part of my family, and I cherish you all. You are today's modern heroes, and I recognize you as such. I feel the same way about the participants of Hoskins Park. You are fine men who I respect. I am also grateful to my past and present board of directors who supported me through this entire process- with a special thanks to Tom Emmerich, Dan Janick, and Scott Dahlgren for being honest friends who helped in times of need.

Thanks to those of you who bought and read *Bottom Fishing*, the original name of *Second Wind*. That support made this new book a reality. The same is true of HigherLife Publishing. You have a great team and took my writing to another level — thank you.

Without God, I would have no ability to write anything worth writing. I owe Him my life and any good thing that I am. Thank You, Jesus, for allowing me to participate in Your kingdom's work. I pray this honors You above all else.

Cover design and artwork: Rachel Lopez

Editing: Content - Chris Maxwell, initial copy edit - Douglas M. McCarty, Ph.D.

TABLE OF CONTENTS

Part Four: Time for That Second Wind

Introduction

Never Enough

On an occasional Saturday, my best friend and I would hop into my Cessna 172 airplane, parked just behind my house, and fly it to Manassas, Virginia. There we would rent a Robinson R22 helicopter, tour Washington, D.C., and hover around our hometown of Annapolis, Maryland. We would complete our day by returning the aircraft to their respective airports, then race to the downtown Annapolis bars in a speedboat. Our night was spent partying. Although many admired this lifestyle, something about it still left me wondering if I wasn't missing something even better. Life was not working out as I expected — I just couldn't figure out why.

Has your life worked out the way you thought it would? Mine hasn't. My expectations of life have always exceeded its reality despite my successes. At one point, life was so hard for me that I wondered if it was worth living. Maybe you have found yourself in that same place ... or are you there now? Despite how hard you have tried to make yourself happy, happiness still eludes you. Or maybe you have learned to endure the hardships of life with a smile, a good attitude, and a busy schedule? You know something is wrong, you just don't know what it is, and you'd prefer to ignore it rather than deal with it.

But when you are alone with your thoughts, you wonder, *Is this all there is?* If this *is* you, then consider this book to have been written *for* you. A book that explains the reality of the battle we are all fighting spiritually, and the truth about the air you need to breathe to get back to the surface and then to keep breathing. You, too, can find hope – the same hope I found.

Christmas philosophy

As a kid, I thought life was like Christmas. I would make a list of things I wanted, and getting them made me happy — for a while. Even if I didn't get everything I wanted, my expectation of receiving them kept me satisfied. As I grew up, I continued to believe in this "Christmas" mentality although my toys became much more expensive, and I became my own Santa Claus. For instance, I bought my Cessna on a quarterly bonus check I received from my employer, Apple Computer, Inc. I thought becoming a pilot with my own airplane (at twenty-six) would make me happy. And for a while, it did.

How many guys in their twenties could fly back to their alma mater for alumni weekend in their own airplane? How many could fly to the beach for dinner when they had an urge for seafood? Nobody I knew.

But I could.

Eventually, I got tired of my airplane, so I started flying helicopters. I remember, after my father became a fixed-wing airplane pilot, I took him up in a helicopter to show him how cool they were to fly. We were traveling about 50 mph in the helicopter when I just reversed it, on a dime — no notice! One moment we were going north, the next south. I just thought that was the coolest thing! I turned to my dad in the passenger seat and said, "Try that in your airplane," with a trace of youthful arrogance. Dad's fatherly reply, "Son, why would I want to?" Right. Why would he want to? Anyway, the thrill of flying helicopters for kicks also wore off.

I can't get no — satisfaction

While all of this was going on, I still thought I would marry my high school sweetheart. For ten years we had an on again, off again relationship. I finally proposed, knowing we needed to settle the matter once and for all. She said no.

That broke my heart.

But I had to get on with life. In fact, those were my most successful years at Apple. I traveled to Hong Kong, China, Germany, and Australia on an expense account. And these were trips I won for outstanding sales performance, not business trips — they were vacations. But I was still broken-hearted. Trips couldn't fill that hole in my heart, even while exploring the world and challenging myself physically:

Witnessing the elimination of the Berlin Wall in Germany and taking down part of the wall with my dad.

Exploring the Great Barrier Reef in Australia with my brother Sam.

Hiking the Great Wall in Beijing, China, with my brother Pete.

Swimming across the Chesapeake Bay.

Lifting weights excessively.

Participating in one of the first sprint triathlons.

It was never enough.

Entrepreneur

To discover the "American Dream," I resigned my lucrative job with Apple to see if I could find satisfaction as my own boss. It was just one more example of my life expectations exceeding life's realities. Starting that business in a recession, just before the country was involved in the first Gulf War, was much harder than I imagined. But I got what I wanted. I was in charge. Unfortunately, the partner who was going to build all these great products to help the education market was a US Marine and was called into military service. While my other partner and I adjusted to our circumstances, managing the company to a couple million in annual sales, I still was not satisfied. Being in charge was not as satisfying as I had thought. That was about the time a good friend insinuated that successful people are unable to be fully satisfied because it is their drive for more that makes them successful. Hearing his remark was troubling for me. I thought that the entire purpose of life was to be happy, comfortable, and satisfied. But I wasn't happy, comfortable, or satisfied. Perhaps you, too, are wondering why everything you've tried just isn't enough.

The vices.

The jobs.

The relationships.

Life.

In the middle of the night, you silently ask the same question I did: Is this all there is?

Living forever

So, I began looking into things I once considered far-fetched or obsolete, like different religious beliefs.

Books about life after death and reincarnation. I still didn't know what to believe, but I knew I was on the right path. I was getting some answers. Those books jarred a childhood memory that I had about death. I remembered being scared thinking about the finality of death at 6 years old. That fear was quickly followed by a thought that I would never die. At that early age, I somehow knew that I was not my physical representation but a spirit inside of me. I say that I "somehow" knew this because although my family went to church, church was a Sunday tradition when we could fit it in, rather than a belief system that ruled our lives.

Who will I believe?

I had no plans of getting duped by other people's well-intentioned opinions either. I observed people talking about subjects as if they were experts without knowing much about the subject at all. Often times it appeared people thought they knew more about what was best for me than I did. Perhaps you know what I mean?

I recall my dad once saying he wondered if God really existed. I felt like the wind was knocked out of me when my father said that. If God didn't exist, I reasoned, there was no hope. Though I sat in silence, gasping for air in my inner self, those comments woke me up. I chose to read and study the Bible myself, praying for God to reveal its truth to me personally, rather than hear someone else tell me what it said or what they thought about it.

I wasn't afraid to find out the truth about the Bible — one way or another. If the Bible was false, it would be good for me to establish that for myself now, rather than believe a lie for the rest of my life. So, I pursued my doubts about the Bible and Christianity while being open to its truth. I concluded that the Bible was true. And the Bible says that God is not only real — He is personal, active, loving, holy, and He is in control. It implies that God is the air we need to breathe in order to persevere. He is our second wind and He has a plan for our lives. It also testifies to the existence of a real devil who is causing havoc on earth and who is our real threat. He is the one trying to destroy our lives.

I also learned that it was at my lowest point that I was most useful to God. During his induction speech, Dr. Tim Laniak, the Dean of Gordon-Conwell Theological Seminary (Charlotte branch), said that while most of us consider things that are broken to be of no value to us, God might consider people who are not broken to be of no use to Him:

> *My sacrifice, O God, is a broken spirit; a broken and contrite heart you, God, will not despise (Psalm 51:17).*

When we finally get the wind knocked out of us by doing things the world's way — our way — we are in a position to heed the words of the Bible — words that tell us to turn to God for air. Air that will refresh us, restore us, like a cool breeze on a scorching summer day. Fresh air.

We all want to know God

My life wasn't turning out as I expected because it was never intended to be lived the way I had been living it. I didn't know it, but I was desperate for the God who created me rather than the things I pursued. All of those things were a cheap substitute for the real thing — God. The Bible says:

> *[God] has also set eternity in the hearts of men (Ecclesiastes 3:11).*

God stamped a part of Himself on all of us. Until we find Him, we have a void in our hearts — a void many try lifelong to fill through cheap substitutes. In essence, we are lost and searching. But once we do find Him, He teaches us what is really going on down here. And that's our point. We are in a war on earth, and our eternity is at stake:

> *Then the dragon was enraged at the woman and went off to make war against the rest of her offspring — those who obey God's commandments and hold to the testimony of Jesus (Revelation 12:17).*

According to that scripture, the dragon is Satan, the woman is Eve, and we are the offspring. The Bible explains that we are in a war. Behavior is often the result of a spiritual battle with an enemy, Satan. Blaming people for the mistakes they make isn't enough. Those who do these awful things may simply be following the devil, rather than God. I know it can be difficult to understand or even believe, but it's true. Satan's main objective is to separate us from God, so that we follow him right to hell.

Jesus

Since God longs to spend eternity with us in heaven — our originally intended destiny — He sent His Son to bring us home. Without Jesus Christ as our Lord and Savior, we all end up separated from God for eternity. Jesus is who we need. He is our ticket to heaven, not our good deeds. In fact, depending on good works to get us to heaven, according to the Bible, gets us nowhere. While we complicate the message down here on earth by all of our scholarly approaches to life and the Bible, the message is fairly simple. Because God loves us so much, He sent Jesus to die in our place to satisfy the problem of His holiness and our sin. When we believe in His plan for our salvation, we receive the resurrected Spirit of Jesus Christ and live with Him forever after our physical death. Because Satan hates God so much, his objective is to get as many people as possible to stand in defiance against God by rejecting Jesus.

As controversial as it might be to some, our actual destination is eternity. Life on earth is merely a stepping stone. We are not physical people deteriorating day-by-day until death takes us to the abyss as many believe. We are souls being advanced moment-by-moment until God takes us home or until we choose to be led astray. Hard to believe, isn't it? It was for me, too. That is, until my life didn't work out as expected.

Second Wind

It seems most of us take life for granted until our good life, the life we expected, is shaken up or knocked out of us. Then many of us wonder if we've missed something along our life journey. Something important in our search for the truth. In our search for purpose. In our search to understand why on earth we are here. Because the basis for my beliefs is the words of the Bible and because those words have become so distorted by those who try to make it say what they want despite what it says, I have used select movie clips and my own personal stories as modern-day parables to simplify its truth. If you feel like you've had the wind knocked out of you, my hope is that *Second Wind* clarifies the mystery of life on earth, what is at stake for our eternity, and the solution to many of our unanswered questions, according to the Bible. I also hope that despite your current situation in life, you will find renewed hope. Because, despite the war we find ourselves in, God wins.

We just have to choose His side.

And that becomes a matter of faith for all of us — including you.

Thanks for reading *Second Wind*.

May God bless the reading of this book and use it for His purposes and glory. Amen.

— PART ONE —

NEEDING A
SECOND WIND

The whole world is under the
control of the evil one (1 John 5:19).

— CHAPTER 1 —

EPIC BATTLE

P ow, pow, pa pow, pow, pow.

The sounds outside my bedroom window startled me from a deep sleep. Jumping up on my knees, I cracked the blinds to see who was setting off firecrackers, disrupting the dawn's silence. Nothing. I leaped to another window, cracked the blinds, and saw a pickup truck idling in Johnny's driveway in the Hoskins/Thomasboro area. I dodged from one window to the next looking for the culprit, as the truck vanished.

The early morning silence returned. *What is wrong with these people?* was my last thought before I drifted back to sleep in my new neighborhood.

"Good morning Johnny," I said to my new neighbor several days later. "Did you hear those firecrackers Sunday morning here in the driveway? They lit them off right outside of my window!" I casually said with some emphasis, as if it were small talk to start the day.

"Firecrackers?" Johnny responded with a chuckle. "Do you mean the gunshots? Shot a hole right through Ronnie's window. Bullet missed him by inches, probably over drugs. Looks like our blessed Ronnie might not be practicing what he preaches!"

Johnny showed me the window with the bullet hole. "What?" I said with the shock Johnny expected. "Gunshots! Is Ronnie OK?" Chuckling again, Johnny said, "Yeah, and I think that might have cured his drug use."

"I thought Ronnie was clean," I said naively, without understanding the reality of addictions, the lies addicts tell, and the masks they wear. "Did you call the police?"

Johnny responded matter-of-factly, "Nope, wouldn't do no good. This kind of thing happens all the time, and they can't really do anything about it, or maybe they just won't."

"But at least they would know it happened!" I said, surprised by his casual attitude.

Welcome to the hood, I thought silently to myself. *What have I gotten myself into this time?*

I walked away, shaking my head, thinking, *War. This is a war.* (Author's journal entry, April 7, 2003)

> *And there was war in heaven. Michael and his angels fought against the dragon, and the dragon and his angels fought back. But he was not strong enough, and they lost their place in heaven. The great dragon was hurled down— that ancient serpent called the devil, or Satan, who leads the whole world astray.... But woe to the earth and the sea, because the devil has gone down to you! He is filled with fury, because he knows that his time is short (Revelation 12:7-9, 12).*

The fight between good and evil

We are in the fight of our lives. We are in a war. I am not talking about the war that took more than 4,400 American Troops in Iraq, the war in Afghanistan, the massacre in Syria, or the continual fighting in other parts of the Middle East. I am referring to the war where the primary battlefield is on our turf — the spiritual battle between good and evil. War expresses itself on those physical battlefields, but also the battlefields in our own homes, businesses, schools, communities, and minds. For instance, what possessed twenty-one-year-old Adam Lanza to kill 20 first-graders in Newtown, Connecticut? Or why would a twenty-two-year-old man shoot a congresswoman at point-blank range in Tucson, Arizona — similar to what happened at Columbine and Virginia Tech? Or what was really behind the random killing of 12 people by James Holmes while movie-goers were watching the latest Batman movie? I am referring to that war, the one that crosses all social, economic, educational, religious, and political boundaries. The one that crosses into the lives of politicians, religious people, businessman, professional sports personalities, students, and educators, regardless of age, gender, race, or title. It's the same war you are fighting in your own life that may have knocked the wind out of you.

Religious results

The story of Ted Haggard is an example of this "other" war. In 2006, Reverend Haggard was the respected senior pastor of New Life Church, which had a 14,000-member congregation. Many leaders, including President George W. Bush, sought his counsel. Haggard passionately preached the gospel (good news) of Jesus Christ while being adamantly against issues such as homosexuality. In November of that same year, a homosexual prostitute, Mike Jones, became unhappy with Haggard's opposition to same-sex marriage. Jones revealed he had been having a homosexual relationship with Haggard.[1] We know of other sexual incidents with Catholic priests and other spiritual leaders, as well, whose behavior puts their entire careers and reputations on the line.

Political and professional examples

Governors Eliot Spitzer, Rod Blagojevich, and Arnold Schwarzenegger made headline news for their behavior. Eliot Spitzer resigned as governor of New York after being involved in a high-priced prostitution ring.[2] Rod Blagojevich was removed from office in Illinois after being convicted of corruption.[3] Arnold Schwarzenegger finally disclosed that he secretly had a ten-year-old child with one of his personal servants. Another politician, Senator John Edwards, fathered a child with his mistress while being named "father of the year" in 2007. Dominique Strauss-Kahn was considered the next favorite to be elected president of France until a sex scandal got him arrested in 2011.[4] Bernard Madoff was sentenced to 150 years in prison because of his multi-billion dollar securities fraud, the largest in US history.[5] Going back a few years to make sure we know this isn't new news, President Clinton denied having a sexual relationship with his intern Monica Lewinski — before he admitted to the affair.[6] Richard Nixon was the only US president to resign the presidency after his staff broke into the Democratic National Committee headquarters, and he covered it up. Same war.

Everyone is at risk

Jerry Sandusky sexually assaulted at least eight boys putting the entire Penn State Football program in turmoil (CBS News, Grand Jury Report / Washington Post Sports, Steve Yanda, July 23, 2012). After lying about it for a decade, Lance Armstrong finally admitted to using performance enhancing drugs and bullying anyone who tried to stop him - hurting the entire cycling community. Kansas City Chief football player Jovan Belcher murdered his girlfriend before committing suicide at Arrowhead Stadium (Kansas City Star, Glenn E. Rice, December 1, 2012). Amy Bishop, a biology professor at the University of Alabama, shot and killed ... three of her colleagues at a faculty meeting after being denied tenure.[7] A grandmother is reported to have sold her eight-week-old grandson for $75,000 to a stranger.[8] Same war. There are also approximately forty-two million abortions worldwide each year, making it more of a casualty on human life than "war" itself — regardless of our own personal thoughts about the right to abort a life.[9] And there are thousands of rapes and sexual assaults, robberies, murders, cases of abuse (both domestic and political), and other crimes in the US each year. Over twenty-five percent of women experience domestic violence.[10] A report on US sex trafficking estimates up to 18,000 women and girls are trafficked for sex in the US each year, while another 300,000 are at risk of being involved.[11] Over thirty million children are estimated to have been sexually exploited worldwide.[12] Human trafficking has become a $32 billion worldwide industry, claiming up to twelve million sex slaves each year.[13] Pornography is a multi-billion dollar worldwide industry.

Including me

We are not excluded from this war.

I mentioned some of my personal story in the introduction without mentioning my own dark side. I have one, though. In my younger days, I was a recreational drug user and a binge drinker. I would drink and drive. I once started a barroom brawl and was arrested for assault and battery. I got a ticket for reckless driving and had my license suspended because I was doing exactly that, driving recklessly. As a single man, I had sex outside of marriage as the norm. I have been involved with pornography without conviction. Years ago, I stole money from a former employer because I figured out an easy way to do it. I justified it as not such a big deal (I ended up writing my employer a check for what I thought I had taken after God brought that old memory to my mind. I also admitted to my former employer what I had done.) I ran out on a check without paying after running up a fairly large tab at an expensive restaurant — while I was on an expense account. I just wanted to see if I could get away with it, and I did. Although this doesn't begin to describe the extent of my list of faults, it gives you an idea of the dark side of my own life. I have one. Just like the other people I've mentioned. Just like you.

Haven't you ever behaved contrary to your character? That's what I mean.

The invisible battle

Why do we do things that could hurt or ruin us? According to the Bible, you and I are in a real war against a real enemy — a war often invisible to the naked eye, a war misunderstood as someone playing with fireworks when it's really gunfire. Few understand this war. Most of us face its consequences rather than fighting as soldiers. We are participants in an unseen cosmic battle that is happening all around us. We are living behind enemy lines.

That's the bad news.

But before you write this off as Hollywood fiction, or explain it away as too farfetched, consider other forces that we deal with every day and which we take for granted as normal. Most of us know that electricity is the primary force running our television sets, lights, electrical appliances, phones, computers, and other devices we use on a daily basis. It's the same with wavelengths that are sending signals to and from your television set or the wavelengths that connect voices to your cell phone. We cannot see electricity or any of these wavelengths. Yet, we depend on them daily. The same is true with wind. We talk about hurricanes as tragic events, though we cannot see the enormous force until it hits. But we see the results. While this invisible spiritual war might be difficult to fathom, it still exists. We really do have an enemy. Though he's often jokingly referred to as "the devil," this one is real.

Footnotes

1 Wikipedia, Ted Haggard. It should also be noted that per Ted Haggard's website and testimony, he did not have an affair with his accuser, rather an encounter.

2 Fox News, New York Governor Eliot Spitzer Resigns Effective Monday Amid Links to Prostitution Ring. Wednesday, March 12, 2008.

3 CNN Politics, Blagojevich convicted on corruption charges, June 27, 2011.

4 CNN World. Dominique Strauss-Kahn: A brilliant career, a stunning accusation, May 16, 2011. Alan Silverleib, CNN.

5 The New York Times, Madoff Is Sentenced to 150 Years for Ponzi Scheme, Diana B. Henriques, June 29, 2009.

6 Wikipedia, Lewinsky scandal.

7 Wikipedia, 2010 University of Alabama in Huntsville shooting.

8 Cops: Grandma Tried to Sell Baby for $75k, abcNEWS/U.S., Dean Schabner, 11/6/10.

9 The Center for Bio-Ethical Reform, Abortion facts, http://www.abortionno.org/Resources/fastfacts.html.

10 National Coalition Against Domestic Violence, Domestic Violence Facts, http://www.ncadv.org/files/DomesticViolenceFactSheet(National).pdf.

11 International Crisis Aid, Sex Trafficking in the United States, http://www.crisisaid.org/ICAPDF/Trafficking/traffickstats.pdf.

12 Ibid.

13 Ibid.

— CHAPTER 2 —

WHO IS OUR ADVERSARY?

Martin lived in a cemetery for years before arriving at my door. While I came to appreciate him for being honest and frank, he remained an angry man during his years at Hoskins Park. He fought the gospel we preached, believing truth is relative and that his way was as good as the next.

Martin is still adamantly fighting Christianity, saying we are trying to force him to believe something he does not believe, and he is offended. He completely misses the part where he has been given room, board, food, kindness, and care for 18 months ... without having to pay much of anything. And when he did pay, we had provided the work. I told Martin to either change his attitude or change his address. He is looking for a new place. (Author's journal entry, August 11, 2004)

While Martin may have believed in some form of a devil, he never understood the reality of the war he was in — with Satan:

> *When Jesus stepped ashore, he was met by a demon-possessed man from the town. For a long time this man had not worn clothes or lived in a house, but had lived in the tombs. Jesus asked him, "What is your name?" "Legion," he replied, because many demons had gone into him. And they begged Jesus repeatedly not to order them to go into the Abyss (Luke 8:27, 30–31).*

The last time I saw Martin, he was staring out a window at the winter shelter on 3rd Street, while I was there to bring donated blankets. I tried to find him inside but could not. Later, I heard he had gone back to the cemetery.

> Be self-controlled and alert. Your enemy the devil prowls around like a roaring lion looking for someone to devour (1 Peter 5:8).

Is the devil real?

Statistically speaking, sixty-three percent of us *do not* believe in a real devil.[1] Many people humor us by explaining our poor choices are a result of having a devil on one shoulder whispering bad things for us to do, while an angel sits on the other shoulder whispering good things for us to do; we have to constantly choose between the two voices. The late Flip Wilson used the character Geraldine on his own comedy show back in the early '70s to nationalize the expression "The devil made me do it!" But perhaps it is not as funny as we think. Many people, particularly the homeless, those addicted to drugs or alcohol, those who are in prison, or who are involved in criminal or destructive behavior believe that might be more fact than fiction. Rarely do I have to explain the reality of Satan to the homeless. They know he lives although they may not fully understand his tactics. Perhaps they are the other thirty-three percent from the study who do believe in an actual devil, just like the Bible says.

Star Wars

They also know that their struggle is similar to that depicted in the movie series *Star Wars*. Two of the main characters of the film *Return of the Jedi*[2] reveal this encounter between the forces of good and evil in a personal way. Anakin Skywalker (Sebastian Shaw), persuaded by the power of the dark side to become the supposed nemesis of good in the character Darth Vader, portrays evil. Luke Skywalker (Mark Hamill), Anakin's son, although tempted by the dark side, remains firm in his predilection for goodness. In fact, his force of goodness prevails over evil and saves the day. As part of his Jedi[3] training, Luke enters the tree on Dagobah and comes face to face with a vision of Darth Vader, which appears real to him. Luke fights Darth Vader (in this vision), cuts his head off, and sees his own face in place of Vader's, suggesting he has a choice, just as Vader did. We also have our choice to make — to follow God and the Bible, or to ignore God and follow Satan. To what degree we follow either is another story, but the choice is the same. And once we give in to "the dark side," or Satan, he has power over us.

My encounter

I watched the movie *The Exorcist* years ago. I laughed in the theater, as I watched those far-fetched scenes of the little girl possessed by the devil. The film showed the little girl's head spinning around, supernatural strength, violence, cursing, voice changes, and so on. But I remember walking out of the theatre scared. Deep down, I believed it was true — I was about eighteen years old and not religious at all. I did not consider whether I believed in a devil at that point, but I did believe in an evil spirit that could take over people. Furthermore, since then, I have encountered what I believe really was the devil. Years ago, I heard a voice in my head tell me that he (and I believed it was the real devil) had ruined my life, after I had done something unsuitable to my character. Until I discovered the reality of this message, and the spiritual war we are all in, he had ruined part of my life. Recently, after having a vividly detailed dream suggesting the devil was going to destroy me, I heard that same voice say, "You're going down, now." I ended up having what some might say was a nervous breakdown. Bottom line? The dream came true. I took two months' leave from my work, received months of intense Christian counseling, and was prescribed an anti-depressant. I pressed into God with all my heart, soul, and mind, trying to find my own second wind. I was freed from the grip of Satan. Those I help off the streets believe there is a devil, too. And I believe he is tempting us to choose evil behavior, which oftentimes manifests itself into the aforementioned statistics.

The fall of mankind

Biblically, the devil is called the serpent, Satan, the tempter, the evil one, a roaring lion, and a dragon or ruler of the kingdom of air, among many other references. And he is not a happy camper. His pride came head to head with God's sovereignty, and he was hurled to earth from heaven as punishment.[4] Responsible for the fall of mankind, he is alive, well, roaming the earth hungry for someone to devour. While this act of disobedience is often ignored as a myth or inconsequential, the Bible states that it severed our relationship with a perfect God. It is where we lost our true identity in God:

> Now the serpent was more crafty than any of the wild animals the LORD God had made. He said to the woman, "Did God really say, 'You must not eat from any tree in the garden'?" The woman said to the serpent, "We may eat fruit from the trees in the garden, but God did say, 'You must not eat fruit from the tree that is in the middle of the garden, and you must not touch it, or you will die.'" "You will not surely die," the serpent said to the woman. "For God knows that when you eat of it your eyes will be opened, and you will be like God, knowing good and evil." When the woman saw that the fruit of the tree was good for food and pleasing to the eye, and also desirable for gaining wisdom, she took some and ate it. She also gave some to her husband, who was with her, and he ate it (Genesis 3:1–6).

God gave Adam and Eve one command — not to eat from the tree of the knowledge of good and evil (Genesis 2:17). So what did the serpent, Satan, do? He got them to do the only thing God asked them not to do, to eat from *that* tree. He did that by causing them to doubt God's Word and listen to him instead of God. The devil tricked Eve into eating from the tree she was told not to. She gave some to Adam, who ate as well. As descendants of Adam and Eve, we inherit their sinful DNA. Our relationship with God was broken and our true identity lost – by their choice.

Job

It is common for the devil to harass us by manipulating our circumstances and tempting us to doubt God and do things contrary to God's original intent. Besides the Genesis account, this is found throughout the Bible, including the story of Job. Satan approaches God and challenges the allegiance of Job, who was an upright, God-fearing man, of whom God was proud. Satan says Job's faithfulness is only because God is blessing Job. If God takes away His protection, Satan said Job would curse Him:

> "Does Job fear God for nothing?" Satan replied. "Have

*you not put a hedge around him and his household and
everything he has? You have blessed the work of his hands,
so that his flocks and herds are spread throughout the land.
But now stretch out your hand and strike everything he has,
and he will surely curse you to your face" (Job 1:9–11).*

Job is put through various trials, yet remains faithful despite his wife's
suggestion that he curse God for their pain. Satan was the instigator
behind the harm done to Job, yet Job remained loyal to God.

David, Jesus, Paul, and Peter

Satan also rose up against all of Israel when he caused King David to
take a census of the people, something God did not want (1 Chronicles
21:1). Most of us know Satan also tempted Jesus in the wilderness,[5]
and we read that the apostle Paul was prevented from going to
Thessalonica because the Bible says "Satan stopped him."[6] Then there
is the apostle Peter (or Simon). Jesus told him Satan had asked if he
could sift (or separate) him just before Peter denied he knew Jesus to
save his own skin:

> *"Simon, Simon, Satan has asked to sift you as wheat" (Luke
> 22:31).*

As the story goes, Satan did just that. Clearly, Satan was involved in
the harassment of those people's lives.

Mother Teresa and the tempter

Mother Teresa understood the reality of Satan as the tempter. This
quote is from her journal as presented in an authorized biography,
written just before the Missionaries of Charity were founded:

> *I went to meet the landlord of 46 Park Circus. The man
> never turned up. I am afraid I liked the place too much —
> and our Lord just wants me to be a 'Free Nun' covered with
> the poverty of the Cross. But today I learned a good lesson
> — the poverty of the poor must be often so hard for them.
> When I went round looking for a home, I walked and walked
> till my legs and arms ached. I thought how they must also
> ache in body and soul looking for home, food, help. Then
> the temptation grew strong. The palace buildings of Loreto*

came rushing into my mind. All the beautiful things and comforts — in a word everything. 'You have only to say a word and all that will be yours again,' the tempter kept on saying. Of free choice, My God, and out of love for you, I desire to remain and do whatever be Your Holy Will in my regard. I did not let a single tear come, even if I suffer more than now. I still want to do your Holy Will. This is the dark night of the birth of the Society. My God give me courage now, this moment, to persevere in following your Will.'[7]

Mother Teresa chose to follow God and resist the enemy's tempting to do otherwise. This excerpt from an interview with *Time Magazine*[8] reiterates that point:

Time: Are you ever afraid?

Mother Teresa: No, I am only afraid of offending God. We are all human beings, that is our weakness, no? The devil would do anything to destroy us, to take us away from Jesus.

Time: Where do you see the devil at work?

Mother Teresa: Everywhere. When a person is longing to come closer to God, he puts temptation in the way to destroy the desire. Sin comes everywhere, in the best of places.

While many people continue to debate the existence of a devil, they do so at the denial of the Bible for which many say they believe, and at the denial of people like Mother Teresa.

Satan gets under our skin

Not only does Satan harass people, he has the ability to inhabit them. Remember Judas? The Bible says he didn't betray Jesus until Satan entered him:

Then Satan entered Judas, called Iscariot, one of the Twelve. And Judas went to the chief priests and the officers of the temple guard and discussed with them how he might betray Jesus (Luke 22:3–4).

There are other examples of Satan inhabiting people as well. A story in the Gospel of Mark is about a man who was possessed by a legion of demons. What I found fascinating is that Jesus did not address the actual man; He addressed the evil spirit living inside of the man:

> When Jesus got out of the boat, a man with an evil spirit came from the tombs to meet him... He shouted at the top of his voice, "What do you want with me, Jesus, Son of the Most High God? Swear to God that you won't torture me!" For Jesus had said to him, "Come out of this man, you evil spirit!" Then Jesus asked him, "What is your name?" "My name is Legion," he replied, "for we are many." And he begged Jesus again and again not to send them out of the area (Mark 5:2, 7–10).

Jesus did something similar when Peter objected to Christ's foretelling of His crucifixion:

> Jesus turned and said to Peter, "Get behind me, Satan! You are a stumbling block to me; you do not have in mind the things of God, but the things of men" (Matthew 16:23).

Then there is our reality. Perhaps you have given some thought to the question I asked earlier: Why else would a twenty-two-year-old man shoot a congresswoman at point-blank range if not tempted by Satan? In her speech at the Tucson memorial, Governor Jan Brewer said it was "one madman's act of darkness." Perhaps she is right, but what made him go mad? Why else would kids be blowing themselves up as suicide bombers to get to "paradise"? Did you know that many of the suicide bombers are between twelve and seventeen years old?[9] Perhaps you have done something unbecoming of you and are asking the same question about your own actions: *Why?* Though we may not completely understand how Satan is able to get inside of people, he can.

And he does.

The hurricane

As these stories testify, Satan also has a voice. There is a modern-day example in the movie *Hurricane*,[10] the story of Rueben "Hurricane" Carter, played by Denzel Washington. Rueben Carter was a middleweight boxer with a triple-murder conviction that was rescinded after he had spent almost 20 years in prison. Although the movie has been criticized as fictitious in many areas, its overall accuracy has been accepted by most. Regardless, there is a powerful scene that might give us an idea of how Satan works in the spiritual realm. Upon his arrival at prison, Carter is put in solitary confinement because of his immediate disrespect for authority. He doesn't want to wear the typical prison garb because of his proclaimed innocence. In a poignant scene, Carter appears to have been alone in his cell for enough time to grow a beard. But, he's still wearing the same white shirt. You can imagine what someone might look like having been in solitary confinement for weeks without a bathroom or any light. It's bad. In this scene, he is having a conversation with what appears to be two versions of himself — an inner spiritual battle. He is sitting on the concrete in the middle of the small cell, with his hands on bended knees. His angry self on his right and his broken self on the left are conversing.

Solitary confinement

The angry Hurricane, standing, swearing, punching his wrapped fists into the air as if shadow boxing, while glaring out in the distance with absolute hate in his eyes, says with a soft, but husky, voice and words that run together in one long sentence, while the broken Rueben Carter is sobbing:

> **Angry Hurricane:** *I can feel the hate ... can you feel it ... can you feel the hatred movin'? Don't you just want to hurt somebody ... feel like I want to kill somebody, except there ain't nobody in here to kill [short pause as he stops punching the air, stands straight up, glares right at Rueben Carter with all that hate in his eyes], except you boy, how about it Rube?*

> **The Real Hurricane:** *Get away from me! [After repeatedly telling the voice to shut up]*

> **Broken Hurricane:** *[Sobbing with his head on his knees] I'm scared. What are we going to do now? Huh?*

Rueben Carter had a battle going on in his mind that only he could hear. He had to choose which voice to listen to, and he chose the broken one.

Larry

It doesn't just happen in movies. It happens in life. One of my former residents can relate.

I met Larry when I worked at the Shelter as a supervisor. He was one of the nicest people I had met. A talented carpenter, I learned more about his struggles when he moved into my house at Hoskins Park. Larry's mom was a drug addict who got pregnant with Larry at fifteen years old. The young mother prioritized men over her son, so Larry's grandmother raised him. She taught him to fear God, literally. Once, when there was a storm, she put Larry and his half sister in the middle of the room and told them to keep quiet so God would spare them from His wrath. Larry's grandmother would tell him, just before bedtime, that if he was bad, something was going to get him and drag him off, something he still believed at thirty years old. Those experiences also taught him to fear the dark. He grew up poor — something he didn't learn until one of his schoolteachers gave him a bag of clothes to take to his grandmother. He understood what that meant. Aside from his grandmother, everyone in his extended family remains chemically dependent. He never mentioned his own father except to say that his half sister's dad molested her and was serving time in jail. Nobody in his family had the same mother and father.

Split personality

At around twenty-five-years-old, Larry moved in with his mom because a drug dealer shot up his grandmother's house trying to kill Larry for stealing all of his cocaine. While transitioning from her house, his mother asked Larry to get his dog. He didn't, so she killed his dog to make a point. According to Larry, the result of all of these factors was the existence of a split personality, the old Larry and the new one. The old one wants to protect Larry from further hurt, criticism, feelings of worthlessness, and from feeling unworthy of being loved. That is the volatile Larry, the confused one, the one who seeks out women for his self-worth, the one who wants revenge for those who hurt him, and the dangerous one willing to risk his life for kicks. The other Larry is trying to believe that God loves him like the Bible says and that he is lovable without having to earn it. This quote reveals how he's trying to make sense out of life:

I had to be pretty strong to keep going for this many years. I've beat Larry up enough. So when other people do it, I want to defend him because I think I am a pretty good guy. But I am not good. But, I'd do anything for anybody. Somehow, Larry thinks you have to earn love, but I guess you can't. I guess that is why everyone thinks [love] is a feeling. I'm trying to figure out why Larry is doing these things because nobody else cares enough to help. But, I can't figure it out. I have read all the books I can, I have talked to all the psychiatrists I know to talk to, but I can't figure out how to fix Larry, you know? When I am talking to people about these issues, they think I am debating or arguing, but I am just trying to make sense in my own head. And you know what, Tom? I read this in a book. It said if you love somebody, you care about his spiritual growth. And you know what I always thought. I thought I hated Larry. One time, I physically beat myself up. I blackened both of my eyes, broke my nose, and put 15 staples in my neck - my first of many trips to the crazy house. But, I care about my spiritual life and that means I do love myself. It's just hard for me to believe God loves me as much as He loves Jesus.

It makes sense that Larry struggles with self-worth, gets his identity from women, struggles with addiction, believes he needs to earn love, sabotages potential success, and struggles with the Biblical character of God — I would, too. *(Author's journal entry, March 16, 2005)*

Battle in our minds

We're all familiar with the battle that goes on in our minds — the choice to do what is right or wrong. But we might not realize the source of these thoughts, ideas, or voices. We can explain it away through other means like blame the person (even if that means blaming ourselves) or condemn them (or ourselves) for all those thoughts and choices. But condemnation of the person is what leads to further condemnation and ultimately expresses itself in the evil behavior we are describing. When people believe they are nothing, trash, or not capable of being loved, their behavior typically follows those thoughts.

It's self-perpetuating. That is Larry's story. On the other hand, when we understand that Biblically it's a spiritual battle and the devil is the one condemning us, not God, everything changes. We get hope in the midst of the war because we know God is with us, God is for us, God cares about us.

But there are things we need to learn about this battle. Is it really true? How does the opposition pursue his primary opponent? Do we sit and wait, doing nothing? Is knowledge enough? Or, is there a plan to find victory in this mystic battle? Let's take a closer look.

Footnotes

1 Although this number might be more arbitrary than accurate since some polls indicate just the opposite. See http://www.religioustolerance.org/chr_sat1.htm

2 Mamill, Mark, perf. Star Wars Episode VI: Return of the Jedi. Dir. Steven Spielberg, Lucasfilm, 1983.

3 A Jedi is a warrior with telekinetic power referred to in the movie saga as "the force."

4 Revelation 12:7-9 & 12.

5 "Then Jesus was led by the Spirit into the wilderness to be tempted by the devil" (Matthew 4:1-11).

6 1 Thessalonians 2:18 respectively.

7 Mother Teresa, Navin Chawla, (Element Books, Rockport, Massachusetts, 1992), pg. 47.

8 Edward W. Desmond in 1989 for Time magazine.

9 Suicide Attack Continues Afghan Trend, The New York Times, Asia Pacific, February 26, 2011, Alissa Rubin. http://www.cnsnews.com/news/article/14-year-old-suicide-bomber-pakistan-want

10 Washington, Denzel, perf. The Hurricane. Dir. Norman Jewison, Azoff Entertainment, 1999.

— CHAPTER 3 —

IS THIS WAR REAL?

Today, the World Trade Center Twin Towers collapsed after terrorists hijacked and flew jets into each of them. Another jet hit the Pentagon while another was crashed into the ground in Pennsylvania. It's hard to describe it all. I watched the second aircraft hit the tower on television and then both of them collapse. I was on my bed reading the book *13 Seconds Over Tokyo* about the Dolittle raid after Pearl Harbor. I finished the book, picked up the ringing phone, and a friend told me to turn on the news. I am in shock. I am grieving too, but not for the same reason as others. I am more scared for my family and friends not knowing Christ than I am sad about the loss of their physical lives. I feel like our country just doesn't understand their need for Jesus, so our focus continues to be on the physical tragedies of life rather than on the spiritual ones. Does anyone realize our eternity is at stake in the real war raging for our souls? We're all going to die a physical death, but where we end up spiritually is dependent on a choice we make that most people still don't believe. Tragic. *(Author's journal entry, Tuesday, September 11, 2001)*

The god of this age has blinded the minds of unbelievers, so that they cannot see the light of the gospel of the glory of Christ, who is the image of God (2 Corinthians 4:4).

Eliminate the idea of a war

Satan's primary objective is to blind us to this conflict and eliminate any discussion of an enemy. He often succeeds by rendering the Holy Bible — the only book that clearly identifies him as the enemy — impotent. We must believe we are at war in order to know we have an enemy and then choose to fight. Most people don't believe in this invisible war. Just about everyone I know would prefer to blame a person for trouble, rather than the devil. Do you remember hearing a tragedy on the news that gives serious credit to Satan for the outcome? It is hardly a serious consideration, although then republican presidential candidate Rick Santorum specifically talked about Satan to a university audience in 2008 when he said:

> Satan has his sights on the United States of America! Satan is attacking the great institutions of America, using those great vices of pride, vanity, and sensuality as the root to attack all of the strong plants that has so deeply rooted in the American tradition.[1]

Commentators considered his remarks inappropriate because he wasn't making light of Satan. Santorum was calling Satan for what he is Biblically — the master of lies. We should, too.

We don't take our enemy seriously

On an episode of American Idol, I watched years ago, I heard one of its judges, Steven Tyler (lead singer for the group Aerosmith), praise a participant because he felt like the performer had finally "danced with the devil," as if it were a good thing. That's what I mean. Nobody questioned his comments at all. We just don't take this war seriously enough. While deep down we may believe in some form of evil, most people consider people or other factors to be the problem. Satan succeeds with his schemes by first attacking the Bible. Have you ever considered how many critics there are of the Bible who have never studied or read it? Doesn't that seem odd? But if you were the enemy trying to keep a lie going, wouldn't you do everything you could to keep people from the truth? Satan seeks to prevent us from reading, believing, and following the Bible.

The Word

Jesus verifies this point in His parable about a farmer planting seeds.

Farmers know that not all the seeds take root. Jesus explained the parable to His disciples as a story about God's Word and the enemy's plan to eliminate its fruition in a person's life. He offered this explanation:

> *This is the meaning of the parable: The seed is the word of God. Those along the path are the ones who hear, and then the devil comes and takes away the word from their hearts, so that they may not believe and be saved (Luke 8:11–12).*

Satan first tries to render the Word of God, the Bible itself, unworthy of any attention. If that doesn't work, he comes against anyone who reads the Bible, trying to distort its truth, to render it fiction or just "relative." He causes us to doubt. If that doesn't work, Satan confuses us to the point of frustration, so we stop reading the Bible. He gets us to quit. Don't you also find it interesting how you've been so easily distracted when you have read and studied the Bible? Life often gets in the way. Our daily grind keeps us too busy for Scripture. Once Satan devalues the Bible, or eliminates it, he separates us from God. That's his ultimate goal. So we blame people (or God) for all our problems, while diagnosing our issues through human terms. It is a subtle process, and he gets away with spiritual murder.

Addictions

Those spiritual murders bring various results. Consider addiction and mental illness.

When someone is addicted to a certain type of drug or behavior, we understand that to mean that the drug or behavior has taken control of his or her life. Some definitions even say addiction is *defined* by our inability to control a habit. The American Heritage Stedman's Medical Dictionary defines addiction this way: "Habitual psychological and physiological dependence on a substance or practice beyond one's voluntary control." That's the first thing many addicts learn in Alcoholics Anonymous — that they do not have the power to overcome their addiction alone. They are slaves to the addiction. That's true, but this question is rarely answered spiritually: Why are they addicted to destructive behavior? Many think it's just genetics. Others think it's an irresponsible lifestyle. Few think it has anything to do with a spiritual matter. So what do we do? We blame and treat the person, physically or psychiatrically.

Mental illness

I heard on National Public Radio (NPR) that a group of scholars were trying to determine the cause behind the 2010 attacks on school children in China. They believe the attack was rooted in mental illness, which is probably true in more cases than the ones we actually identify from a medical perspective. But that still does not get at the root of what is causing the mental illness. I also heard that many experts believe all destructive behaviors can be fixed through psychiatric treatment without regard to the Bible. While we look for psychological roots that caused trauma in someone's life resulting in mental illness, addiction or other perverse behavior, we completely ignore the spiritual issues. In fact, saying something like homosexuality is a spiritual issue is nonsense to most people, including organizations like the American Psychological Association (APA). This group unanimously approved a resolution supporting full marriage equity according to USA Today.[2] They believe some people are wired "gay" and should be free to live as they please. Since they have dismissed the Bible as nonsense, anyone who discusses this topic, as I am right now, is considered judgmental. As for Satan — Who?

The Bible is irrelevant

So, even though many of us may recognize something unexpected is going on down here on earth, we continue to minimize it as "life." We deal with it in the physical realm, rather than seeking to comprehend it in the spiritual realm. For those people whose behavior was illegal, we categorize them as criminals. For those who were sexually unfaithful, they are adulterers. For those who overdose using drugs, they are drug addicts. The mentally ill are mentally ill. Those attracted to the same sex are "gay." If it has something to do with our government, then it is just political. According to the wisdom of the world, there is no war, unless it is on terror, drugs, or some other physical reality. So, if you find yourself on the bottom living a life that is not working out as expected, according to the world we live in, you've just got to pick yourself up and try harder. Moreover, some of those who follow this mentality will wrongly quote scripture by telling you the Bible says, "God helps those who help themselves." The Bible doesn't say that at all. As for any real spiritual battle, they might patronize you by suggesting it is something to consider, as is the case with Adam Lanza, the Sandy Hook Elementary school shooter, or James Holmes, the Colorado theatre shooter, while concluding it is too much of a mystery to deal with in our reality. But the Bible attributes the chaos very differently — suggesting our worldly wisdom is foolishness:

> For the message of the cross is foolishness to those who are perishing, but to us who are being saved it is the power of God. For it is written: "I will destroy the wisdom of the wise; the intelligence of the intelligent I will frustrate." Where is the wise man? Where is the scholar? Where is the philosopher of this age? Has not God made foolish the wisdom of the world? For since in the wisdom of God the world through its wisdom did not know him, God was pleased through the foolishness of what was preached to save those who believe (1 Corinthians 1:18–21).

I have identified nine false belief systems or tactics in the upcoming chapters, which I consider the primary ways the enemy gets us focused on everything, but him and "the" God found in the book most have dismissed, the Holy Bible. As we enter a discussion about those topics, let's allow my honest reflections to keep our discussion real. I'm not only arguing my case and proving my points. I am inviting us all to choose a second wind — even by realizing we're really at war. These journal entries allow you to share my own experiences.

Take time to read them.

Take time to consider your own.

And prepare for a journey of change, a way, an explanation for life's chaos, a second wind.

Gordon, one of our residents I had very high hopes for, used drugs again. He went to mental health, was admitted, and evidently escaped. The police were looking for him today at Johnny's. It is amazing to me that some of the men who are the most clean cut and polite are often the hardest to help, perhaps because people do judge them by their cover thus enabling them to stay off the bottom longer than those who look the part. (Author's journal entry, May 21, 2005)

Did I mention a guy got shot and killed on Rozzelle's Ferry Road on the other side of the railroad tracks? It happened a couple months ago in front of the house of ill repute (drug/prostitution house), right across the street from our ministry. (Author's journal entry, August 16, 2004)

There were gunshots fired just outside the house the other night. I heard them nearby about midnight. Didn't see anyone when I looked out though. Henry said a police car was roaming up and down the street just after we heard the shots. (Author's journal entry, October 31, 2002)

Last night, at the neighbor's house across the street, there was a beating and stabbing. Evidently, the guy who lived there, Juan, tied up a woman and was beating her when another man came in to help. They beat and tied him up, stabbed him in the stomach and sliced his face two times. Somehow, he lived. I did not know about it until I saw the police over there. I went over and prayed for the folks involved. I spoke to Juan, too, but did not know what he had done. Neither did the police. The people are Hispanic and that may have helped this guy get away ... had the police understood what had happened, they may have been able to arrest him. But none of them speak very good English and none of the police spoke Spanish. At least, this is what I have heard from the other neighbor, who I just visited. Anyway, it was a bad situation, and Juan is a wanted man. I sent out a request for prayer to about 70 people. (Author's journal entry, August 24, 2003)

Reality. It can't be swept under the rug forever.

Footnotes

1 Politico, Rush Limbaugh on Santorum and Satan, Mackenzie Weinger, 2/21/12, http://www.politico.com/news/stories/0212/73137.html

2 USA Today, Citing new research, psychology group supports gay marriage, Sharon Jayson, 8/4/11.

PART TWO

WHAT'S IN THE WAY?

NINE TACTICS THE ENEMY USES AGAINST US

Now the serpent was more crafty
than any of the wild animals the
LORD God had made (Genesis 3:1).

— CHAPTER 4 —

IT'S ABOUT WHAT WE DO!

I listened to Denny play the piano and sing several times at the Uptown Men's Shelter, wondering how I could help him get a successful recording contract, even though I had no experience in the music industry. He was that good.

He also struggled with mental illness and crack cocaine, a deadly combination. Can someone with this much talent be unable to use it because of a disability? Denny eventually moved into my house as part of Hoskins Park Ministries. That is when I began to understand him a bit better. It seems that because people had always focused on what he could do as a musician, he became resentful of the very music that could help him prosper. Denny wanted to be loved as a person first, rather than as a piano player. Even as a child the focus was always on his musical abilities, as opposed to the person. Denny became a dear friend of mine. One thing is for sure, if people just love Denny's music, Denny will never really believe they love him.

> For it is by grace you have been saved, through faith — and this is not from yourselves, it is the gift of God — not by works, so that no one can boast (Ephesians 2:8–9).

Convince us it's all up to us, individually

The first tactic or false belief system undermining the Bible's relevance is the performance-based belief system. It is the one that says we are what we do. What we do defines us. This belief system is about our ability to control our lives. It considers circumstances as circumstantial.

Our success or failure is about how well we do what we do. It is all up to us, and we are judged accordingly. For the most part, God is left out of this performance-belief system, since we become our own gods in control of our own lives. We compare ourselves to one another. We grade ourselves by how we match up.

There are those who say despite our circumstances, we need to pull ourselves up by our bootstraps and "just do it." Some call it survival of the fittest,[1] and it begins at birth. We are either good or bad babies by how we behave. If we cry often, we are not as good as those babies who cry less. From the moment we're born, we are designated as weak or tough, smart or not, cute or not, fat or skinny.

Philip Yancey, in his book *What's So Amazing About Grace?*, says this about our performance living lifestyle in the US:

> *As early as preschool and kindergarten we are tested and evaluated before being slotted into an "advanced," "normal," or "slow" track. From then on we receive grades denoting performance in math, science, reading, and even "social skills" and "citizenship." Test papers come back with errors — not correct answers — highlighted. All this helps prepare us for the real world with its relentless ranking, a grown-up version of the playground game "king of the hill."[2]*

Our achievements define us. On and on it goes, until we are at our funeral with people talking about what we did. Our success in life is how high up on the scale we get in comparison to others. And the higher we get, the prouder we should be — particularly if our circumstances have been more difficult than the norm.

Discrimination

While there is nothing wrong with achievements, our achievements often come at someone else's expense. That is what often flames racial issues and segregates us as people. But not just on issues of race. I am appalled by how we have historically handled racial issues, but most of us are old enough to know that if you take away race as an issue, we will focus on something else.

Race may have been a factor in the shooting of seventeen year-old Trayvon Martin and subsequent controversy regarding George

Zimmerman, but there were a lot more murders that same day that had nothing to do with race — but someone still died at the hand of another (as is most often the case — murders are typically committed within their own race).[3] For instance, a black man, Trevor Dooley, shot an unarmed white veteran, David James, in Florida the month previous to the Trayvon Martin tragedy and to my understanding, race was never used as an argument.[4] A Hispanic man recently interviewed on NPR said that Marco Rubio, a highly visible and respected Hispanic Senator in Florida, could not relate to the man being interviewed regardless of his race. It was his political association that caused division amongst two Hispanic men. We also elected and re-elected the first African-American president ever. We just use race as another means of judgment, among many. Gender issues, for instance, is what was behind a class action suit against Wal-Mart on behalf of some 1.5 million women.[5] If you take away gender, we will compare ourselves on the basis of our financial status. That being equal, we will be measured on our level of education. The list goes on and on with factors such as weight, looks, age, physique, personal mannerisms, hair length, athleticism, knowledge of a specific task at hand or religion. Seth Walsh, thirteen years old, is reported to have committed suicide because his classmates were bullying him over his sexual orientation — not race.[6] Another thirteen-year-old, Jon Carmichael, hung himself because he was picked on for being small.[7] Race is just one of the starting points of discrimination, but all of us might be guilty of discrimination to some degree.

Uniquely made

During football season, I was at a FedEx copy center and mentioned Ohio State's victory in football that day. It was just something to say to start a conversation, since I am not that much of a college football fan. But the fellow I said it to was a Michigan fan, who gazed back at me saying, "Are you trying to start a fight?" I quickly learned they are big rivals. Now, he was sort-of kidding, but there was a slight tone of seriousness in his words.

We all have different tastes. That is what makes us unique. Do we really think that because we like a certain color, flavor of ice cream, or style of car that that color, flavor, or style is best for everyone? Sometimes I catch myself saying, "I would never buy something like that!" Well good for me! But that is very naïve thinking! The fact that we

41

don't like tattoos, earrings, long hair, getting up early, the mountains, etc., does not matter to those who do like those things. Those whose belief systems are based upon performance are always competing, thinking their ways are best for everyone. That is why I said we all might be more polarized in our thinking than we realize.

When we live in the performance driven world, even a simple disagreement with another person can cause division. We can blame it on whatever we would like, starting with the easiest place to point a finger when it is applicable: race.

But the reality is this: The heart of man is corrupted (Jeremiah 17:9).

It's just judgment.

It's our attempt to make ourselves feel better about ourselves at the expense of someone else.

This is part of living in a performance-driven world.

This does not eliminate truth, either. Truth is not about our tastes. It is about the truth. But, even if we disagree with the truth, we should do so without judging others who believe differently. Those who know the truth can share it with others. It is up to others to decide what they believe is the truth, even if they never choose to believe it is true. But as for personal tastes, none of us should think our tastes put us in a higher, worthier class above others. That is the issue of competitiveness that leads to discrimination. It is a tactic of our enemy.

Comparison in sin

Performance-based living also applies to sin. Many people regard some sins as worse than others. I have heard even criminals judge one another accordingly. For instance, someone who is a petty thief is nothing compared to someone who has committed armed robbery. A person busted for marijuana is not as bad as someone busted for heroin. Rape is not as bad as murder. And a murderer is felt to be preferable to a pedophile. I actually saw a bumper sticker that read something to the effect of, "Improve society, kill a pedophile." In a performance-based society everything is judged, even in criminal activity.

Morally upright people can fall prey to this belief system as they tend to judge immoral people by their own standard of morality. That is what the Pharisees did in Jesus' day. While pointing out the flaws of the obviously flawed, they did not know the extent of their own sin against a holy and perfect God. Remember Jesus' words when the Pharisees brought an adulterous woman before Him just before stoning her? He said:

> *"If any one of you is without sin, let him be the first to throw a stone at her" (John 8:7).*

While we look out for number one, we might miss the fact we are all implicated by our own value judgments. If everyone is compared to everyone else, then others are judging us all. Sure, some of us are judged more harshly than others; still, we all stand under judgment. That leads to further judgment. It is an unending cycle that demands an answer to the question, "What have you done for me lately?"

Ted Williams

Two stories further clarify this point about judgment: the story of the homeless man with a unique voice and LeBron James. Ted Williams was homeless, living on the street until someone recognized his distinctive voice and believed him when he said he was two years sober. It had less to do with him being just a person who needed help; rather, it was his voice and new direction that appeared to make the difference. Twenty-four hours after someone discovered his voice and believed he would do something with it, he was on the *Today* show. He was a hero. He relapsed soon thereafter and was back to drinking — so to many he became a zero (again). It was all about his voice and ability to stay clean — so he could be somebody. Somebody like us, you know, the ones who appear to have it all together, whether any of us do or not. As this reasoning goes, if he didn't use his voice, he was wasting his gift. But who was Ted Williams without his voice? To many, he was just another drunk homeless man who was getting what he deserved. In our performance-based society, he was a loser. I am well aware of this view since I work closely with the homeless. Most people judge them by their homelessness without ever knowing them as people.

LeBron James

The other story is the highly visible and prominent basketball player LeBron James, who was accused of abandoning Cleveland by choosing to play for Miami. Here is one of the greatest and most gifted basketball players of all times being judged by an entire city because he chose to leave. That, my friends, is judgment. His level of success had nothing to do with it. I wonder how the other Cleveland players felt about the city abandoning their hopes of winning a trophy because their hopes were in LeBron James rather than the team. The right coach and players don't always need the best ones, as was proven by the Dallas Maverick's defeat of the Heat in the 2011 NBA championships. Hopefully, you are starting to get the point. Can you imagine Ted Williams and LeBron James judging our decisions? I doubt they would agree with all of our choices. But who are they to judge us? The Bible says:

> *"Do not judge, or you too will be judged. For in the same way you judge others, you will be judged, and with the measure you use, it will be measured to you. Why do you look at the speck of sawdust in your brother's eye and pay no attention to the plank in your own eye? How can you say to your brother, 'Let me take the speck out of your eye,' when all the time there is a plank in your own eye? You hypocrite, first take the plank out of your own eye, and then you will see clearly to remove the speck from your brother's eye" (Matthew 7:1–5).*

Does it work?

This judgmental type of life is self-incriminating and does not appear to work. At its worst, it breeds selfishness, indulgence, immorality, addiction, blame, division, and condemnation. That is why many of the homeless remain in their same situation; they feel condemned by society. Then they turn to something for relief from the pain, often times it's drugs. They just don't have the financial stability to mask their problems like many of those of us with means — many of us who might have a home, but are still homeless deep down.

That is also why many successful people fall prey to its madness, because in a performance-driven society, you are only as good as your last performance. Michael Jackson, for instance, is dead. His death has been attributed to an overuse of drugs that helped him cope, regardless of whether his doctor erred. But, he was considered one of the best performers of our time and known as the "King of Pop." Why did he need drugs to cope with success? The same is true with Whitney

Houston — although she was said to have been on the rebound months before her death — cocaine still appeared to be the culprit for her drowning. Amy Winehouse had substance abuse problems and issues with self-harm, and struggled with eating disorders and depression.[8] Tiger Woods was divorced (from a supermodel) because of his immoral behavior. Heath Ledger died of an accidental overdose of prescription drugs while playing the role of Joker from the movie *Batman*.[9] What makes this of even more interest is that Jack Nicholson, who played the role of Joker in an earlier Batman movie, supposedly warned Heath Ledger not to take the role. In fact, Nicholson was said to have been furious he had not been consulted about the role before he accepted it himself years ago. When told of Ledger's death he is said to have replied, "Well, I warned him." That was it. Warned him of what, a performance in a movie? Coincidently, this was the same Batman movie series that was playing in a Colorado theatre (The Dark Night) when James Holmes opened fire on the audience killing 12 movie- goers and injuring 58 others. When caught he claimed to be "the Joker" (New York Daily News, Monday, July 23rd, 2012).

Not a new idea

We remember Elvis Presley, Marilyn Monroe, and other celebrities whose successful performances were insufficient to ensure their happiness. So, if performance is the key to happiness, why isn't it enough? Since it doesn't appear to be working, why do we keep living in that world? Henri Nouwen, a Catholic priest who served the poor, said:

> As long as we continue to live as if we are what we do, what we have, and what other people think about us, we will remain filled with judgments, opinions, evaluations, and condemnations. We will remain addicted to the need to put people and things in their 'right' place. To the degree that we embrace the truth that our identity is not rooted in our success, power, or popularity, but in God's infinite love, to that degree can we let go of our need to judge.[10]

Performance is what fuels racial tensions and other issues of discrimination because it is based upon doing, which is based upon judgment.

Bottom line

If we think it is all up to us, then we cease to think of God as our protector or our ultimate authority. We disregard Satan as our true enemy, and we put faith in people. Since people are easily corrupted by money, power, or sex, many of those in whom we place our trust are not worthy — including us. So a cycle is created, a cycle of fix and blame. Let me use technology as an example. When we are threatened, we utilize all the resources we can muster up to protect us from "bad people," including the use of technology. But, so do those same bad people. Nuclear weapons, for instance, have been a deterrent to those who want to cause harm, since control over them has been fairly good up to this point. However, the wrong people are now gaining the ability to create these terrible weapons, and they might just use them. So, it is a cat and mouse game. While we continue to develop technology, we escalate the need for it. Then we become more dependent on someone to protect us from it. If not God, ultimately, that protective entity is our government.

Socialism

After 9/11, we wanted the government to increase control over security at airports because of threats — we wanted them to fix our security system. We also wanted them to stop terrorism. Most believe the threat has been reduced, even though many might not know it cost the United States at least a trillion dollars to do so and might have put us over the financial edge. Some airports have body scans, which infringe on our privacy, and many people think the government has gone too far. After the Newtown, Connecticut shooting, the debate on gun control escalated to an unprecedented level. Many people are willing to sacrifice more of our freedom for protection. But if the government goes too far, many will complain. So, one day we are screaming at the government to protect us, while the next we are blaming them for taking our freedom from us and bankrupting our country. As the cycle goes, man-made technology continues to advance, escalating the need for it. But we cannot have it both ways when we depend on man to save or fix us. So we all become political, giving the government more and more authority to protect us at the expense of trusting God with that job:

> *Trust in the LORD with all your heart and lean not on your own understanding (Proverbs 3:5).*

We must trust the Lord at the expense of our own wisdom and understanding.

As Christians, that means remembering we are "one" in Christ:

> *There is neither Jew nor Greek, slave nor free, male nor female, for you are all one in Christ Jesus (Galatians 3:28).*

Further translation of that scripture means there is "neither" white nor black, rich nor poor, educated or uneducated – for those who have put their faith in Jesus Christ. We are one – in Him. We must all trust in the God of the Bible we claim to know instead of trusting in the god of this age who asks, *What have you done for me lately?*

Footnotes

1 A term coined by British philosopher Herbert Spencer and later used by Charles Darwin.

2 Yancey, Philip, What's So Amazing About Grace? (Zondervan, 1997), pg. 36.

3 Encyclopedia of death and dying. http://www.deathreference.com/Gi-Ho/Homicide-Epidemiology-of.html#b

4 KSDK.com, Iraq War veteran killed; widow says Florida's "Stand Your Ground" law is free pass for murder. Kevin Held. March 22, 201.

5 USA TODAY, Woman take case against Wal-Mart to highest court, Joan Biskupic. The Supreme Court refused to expand the lawsuit and blocked the case from further litigation on 6-20.

6 cbsnews.com, Seth Walsh: 13-Year-Old Who Endured Gay Taunts Memorialized After Suicide, October 4, 2010, Edecio Martinez.

7 cbsnews.com, 13-Year-Old Jon Carmichael Commits Suicide Following Bullying, March 31, 2010, Edwcio Martinez.

8 Amy Winehouse, Wikipedia.

9 msnbc, Heath Ledger died of accidental overdose, Associated Press, February 6, 2008.

10 Nouwen, Henri, The Heart of Henri Nouwen (Crossroad Publishing Co., New York, NY, 2003), pg. 47. Henri Nouwen died in 1996.

— CHAPTER 5 —

IT'S ALL ABOUT OUR HAPPINESS!

S Surrender your rights, you were bought for a price (1 Corinthians 6:20).

"Hey, where are the beds?" I asked a resident after walking away, wondering why I had decided to check myself in to this shelter in the first place. He pointed in the direction of the largest room in the shelter. I thanked him and followed his directions. Oh my gosh, I thought as I walked into a room that reminded me of an army barracks for unruly boy scouts. My deep sigh was shortened by a stench that would have clogged up a bathroom sink if solidified. My face reflected my discomfort as I found my bed amongst the other 200. Surrendering once again to the reason I was actually in the shelter, I got into my single bed only to discover the smell worsening. "Lord, please protect me and help me get through this night," I prayed on and off for hours, wondering if some little creatures weren't crawling all over me. All the while, the snoring, belching, grunts, groans, and any other disgusting bodily sounds known to men were heard as loudly as if I were in a forest alone with the crickets. I watched the clock all night long as it slowed to a near crawl: tick ... tock ... tick ... tock ... tick ... tock. Then at 3 a.m., the clock went backwards an hour. Of all the days — it was Daylight Saving Time. Finally, the night was over — praise the Lord!

"Man. That was one of the longest nights of my life!" I said to my new friend Mike, exhausted from having had no sleep and once

dressed.

"What's the matter?" he politely asked, as if he was used to all those things that made me uncomfortable.

"The smell in my bed was enough to make me puke," I responded. "I felt like things were crawling all over me all night, too."

"What? Did you change the sheets?" he asked, surprised by my comments.

"No, was I supposed to?" I asked, waiting for the punch line.

"Of course! This isn't the Holiday Inn!" he said as he began laughing hysterically. Embarrassed, but relieved I didn't have to relive that part of the experience again, I was reminded of the reason I was in the shelter in the first place — and it wasn't for my happiness. (Author's journal entry, October 30, 2000)

In those days Israel had no king; everyone did as he saw fit (Judges 21:25).

If it feels good, do it!

The feelings-based belief system is the second false belief system I want to discuss. It is the system that says, "If it feels good, do it." It is based upon the Burger King philosophy of life, suggesting you and I can have it our way. It implies that satisfied feelings lead to happiness. And, while it might take us a few years to figure this out, most of us learn that over time we are dissatisfied in getting what we want. Our feelings are fickle. If we are following them by our desire to have it our way, we will ultimately conclude that this belief system does not work. Or it will kill us. I like McDonald's, but if I ate there every time I felt like eating a Big Mac, I would likely have a heart attack. I know because I tried it once! Over a six-month period of my life, the stress of life got so difficult that I ate everything I wanted without regard to nutrition. Always craving a Happy Meal, I indulged.

And I was happy for a while.

But the unhappy results also came with that choice:

I gained 50 pounds.

I ended up in the hospital.

I couldn't breathe.

Now, not being naïve to the importance of nutrition, I decided to take action. With the help of a friend:

I reversed my diet.

I chose to eat food that was better for me.

I lost the 50 pounds.

I ran a marathon within a year.

I finished an Ironman triathlon.

So, while following my feelings gave me some daily relief from the stress of life, it prevented me from doing other things I enjoy. And it almost killed me.

The healthy versus unhealthy table

Think of it this way. If we were to put two tables before most people, one table full of healthy food — like fresh vegetables, salad, plain nuts, clean water, brown rice, fish or lean broiled meat, fruit, modest sugar — versus an unhealthy table of rich, high fat food or fast food (French fries, hamburgers), soda, alcohol, fried food, sugary desserts (ice cream, candy, cookies, donuts, Twinkies) plus foods with a lot of preservatives (crackers, chips, etc.), which table would you choose? Based upon statistics, most Americans are choosing the unhealthy table, knowing it is the poorer choice.[1] We all know that eating poorly is unhealthy, so why do so many of us eat this way? I'll tell you why — because we like the taste! It makes us happy — even at the risk of death!

That is why the owner of Las Vegas Heart Attack Grill, Jon Basso, told CBS News, when one of his customers had a heart attack after eating his triple bypass burger, "We throw slogans at you like, 'Taste worth dying for' and post signs that read: 'Caution! This establishment is bad for your health',"[2] because many of their customers knowingly risk their health for the sake of their immediate taste buds. It's deadly, but it's good. That is true for many of us. Do you know what our answer is to better eating? Don't — just take a pill. If we eat too much, many of us take medication to settle our stomachs. If we get coronary heart disease, we take aspirin, digitalis, an ACE (angiotensin converting enzyme) inhibitor, or sometimes even nitroglycerin. Most of us once thought nitroglycerin as a bomb-making ingredient in old Western matinees. Now, we are prescribed it for health reasons. I read an article in *The Washington Times* that said British researchers were proposing that fast food restaurants offer a cholesterol-lowering drug to be given with fast food meals to minimize the risk of eating the fatty meal just purchased.[3] If it's that bad for us, shouldn't we just eat healthier rather than take a pill?

Do or die

President Clinton, who would run to McDonald's for breakfast while he was president, underwent quadruple bypass surgery in 2004 and had a stent put in his heart in 2010. He ate from the unhealthy table. Now he lives on fruits and vegetables, has no dairy products at all, and he drinks protein shakes. He said eating this way has changed his entire metabolism. He lost twenty-four pounds and his health improved drastically. He knew it was either change his diet or suffer the consequences, and he didn't want to die yet. I think he took all the pills he could without the results for which he hoped. Furthermore, he referenced a study by doctors Esselstyn and Ornish that said eighty-two percent of people in the study since 1986, who went on this plant-based diet, all reversed their heart disease (The New York Times, Bill Clinton's Vegan Journey, Anahad O'connor, August 18, 2011). According to the book *The Spectrum*, when you remove foods known to devastate and injure veins and arteries, the body will reverse the symptoms. Part of the evidence comes from the Papua Highlanders in New Guinea, the rural Chinese people, the Central African people, and the North Mexican Indians, where there isn't a trace of heart disease.[4] Esselstyn says of heart disease:

> *It's a food borne illness, and we're never going to end the epidemic with stents, with bypasses, with the drugs, because none of it is treating causation of the illness.*[5]

Food is the key to good health. These two doctors claimed that one can reduce the incidence of heart disease and cancer by eating a healthy diet.[6] But, do we? Will we?

But it doesn't work

We might wish we could eat whatever we wanted and be healthy, but we cannot. Following the feelings-based belief system, the one that says you can have it your way and be satisfied by worldly desires, does not work with food. It does not work with what we believe about life either, despite how long we might get away with it. As a young adult, I was led to believe he who died with the most toys wins. I ended up owning my own airplane, speedboat, and home on the water, which qualified me as a contender in this race, but it left me empty. There are many examples of people in the same boat. Many might recall that Deion Sanders, former professional football and baseball great, drove his Mercedes-Benz off a cliff because of his dissatisfaction with life. He was at the pinnacle of his career and "winning at life" according to the culture's definition, and attempted suicide.[7] He ultimately accepted Jesus Christ as his Lord and Savior. We must set aside:

- our instant gratification mindset,
- our happiness,
- our feelings.

Why?

For a greater purpose — one that comes at the expense of *our way*.

For a second wind worth that type of price.

Love

What is interesting is that love requires such a sacrifice of *our way*. The subtle change that has happened in our culture based on this one false belief system or tactic is our redefining of love as lust. Love is about sacrifice for the good of another person. Lust is about getting our own way so that we feel loved. Once again, the statistics prove this point to be true, since over 50 percent of marriages, either Christian or non-Christian, fail. Love, by definition, doesn't. Love is not a feeling — but lust is. I will save some of this for the chapter on the characteristics of God, but for now, consider how love is often defined by feelings rather than commitment. Why? Because we like the taste!

As sad and incredible as it is, we have redefined the very thing we all want at the foundation of our souls: love, which is the essence of God, and made it about us. That is why the right to abort a child has become legitimized — because it is more about the mother's rights, rather than love for the mother's unborn child. While many of us will continue to pursue happiness by trying to get what we want, happiness will be ever elusive.

Despite the worldly philosophy trying to convince us otherwise, we can't have it all.

You can't have it all.

I can't have it all.

Happiness is not the goal

That is why Jesus led a life of sacrifice, including the sacrifice of His life for us. He is the essence of love. And He asks us to follow Him. Happiness is not our goal. According to the Bible, God is. Of course, that does not mean we will not have moments of joy. As Christians, we should have the most joy! While I was in the shelter, I met some of the guys who eventually became my friends. In fact, some of the men I met (and still meet) off the street are some of the most respected people I know. Yes, it was difficult living in their community for the time I did, but there was a joy I got from those years that I cannot explain in words. In fact, I often considered it a slice of the Promised Land in my life. When we know our Creator and destiny — paradise — we can rejoice in the midst of life's grind. We can continue on as Christian soldiers. But happiness typically has the wrong connotation. So, while people pursue happiness, at least the fleeting kind, the kind that makes us comfortable, it is likely to leave us empty or attracted to something that will ultimately ruin us individually and as a society. That also goes for those who claim to be Christians.

Footnotes

1   Statistics: The average American teenage boy consumes 40 gallons of soda each year and will gain at least 20 pounds from soda by high school graduation. Over one billion people drink soda every day (out of about 6.5 billion people world-wide). It is estimated that 25% of the total daily calories of "soda drinkers" comes from soda. According to a CBS news report, we spend over $110 billion on fast food (in 1970 it was $6 billion) each year with about 25% of our population eating at a fast food restaurant daily. CBS News Report, Jan. 18, 2001 Americans Are Obsessed with Fast Food: The Dark Side of the All-American Meal. Over one-third of Americans are considered obese while another one-third are considered overweight. The risk of heart disease, cancer, stroke, diabetes, hypertension, and osteoporosis have greatly increased because of our poor diets. They now account for over 50% of the deaths in the United States, and about 300,000 people die each year from being obese or overweight. Nutrition and Your Health: Dietary Guidelines for Americans, USDA, http://www.health.gov/dietaryguidelines/dga2005/report/html/B_Introduction.htm. About 1.5 million people will be diagnosed with cancer this year and about a half million will die from it. Studies indicate that healthier diets would save billions in medical costs and lost productivity (some estimates say we could save as much as $147 billion). National Alliance for Nutrition and Activity, National Health Priorities, Reducing Obesity, Heart Disease, Cancer, Diabetes and Other

    Diet-and Inactivity-Related Diseases, Costs and Disabilities, 2008, Joy Johanson.

2   CBS THIS MORNING, Apparent heart attack at heart attack grill. February 16, 2012. John Blackstone. http://www.cbsnews.com/8301-505263_162-57379101/apparent-heart-attack-at-heart-attack-grill/

3   http://www.washingtontimes.com/news/2010/aug/12/forget-the-fries-would-you-like-a-statin-with-that/

4   Frontline, Plant-based diet to save the heart, Interview with Dr. Caldwell B. Esselstyn, Volume 18 – Issue 01.

5   CNN Health, The 'heart attack proof' diet? David S. Martin, August 22, 2011.

6   CNN, September 25, 2010. Huffington Post. http://www.huffingtonpost.com/2010/09/25/cnns-wolf-blitzer-intervi_n_739134.html.

7   Power, Money, & Sex, How Success Almost Ruined My Life, Deion Sanders (Nashville: Word Publishing, 1998).

— CHAPTER 6 —

CHRISTIANS ARE HYPOCRITES

"My name is Tom Wheeler," I told the man in charge. "One of your inspectors condemned one of our houses and I wanted to see what we needed to do in order to save it."

After looking up the house in question on his computer, he replied, "The house has been scheduled for demolition in the next thirty days. Once it is assessed to be more costly to repair than rebuild, as is the case with that house, it is automatically condemned. There is nothing you can do."

"Well, I understand that might typically be the case," I said. "But I am a Christian pastor, and we help men get off the streets. I promise I will get this house up to code, if you just give me a chance." I believed that would be enough for him to reverse his decision and extend me an exemption.

"Pastor? You all are the worst offenders," he said matter-of-factly and as if to end the discussion. "I have granted extensions to several pastors who claimed God told them this or that and then never did what they said."

"Well, I understand," I said, stunned, but knowing that he was speaking the truth. "I am not that type of person, but I respect your decision. I am also sorry for those of us who call ourselves Christians and then don't do what we say. We should be the most trustable. I will make an appeal to the City Council," I said, truly understanding, but unwilling to give up on the house.

"I'll tell you what," he responded. "Give me twenty-four hours to think about it. Call me tomorrow and I'll let you know my decision. But the chance of me changing my mind is doubtful."

"OK, thanks," I said before hanging up.

The entire ministry prayed. The next day, he granted us an extension and we completed the house as we said. I am still getting used to the fact that being a Christian pastor doesn't carry the respect it ought to — because we often don't resemble our Lord and Savior as we should.

> *You, then, who teach others, do you not teach yourself?*
> *You who preach against stealing, do you steal? You who*
> *say that people should not commit adultery, do you commit*
> *adultery? You who abhor idols, do you rob temples? You*
> *who boast in the law, do you dishonor God by breaking the*
> *law? As it is written: "God's name is blasphemed among*
> *the Gentiles because of you" (Romans 2:21–24).*

Make Christianity about Christians

This enemy tactic is the one that says you should base your decision about Christianity on Christians. In fact, this appears to be the one that impacted India's former leader, Mahatma Gandhi. Gandhi (1869–1948) is considered one of the most respected leaders of modern history. Known as the Father of the Nation of India, he is one of the only leaders in history to achieve national independence through nonviolent means.[1] Gandhi, a Hindu, is said to have admired Jesus and often quoted the Sermon on the Mount while at the same time rejecting Christianity.[2] He was asked why he didn't become a Christian, and he is said to have replied:

> *Oh, I don't reject your Christ. I love your Christ. It's just that*
> *so many of you Christians are so unlike your Christ.*[3]

According to the missionary E. Stanley Jones, a Methodist missionary in India, a close friend to Gandhi and who wrote a biography on his life, Gandhi tried to attend a church service in South Africa and was prevented from doing so by an elder of the church, who referred to him as a "kaffir," and barred him from the church. This is the account by Jones:

"Where do you think you're going, kaffir?" the man asked Gandhi in a belligerent tone of voice. Gandhi replied, "I'd like to attend worship here." The church elder snarled at him, "There's no room for kaffirs in this church. Get out of there or I'll have my assistants throw you down the steps."[4]

According to this report, it was then that Gandhi decided to adopt what was good about Christianity while also deciding he would not become a Christian, if it meant being a part of the local church. Unfortunately, this happens more frequently than we want to admit.

Miracle cars

I heard a scam on the television show *American Greed*.[5] It happened among the Christian community in the 1990's (and into early 2000's). The scam was started by Robert Gomez, who wanted to become a professional gambler, but didn't have the money. He recruited a friend, James Nichols, to help him with his plan. According to reports, Gomez said that his fictitiously adopted father, millionaire John Bowers (who he claimed had a $411 million estate), had a large number of cars that were available to Christians at a really low price. Intentionally or not, the church became the target when Gomez brought the news to his local church. This congregation embraced the scam as an answer to prayers, and purchased all the cars. I do not recall the specific list of the sixteen cars or prices, but there were late model cars selling for $1,000 or $1,500, to give you an idea of the deal being offered. Because of Gomez and Nichols' success at the church, Gomez told the congregation that, upon further investigation of his fictitious father's estate, there were many more cars to be sold. The list kept growing as fast as Nichols and Gomez could type it up.

I just wanted to be part of the miracle

The news spread across the country's Christian community. It was referred to as "Miracle Cars" after Corine Conway, a trusted and popular preacher, heard the story. She spread the news without checking into its legitimacy. Because of her heralded name, she may have been one of the primary reasons the scam succeeded. Many Christians were convinced it was true. The scam that began at a local church making a few thousand dollars ballooned into a scam making millions for its

wannabe professional gamblers (which they became, by the way).
Former Kansas City Chief football player Ricky Siglar and his wife
invested $180,000 by the time it was over, along with some 4,000
other investors. The list of churches that were involved was long. They
sold over 21 million dollars' worth of phantom cars over a four-year
period. Incredibly, no one ever had any proof the cars existed — it was
all done on faith! Finally, a small town police chief, Cindy Schroeder, of
Higgensville, heard about the cars and began to ask questions, as it
seemed too good to be true. She immediately contacted Conway to
find out who was behind this. Sadly, her questions were considered
"insulting" as she was told, "Sister, you got to believe!" Upon
investigation she learned the truth. There was no John Bowers.

No estate.

No cars.

Many just wanted to be a part of the miracle.

The miracle that was really a scam.[6]

The Good Samaritan

From the Biblical story of the Good Samaritan, it wasn't the religious
folks who helped the man in need, but one of the lowlifes of society.
The Samaritans were considered outcasts, a mixed race, only partially
Jewish as a result of the exile (2 Kings 17). Jesus made the Samaritan
the hero, because he was the only one who took the time to help the
man in need. The others were too busy, even those who said they were
committed to God (Luke 10:30–37). Sometimes the people that are
most helpful to others are those who society shuns — like the homeless
I work with.

Beautiful people.

Attack!

It is also true that all of the apostles deserted Jesus while he was
being arrested. So, after all the miracles Jesus did before their eyes,
they still abandoned Him in His greatest time of need (Matthew 26:56).
While many of us, who claim to be Christians, are hypocritical, judging
Christianity by Christians is not a fair way to judge Christianity. I say that
with regret, since a good role model can be very helpful, but we still

must not miss Jesus when we look at His followers. Moreover, if you were the enemy, wouldn't you want to do the most harm to those who could hurt their own cause the most? Consider Mel Gibson and his movie *The Passion of the Christ*[7] in 2004. That movie had more impact on people than most other Hollywood films, and it gave honor and glory to Jesus Christ. Mel Gibson's life has appeared to be under attack ever since (apparently by his own sinful behavior and choices). Most will just consider him a hypocrite, as it appears he is, but it is likely Satan behind the scenes. My take on it? Satan wants to ruin reputations so people will consider the sin of the man rather than the truth of the message.

God, no!

In fact, this is the reasoning behind a book titled, *GOD, NO! Signs You May Already Be An Atheist AND Other Magical Tales,* authored by Penn Jillette. Jillette, an outspoken atheist libertarian, hypothesizes that because so few Christians (or religious people) live out their faith in their daily lives, they are really disguised atheists. That is one reason he considers himself to be an atheist, at least according to his interview on NPR. His arguments against the existence of God were full of their own contradictions, but, I could not fault the point he made about hypocrisy.[8] Like Gandhi, he listens to what many people preach about their religion and then he watches how they behave. Unlike Gandhi, however, he has chosen to throw out the baby with the bath water, as the expression goes. This is what can happen when we, as Christians, are just talk. People see past our words. They then dismiss the God we claim to know and follow.

Still we must follow Jesus

But irrespective of that, we should not take that bait. Do we consider all doctors corrupt because some of them are? Are all priests child molesters? How about financial managers — are they all like Bernie Madoff? Are all lawyers or teachers corrupt because some of them are? If one bad apple truly spoils the whole bunch, then we are all in trouble.

There are some great examples of Christians amongst us. But people fall short of the glory of God.

I do.

You do.

Mother Teresa did as well.

That is why we need Jesus.

For those of us who claim to be Christians, however, we must remember God is looking for us to be salt and light. We need to lead by example:

> *I discipline my body and keep it under control, lest after preaching to others I myself should be disqualified (1 Corinthians 9:27, ESV).*

> *If my people, who are called by my name, will humble themselves and pray and seek my face and turn from their wicked ways, then will I hear from heaven and will forgive their sin and will heal their land (2 Chronicles 7:14, ESV).*

While the argument that Christians are hypocrites shouldn't cause anyone to dismiss Christianity, I hope it wakes us up. If you are a professed Christian, please join with me. Let's represent Christ in our daily lives — lives that matter more than we think.

Stay the course.

People are watching.

Footnotes

1 August 15, 1947.

2 John Mark Ministries, Gandhi and Christianity, Roland Croucher and others, August 28, 2003. Also Wikipedia, Gandhi. Interfaith Heroes, Stanley Jones, January 20, 2009.

3 Ibid.

4 Ibid.

5 CSNBC television, 8-7-2010.

6 Ibid.

7 Gibson, Mel, perf. The Passion of the Christ. Dir. Mel Gibson. Icon Productions, 2004.

8 npr, Penn Jillette's 'God, No!': An Atheist Libertarian On Tricks, Bacon, And The TSA, August 16, 2011, Linda Holmes.

— CHAPTER 7 —

GOD IS TO BLAME!

arry called me this evening, really hurting. Said he was suicidal and wanted to kill someone. He can't figure out why God doesn't let him live the way he wants to, so he can be happy. I went and met him. He was driving a car without a license and had been drinking. I got him to give me his keys. Doug met me. We asked him if we could take him to mental health, detox, or the winter shelter. He said no to all of our suggestions and asked for his keys back. I wouldn't give them to him. He walked over to Robin's house, a few blocks away, as we followed. She told him to leave and explained to us that she had taken a warrant out for assault — evidently, they got in a fight; her bruises appeared to prove it. We had already called the police over Larry's threats. They arrived a couple hours later. Just prior to Larry being arrested at Park Road shopping center we saw him swallow a bunch of something, which we assumed were pills of some sort. We told the police who said they were taking him to CMC before taking him to mental health or jail. Anyway, it took from 4 p.m. to 10 p.m. *(Author's journal entry, December 2, 2005)*

People ruin their lives by their own foolishness and then are angry at the Lord (Proverbs 19:3, NLT).

Eliminate our problems

Have you ever blamed God? Satan uses that tactic as a final knockout punch. It denies the notion of any war. It implies that if God is big enough to create the universe, then why doesn't He just eliminate the world's problems — including our own? It is along the lines of the performance-driven tactic, but with the blame focused on God, rather than anyone else. That reminds me of a scene from the comedy *Bruce Almighty*.[1] Bruce (Jim Carrey) is a nice guy, a news reporter who appears to get kicked around by everyone. Yet, he never asks God for help, since he is too busy blaming Him for all his problems. His girl friend, Grace (Jennifer Aniston), suggests he try prayer. While driving his car one night, he asks God for a sign. He is interrupted by a very slow-moving truck that pulls in front of him full of signs that say, "Slow Down, Caution Ahead!" Rather than accept the signs as a "sign," he gets mad, steps on the gas and flies by this slow truck, crashes, and then blames God for the wreck! In fact, he calls God a mean kid with a magnifying glass and challenges God to smite him! He is through with prayer!

Just after that scene and through a series of supernatural events, he ends up in front of someone claiming to be God (Morgan Freeman). The rest of the movie is about God giving Bruce authority to prove himself better than God, since Bruce obviously thinks he is. Bruce finds out it's not so easy dealing with people's wants as things fall apart under his watch.

Sound familiar? Many of us blame God for our problems, assuming we could do better at His job:

> *Then the LORD said to Job, "Do you still want to argue with the Almighty? You are God's critic, but do you have the answers?" (Job 40:1–2, NLT)*

You fix it! What's it got to do with me?

Since we think He caused our problems, we think He should solve them, along with all the other problems we see in the world. If He doesn't, we accuse Him of sleeping at the wheel. Perhaps that is why Henri Nowen wrote:

> *Most of us distrust God. Most of us think of God as a fearful, punitive authority or as an empty, powerless nothing.*[2]

Haven't you wondered why God allows the suffering and evil we see in the world? Surely He would do something about the starving children if He knew about them, wouldn't He? Or He would heal us if He knew how sick we were. Or He would end homelessness. Many of us use that as our excuse to believe He is not active in the lives of people. But what if we are the cause of much of the suffering we attribute to Him because of our lack of belief in this message? We find this word in Deuteronomy:

> See, I am setting before you today a blessing and a curse
> — the blessing if you obey the commands of the LORD
> your God that I am giving you today; the curse if you
> disobey the commands of the LORD your God and turn
> from the way that I command you today by following other
> gods, which you have not known (Deuteronomy 11:26–28).

We may have a nearsighted view of the truth of the Bible, but that won't alter its truth. Those who follow God will be blessed. Those who do not are automatically cursed because they are trying to live apart from the Creator. So, what is Satan's role? To get each of us to believe that God — the one who says you are blessed if you obey Him and cursed if you do not — is unfair by being so absolute in His desire for us to serve Him only.

Put the gun down

Metaphorically speaking, we all have access to our own handgun. When we choose to do something that is contrary to God's will, we are picking up a figurative gun, shooting at ourselves and others. We might shoot ourselves in the foot, as the expression goes, or somewhere else. I often remind those I serve that if they continue to abuse drugs, they are potentially killing their brains and other body parts. Since misuse of drugs destroys their brains, they are taking their loaded gun and shooting themselves in the head. It's the same with those who drink and drive or have sex outside of marriage. When you carry around a loaded gun, eventually it goes off.

I miss my friend Paul. A diabetic, Paul had his leg amputated inches below his knee. It breaks my heart, but I personally warned Paul several years ago that if he did not stop using drugs and lying about it, he would start to lose body parts. He didn't stop. It cost him a toe, a finger, his leg, and sadly his life on October 6, 2011.

I also warned another young fellow from our ministry. Because of his involvement in illegal drugs, he had been shot five times and lived to talk about it. He was still being recruited by well-respected colleges to play football. I referred him to this passage as something to consider:

Later Jesus found him at the temple and said to him, "See, you are well again. Stop sinning or something worse may happen to you" (John 5:14).

He ignored the message and was soon shot for the sixth time. There was no metaphor in his situation. A real gun shot him. The message is the same for all of us. If you overeat, your body pays for it by the stress you put on your bones, joints, and organs. Our hearts can only stand so much abuse. The same is true for those who smoke. If you have a sexual addiction, you are implicitly choosing sex over relationships, even though we all crave relationships. Folks can say what they want about the AIDS epidemic, but AIDS may never have existed if we stuck to God's guidelines for abstinence before marriage, then to His design for sex to stay between a man and woman only. If you do the crime, you will likely do the time, despite those who think they can beat the system. Putting the gun down means you recognize that you are actually hurting yourself and others by defying the scripture that is being played out in your life — blessings or curses.

The God of our design

Again, Satan's tactic is to get us to blame the one who gave us life for all the misery in the world, even though God left us a Guidebook. If we read it, believe it, and follow it, He will solve these problems (or prevent them) often while using His people as His tools. That reminds me of what was said about Jesus while He hung on the cross:

The people stood watching, and the rulers even sneered at him. They said, "He saved others; let him save himself if he is the Christ of God, the Chosen One" (Luke 23:35).

Many think God is supposed to act like the God of our opinions rather than the God of His Word. One of the most important things I learned in seminary and through my life experiences is that I am not God, and neither are you! I know; I'm a genius. God is not to blame; we are. So why do we continue to act as if we are God?

Caveat

I want to mention another caveat for those whose circumstances do not appear blessed, even though they might be following God. We all know that people still get sick, suffer, and die even though they do cry out to God and obey Him. As Christians, we are told we will suffer like Jesus because no student is greater than his master (Matthew 10:24), and we are the students. In those instances, just like Job, we must remain faithful, and we must trust God to get us through. We have to stay the course. But we need to understand that in the midst of our battle, we still have a real enemy. And that enemy might be the reason for our circumstances. Even so, while it might seem reasonable to doubt God when things are not going well, for whatever reason we choose to doubt Him, where then do we place our faith - in people? We know people let us down, including ourselves, so that is not a viable option. Or should we just give up?

Quitting

We all know that quitting is typically the worst thing we could do. I read about a man who was born into poverty and faced defeat for most of his life — but he never quit. He confessed these words in his thirties:

> I am now the most miserable man living. Whether I shall ever be better I cannot tell; I awfully forebode I shall not; To remain as I am is impossible; I must die or be better.[3]

That does not sound like a happy man. His list of failures was extensive. In 1831, he failed in business. In 1832, he was defeated for Legislature. In 1833, he failed in business again. In 1836, he suffered a nervous breakdown. In 1838, he was defeated for Speaker. In 1840, he was defeated for Elector. In 1843 he was defeated for Congress. In 1848, he was defeated for Congress again. In 1855, he was defeated for Senate. In 1856, he was defeated for Vice President. In 1858, he was defeated for Senate. It wasn't until November 6, 1860, that Abraham Lincoln's persistence was rewarded; he was elected the sixteenth president of the United States of America.[4] His most significant achievements in life might have come because of his experience with failure and his persistence to continue on despite the odds.

None of us know where we are in the history of our lives — only God does. Maybe we will live another day or two, or another hundred years — we don't know. Therefore, while He may want us all to give up our way, He doesn't want us to quit. That sure doesn't mean we won't want to — we just shouldn't:

> Let us not become weary in doing good, for at the proper time we will reap a harvest if we do not give up (Galatians 6:9).

God isn't to blame. He is faithful to complete the plans He has for our lives. We simply have to trust Him to do it:

> The one who calls you is faithful and he will do it (1 Thessalonians 5:24).

And He will — in His time.

Footnotes

1   Carrey, Jim, perf. Bruce Almighty. Dir. Tom Shadyac, Universal Pictures, 2003.

2   Nouwen, pg. 98.

3   McMan's Depression and Bipolar Web, Lincoln and His Depressions, John McManamy.

4   The Edge. Pg. 6-25, http://www.mcmanweb.com/article-225.htm

— CHAPTER 8 —

IT TAKES TOO MUCH FAITH!

L ast night around 10 p.m., we heard shots fired just outside my door. I rushed to see what was up, a normal occurrence in my new life. My neighbor across the street was standing in his side lawn, saw me at the door and asked in a loud voice, "You got any problem with what I just did?"

"Well I don't know what you just did," I said, certain he had fired the shots. "I just came out to see if everything was OK and everyone was still alive." He assured me everything was fine. I heard the neighbor behind him asking the same thing as I went inside. I guess he just decided to take out a pistol and start shooting. Thankfully not at me! I walked away shaking my head — again. *(Author's journal entry, August 16, 2004)*

"For my thoughts are not your thoughts, neither are your ways my ways," declares the LORD. "As the heavens are higher than the earth, so are my ways higher than your ways and my thoughts than your thoughts" (Isaiah 55:8–9).

Christianity contradicts our intelligence

The next tactic Satan uses is the notion that it just takes too much faith to believe in Biblical Christianity because Christianity defies the intellect. While this is similar to the primary objective of Satan to render the Bible irrelevant, it is different. Moving beyond simple dismissal, it makes intelligence the central issue. Many Christians have tried to defy science by depending solely on faith, but science does not defy Christianity (or vice versa). Sometimes those who call themselves Christians try to defend indefensible issues and are then disproved by science. The Genesis account, for instance, says that God created the earth in seven days. If that is true, the earth can be calculated to be six thousand years old based on the Biblical account.[1] Scientists, however, have determined that the earth is approximately 4.5 billion years old.[2] Because of this discrepancy, it would seem natural to believe that either the Bible or science must be wrong. However, the Hebrew word for *day* that is used in Genesis is *Yom*, which can mean a segment of time rather than a twenty-four-hour day. A segment of time could be anywhere from a second to any number of years. For instance, *Yom* could mean the day of the dinosaur, referring to the time in history when dinosaurs roamed the earth.[3] Therefore, the Bible and the Genesis account of creation could be completely accurate based on a more, rather than less, literal interpretation of the Bible. There is another possibility. When God created Adam, Adam does not appear to have been a baby. Rather, he seems to have been created with some years on him:

> *Now the LORD God had planted a garden in the east, in*
> *Eden; and there he put the man he had formed (Genesis 2:8).*

That could be true of the earth as well. Perhaps God created the earth as if it were 4.5 billion years old when, in fact, that was not literally true.

I repeat — it's not about Christians!

Not all Christians try to defend apparent contradictions with science. Not all who call themselves Christians threaten to burn the Qur'an on September 11, or actually follow through and burn it later on as Terry Jones is said to have done.[4] Not all Christians protest at the funerals of young soldiers who died in battle because they think God is punishing the United States for tolerating homosexuality.[5] And not all Christians are predicting they know when the end of times is going to be either, particularly since the Bible says we won't know.[6] So, let's take the Bible for what the Bible says, not for what some Christians say about the Bible — as sad and frustrated as it makes me to have to write that for a second time. Those of us who call ourselves Christians should be above reproach. Sadly, we often get caught in Satan's traps just like the rest of the world, because we too take our eyes away from our Lord and Savior. Then we doubt the same message we preach to others. Irrespective of that, many things are a matter of faith and not just faith in Christianity. In fact, everyone has faith, even atheists — the issue is where we place our faith. Take the movie *Contact* as an example.

Contact

Contact[7] is a movie about Eleanor (Ellie) Arroway (Jodie Foster), a scientist and confirmed atheist who has a lifelong belief in intelligent life in deep space. It has been her life's mission to prove it to the world. In one scene, Ellie tells a Christian pastor (Palmer Joss, played by Matthew McConaughey) that while she doesn't have faith in God, she strongly believes in aliens. Moreover, she challenged the faith of this pastor on his own faith in God. In fact, she wanted Palmer to prove there was a God, even though she had no proof of aliens. Here is his response when she asked him to prove it:

Palmer Joss: *Did you love your father?*

Ellie Arroway: *What?*

Palmer Joss: *Your dad. Did you love him?*

Ellie Arroway: *Yes, very much.*

Palmer Joss: *Prove it.*

His point was that proving you love someone can be difficult, even inconclusive, which is the same with God. It is a good point, as it suggests that proof can be somewhat misleading.

Faith of an atheist

What I found more interesting however, was the scene where Palmer asks Ellie about her belief in life on other planets and her explanation for why she wants to get buckled into a craft that would hopefully take her to the aliens she had finally contacted:

Palmer Joss: *By doing this, you're willing to give your life, you're willing to die for it. Why?*

Ellie Arroway: *For as long as I can remember, I've been searching for something, some reason why we're here. What are we doing here? Who are we? If this is a chance to find out even just a little part of that answer ... I don't know, I think it's worth a human life. Don't you?*

Although not outwardly spoken in the movie, Ellie had faith, a lot of faith, since she was willing to die for what she believed in (aliens!). As the movie goes, Ellie does take a trip into space and meets with her deceased father — but, upon her return and to her dismay, there was no physical evidence that any of it happened. She ended up almost contradicting herself by telling people that they had to trust her on faith. As a scientist, she knew how inappropriate that was to say, but for her, it was true! People who turn to the Bible have the same questions as Ellie. We just don't think the answer is lost in space.

Faith in the fog

What does someone do whose faith is in traditional areas when they are surrounded by sharks and caught in the fog, metaphorically and literally speaking? Florence Chadwick wanted to be the first woman to swim the twenty-one-mile strait between Catalina Island and Palos Verde on the California coast. It was cold and foggy the morning of July 4, 1952, when she attempted her swim. Several times, her support crew had to drive the sharks away using their rifles. Despite the encouragement of her trainer and mom, she quit before finishing. Afterward, she is reported to have said that she would not have quit within a half mile of the finish, had the fog not prevented her from seeing the finish:

> *Look, I'm not excusing myself, but if I could have seen land, I know I could have made it.*[8]

Her faith was in her abilities, but when the fog prevented her from seeing the end, she gave up. To her credit, she eventually returned and was victorious. But it appears her faith was in her own abilities, her determination — what she could see, which wasn't enough in the fog. Sometimes our faith has to be tested to see just how much faith we really have in whatever we claim to have faith in. Biblical Christians just believe the Bible, the most influential book in civilization, even if we have become the minority.

Minority

Besides the truth being arrogant, the majority is often wrong about many things, so being a minority is not a surprise. For example, did you know that 12.3 percent of the world's population (and 15.6 percent of the 167 countries in the world) is a full democracy?[9] Although another 37.2 percent of the population (and 31.7 percent of countries) are living in flawed democracies. You — if you live in the United States — live *as a minority*.[10] Furthermore, if you live in the United States, you are one of about 307 million others. But there are some 6.5 billion people in the world. So, less than 5 percent of the world's population lives in America. You are a minority twice over just by living in the United States.

If you have a home and car, you are in the top 3 percent of the wealthiest people on earth. If you eat healthy, you are in the minority. Most of us live as a "minority" if we are living in America. These percentages are something to consider as we switch sides of the fence to defend our opinions. Although living a healthy life does not guarantee a disease-free one, it at least gives us some degree of control over our health. Irrespective of that, it won't stop most of the medical community from focusing on medicine as the cure for health problems, when our diet is often at its root. The Christian Reformation was undertaken by a minority of people who disagreed with the majority and who sought to set things straight. Most causes worth fighting start with a minority opposing the majority. So, while the minority may not always be right, I hope the argument that the majority of people not believing the Bible as an argument against its validity is juxtaposed to the reality that the majority is often wrong.

I don't think Christianity contradicts anyone's intelligence.

Christianity enhances it.

Footnotes

1   Wikipedia, Dating Creation.

2   Wikipedia, Age of Earth.

3   http://www.thefreedictionary.com/Yom.

4   The Christian Science Monitor, Pastor Terry Jones is given car for refraining from burning holy book, Beth DeFalco, Associated Press, October 15, 2010.

5   Mscbc.com, "Dad sues 'Thank God for Dead Soldiers' church," Ben Nuckols, Associated Press, 4/13/2010.

6   Acts 1:7.

7   Foster, Jodie, perf. Contact. Dir. Robert Zemeckis, Warner Bros., 1997.

8   Read more: http://www.answers.com/topic/florence-chadwick#ixzz1W65zYTXr. Answers.com, Florence Chadwick.

9   The Huffington Post, World's Top Democratic Governments: Economist Intelligence Unit's Democracy Index 2010, Curtis W. Wong, 12/14/10. Democracy index 2010, Democracy in retreat, A report from the Economist Intelligence Unit, pg. 1.

10 Ibid.

— CHAPTER 9 —

TRUTH IS RELATIVE!

" I am glad you found your truth," Julie said after I shared my faith in Jesus Christ and my work at Hoskins Park. "I'm glad you are happy." It's the standard answer for someone who wants to clearly convey that while you or I believe Jesus is Lord and Savior, he or she does not. Since nobody they know has died and returned to life, claiming someone knows the absolute truth is naïve to those same people. *Truth is not relative, I walked away thinking. By definition, it isn't. How can intelligent people actually believe that it is relative when they are dealing with the reality of truth every day? (Author's entry, July, 2005)*

Someone ran through our property today being chased by the police. I wonder if he noticed the cross he passed twice — the first time as he was running by as a wanted man, the second time escorted by the police in handcuffs as a found one. The cross, his only hope, I wonder if he noticed the cross. *(Author's journal entry, April 14, 2003)*

"You will not surely die," the serpent said to the woman. "For God knows that when you eat of it your eyes will be opened, and you will be like God..." (Genesis 3:4–5).

What are we doin' here?

Another tactic of the enemy is the agnostic one. It implies that truth is relative and that all religions may be true to one degree or another. Therefore, we should not pretend we know the truth by choosing a religion, then trying to convince everyone of our perceived truth, since we cannot know with certainty. This kind of belief system is ubiquitous in our culture. While this might sound understandable, irrespective of whether it is reasonable, truth is not a matter of degrees. In fact, being just one degree off course can actually cause us to miss our destination completely.

One degree doesn't matter anyway

If we left the coast of California heading for Hawaii one degree off, we would miss Hawaii by about forty-three miles.[1] Being off a degree can also be the difference between life and death. The earth is on a 23-degree axis towards the sun. If the earth were one degree off (closer or farther away from the sun), we would either melt or freeze. So, while we may get away with being a degree off for a period of time, it catches up to us. The longer we travel one degree off, the farther we get from our target.

It is the same with speed. One mile-per-hour might not matter much traveling in the space shuttle or in a car, but if you are riding a bike, it is much more significant. If you are running or swimming, it can be the difference between an Olympic athlete and a casual exerciser. The same is true with a period of time, such as a second. If you are driving your car, one second can be the difference between your safety and an accident. Take our eyes off the road at the wrong moment, and we can be in a life-changing (or ending) accident. That is why it is now illegal to text while driving in many states. It takes our eyes off of the road for too many seconds. So, although a degree, mile-per-hour, inch, or second's importance on any given situation is relative, it can be the difference between success and failure, between life and death, between right and wrong.

Do you wear a seat belt for your comfort or for your safety? Rhetorical question. We wear it because we understand that in a split second, we could be in an accident.

Seconds matter.

Degrees matter.

Individual interpretation

Many don't believe that the message we read in the Bible today is the message intended by its authors despite how close they might have been. Their contention is that linguists cannot always accurately interpret the languages of the Bible into English (or modern-day languages). That means we cannot be confident in what it actually says let alone means. Translated — it is individually interpretable. Since it might be close to its intended interpretation, they believe the Bible has some credibility, just not 100 percent.

It's close.

And that's good enough.

But if someone believes the Bible's content is up for grabs, where do we draw the line? Our third President, Thomas Jefferson, cut up the Bible, disregarding passages of Scripture he did not believe fit accurately with his understanding of the Bible. He believed it was a matter of degrees. But that is dangerous and can lead to serious misunderstandings. Who can be sure what parts are true and false if everyone thinks the accuracy of the Bible is debatable? Some believe that parts of the Bible are more difficult to understand than others. This is actually mentioned in Scripture:

> [Paul's] letters contain some things that are hard to understand, which ignorant and unstable people distort, as they do the other Scriptures, to their own destruction (2 Peter 3:16).

So, although it might be true that parts of the Bible are challenging to understand, it is not difficult enough to render the message inconclusive. Furthermore, this is common in any area of study. There are always parts that are more difficult to understand than others in mathematics, science, history, engineering, economics, etc. But does it give us the right to interpret the information as we please? No, it doesn't. Those who have studied the Bible know that there are few, if any, passages that are inconsistent with its general message. Many may not always like or want to believe what the Bible says, but its overall message is clear.

We also must trust that our scholars, those who interpret the Bible from its original languages, are fairly good at translating documents from different languages (even though there are always some idiosyncrasies).

Unless you doubt the intelligence of our scholars, you must trust that our translators can translate documents well enough to understand them accurately. When I wrote this, I was listening to a live interview between Larry King and the president of Iran, Mahmoud Ahmadinejad.[2] I believe Ahmadinejad was speaking Farsi, with a translator translating what he was saying into English for King and his audience. I would be alarmed if the translator inaccurately translated the conversation — wouldn't you? Wars can be started when people suggest interpretation is a matter of opinion.

Typically, issues regarding the Bible are not a matter of translation — they are a matter of trust. What might have innocently started off as just missing the mark by a degree by our believing the Bible is individually interpretable has now traveled so far away from the target that the target is no longer in sight. That is why the discussion of gay marriage is gaining momentum. People don't think the Bible is clear about homosexuality. The passages that are against it, they reason, are relative when you consider other factors, like how we feel about those passages when they disagree with our chosen lifestyle.

Truth is

Our acceptance of an agnostic approach to religion is another of Satan's tactics to blind us from the truth. It's stinkin' thinkin', as David Chadwick often preaches at Forest Hill Church. But truth does not depend on our opinions or beliefs. Furthermore, while an agnostic approach to religion still might sound reasonable, we don't accept it in our own realities. In the midst of uncertainty, we are all forced to choose. We choose spouses, doctors, lawyers, jobs, financial managers, airlines, diets, accountants, day-to-day behavior, along with some form of religion or belief system. We do so knowing that not all spouses, doctors, lawyers, accountants, airlines, and religions are the same. Some are better or worse than others. That is why intelligent people do research before making important choices, because they want to make the right one. We realize that there will be consequences for our choices, so we aren't haphazard about any of them. Are we?

Truth and consequences

Suffice to say, while the truth might appear to be hidden under the camouflage of relativity for a time, it is still true. Consequently, it will ultimately force us to deal with its reality, including the truth about religion. I listened to Massachusetts financial investigator Harry Markopolos tell how he had warned the SEC about Bernie Madoff's frauds for nine years. He was ignored.[3] Nouriel Roubini, an economist, predicted the housing collapse and worldwide recession in detail, three years in advance of its occurrence; he was nicknamed Dr. Doom and ignored.[4] I doubt he is surprised with the precarious financial situation we find in the world today. It is reported that John P. O'Neil, a top anti-terrorism expert in the FBI, warned superiors of the threat of Al Qaeda and Osama Bin Laden before 9/11, but was ignored. Having become known as a maverick over his warnings, he left the FBI and took a job as head of security at the World Trade Center on August 23, 2001, where he later died by the hand of Osama Bin Laden.[5] The *Titanic* captain was warned of icebergs, yet he sped up, and the unsinkable ship sank.[6] The officials in New Orleans were warned that if a category 5 hurricane hit the city, without upgrading the levee system, it would likely be destroyed.[7] The disastrous proof occurred in the form of Katrina in August 2005. There were warnings about the space shuttle Challenger taking off in freezing temperatures, but it lifted off anyway, just before it came apart.[8] Many alarms have sounded — to deaf ears.

The proof is coming

So, while many may think they are headed to heaven when they die because truth is relative, if they have not put their faith in Jesus Christ as their Lord and Savior, that's not where they will end up:

> *"Not everyone who says to me, 'Lord, Lord,' will enter the kingdom of heaven, but only the one who does the will of my Father who is in heaven" (Matthew 7:21).*

The spiritual "theory of relativity" is at best a theory of contradiction, at worst a fatal attraction. Truth is not relative. Jesus asked His disciples and all of us one important question that we all must answer regardless of our own thoughts about religion:

> *"But what about you?" he asked. "Who do you say I am?" (Matthew 16:15)*

So, who do you say that Jesus Christ is?

And what is the source for *your* answer?

Footnotes

1 In navigation, every mile we travel that is one degree off, we end up 92 feet off course at the end of that mile. Hawaii is about 2500 miles from California. That is 230,000 feet, divided by 5280 feet or the number of feet in a mile, which means we would be off course by about 43.5 miles.

2 9:20 pm on September 22, 2010.

3 New York Daily News, In his new book 'No One Would Listen', investigator, Markopolos says he thought about killing Madoff, Caitlin O'Connell, March 1, 2010.

4 The New York Times, Dr. Doom, Stephen Mihm, August 15, 2008.

5 Frontline, pbs.org., the man who knew, John P. O'Neill.

6 Wikipedia, RMS Titanic.

7 Wikipedia, Hurricane Preparedness for New Orleans.

8 Wikipedia, Space Shuttle Challenger launch decision.

— CHAPTER 10 —

TURNING RIGHT AND WRONG UPSIDE DOWN

"**S**on," my dad said to me after I grimaced at his use of the Lord's name in vain. "When are you going to join the human race?" He asked as if using the Lord's name inappropriately was standard English. "Get your brains out of the closet." Those were his last words before I drove off thinking, *When did someone who actually believes in the book our country was founded upon become the ignorant one? And when did someone who uses the Lord's name in vain become normal?* The Bible says, "You shall not take the name of the Lord your God in vain, for the Lord will not leave him unpunished who takes His name in vain" (Exodus 20:7). I believe the Bible.

> *There is a way that seems right to a man, but in the end it leads to death (Proverbs 16:25).*

> *Jesus didn't trust them, because he knew human nature. No one needed to tell him what mankind is really like (John 2:24–25, NLT).*

The frog is boiling

There has been a study that says you can place a frog in water and boil it alive, if you increase the temperature of the cold water slowly enough. On the other hand, if you place a frog in already boiling water, the frog will supposedly jump out.[1] Satan seems to be a master at this next tactic, but we are the frogs and sin is the pot. Having convinced us that degrees don't matter, Satan makes subtle enough changes over time, so that we appear blind to the obvious, but radical, changes in our culture. Recently, I had another potentially cancerous cell removed from my leg. My doctor, leaning over my ankle, slicing off a piece of my skin for a biopsy, said, "You know, these were all a result of the sun you got twenty years ago, not any time recently. It just takes time for it to develop into cancer." And we all know it is true. You typically don't get cancer from getting sunburned a couple times; nor do you typically get cancer by smoking one cigarette. Nor do you typically gain 20 pounds overnight.

The United States

If we all think back, we can see that the current situation in our country — which is normal to many younger people — is completely out of control to the older generations. For instance, many people today consider something that used to be sinful, premarital sex, as normal. Furthermore, same-sex sex is now being considered normal behavior under the umbrella of tolerance, when it was once considered perverse. While this tolerant approach to behavior appears to be a loving approach to life, it is far from that. It is the same as telling an addict that his addiction is OK. It is not. As a Christian nation, sex before marriage and homosexuality were improper and not God's idea for mankind. Why? Because the Bible clearly says so and we believed the Bible, despite how poorly many leaders interpret it. Read the scripture below and you will understand what I mean, particularly regarding same-sex sexual activity:

> Because of this, God gave them over to shameful lusts. Even their women exchanged natural relations for unnatural ones. In the same way the men also abandoned natural relations with women and were inflamed with lust for one another. Men committed indecent acts with other men, and received in themselves the due penalty for their perversion (Romans 1:26–27).

> Do not practice homosexuality, having sex with another man as with a woman. It is a detestable sin (Leviticus 18:22, NLT).

Now, before getting sensitive to the modern day controversy over this topic, please hear me out. If you have a preference for the same sex, I am not putting you down. I am not condemning you either, although I understand why you might think otherwise, since so many people do condemn you, Christians included. Please forgive us. I recently watched the video of Reverend Sean Harris, a preacher from the Berean Baptist Church in Fayetteville, North Carolina, tell fathers to put their kids in place by "cracking" their limp wrists and punching them at the first sign of feminine traits.[2] That is the kind of condemnation that leads to further acts of condemnation and hatred. It is not Biblical at all and does not represent the Jesus I know. Many people, like that, forget that everyone has tendencies (behaviors) that are different, including that preacher, and they just like to pick on this one. Like I said, heterosexual sex before marriage is not acceptable either, Biblically speaking. One sin is as bad as the other — they miss the mark. Jesus has to change our hearts, people can't.

We all have issues

There is also a sin many Christians completely ignore, while we often focus on sexual tendencies, which is gluttony. It is fascinating to me how many Christians avoid even the willingness to talk about this issue while focusing on more "serious" sin. But this is what the Bible says about our overeating habits:

> Their destiny is destruction, their god is their stomach, and their glory is in their shame. Their mind is set on earthly things (Philippians 3:19).

Pride could be considered our worst sin, since it often prevents us from accepting the message of salvation in the first place. The remainder of the scripture I just referenced from the Book of Romans is below, and it solidifies my point:

> Furthermore, since they did not think it worthwhile to retain the knowledge of God, he gave them over to a depraved mind, to do what ought not to be done. They have become filled with every kind of wickedness, evil, greed and depravity. They are full of envy, murder, strife, deceit and malice. They are gossips, slanderers, God-haters, insolent, arrogant and boastful; they invent ways of doing evil; they disobey their parents; they are senseless, faithless, heartless, ruthless. Although they know God's righteous decree that those who do such things deserve death, they

*not only continue to do these very things but also approve
of those who practice them (Romans 1:28–32).*

I understand your disdain for the condemnation you feel from judgmental Christians. We should not disrespect each other for our personal tendencies — which we all have — nor should we be unloving to our neighbor who we are commanded to love. But, we are not supposed to love people at the expense of God's holiness or at the beckoning of Satan. Think of a child running toward a cliff. As the child nears the edge, he or she does not see the impending danger. The parent's job is to stop the child whether or not he or she wants to be stopped. That is love, although the child might not feel like it at the time. In this case, we are the children and God is our parent. He is desperately trying to warn us from running off that cliff.

The Bible

Many might recall one of the most significant blows to the belief in the Bible came from Charles Darwin's *Origin of the Species,* published in 1859. Another event, the Scopes (monkey) trial held on May 5, 1925, brought Darwin's theory of evolution head to head with the creation theory of the Bible.[3] We know it continues to be debated today, even as Darwin's theory may have become the majority view.

What is interesting about this theory is the fact that all of the species that supposedly evolved into something else still exist. Why didn't all of the species evolve if that theory was accurate?

Have you thought about that?

There is a scientific answer, of course, but it takes faith to follow their scientific reasoning.

Belief in the Bible has been on a steady trend downward. Now, we have taken down the Ten Commandments, we have taken prayer out of the classroom, and many want to sue those who want to do otherwise. This would have been outrageous to our forefathers, who regularly called on days of prayer and fasting for the sake of our country.

George Washington

For instance, George Washington is said to have been responsible for the following prayer, written at Newburgh, New York on June 14, 1783, at the end of the Revolutionary War. It was circulated to 13 governors of the freed states:

> *I now make it my earnest prayer that God would have you, and the State over which you preside, in his holy protection; that he would incline the hearts of the citizens to cultivate a spirit of subordination and obedience to government, to entertain a brotherly affection and love for one another, for their fellow-citizens of the United States at large, and particularly for brethren who have served in the field; and finally that he would most graciously be pleased to dispose us all to do justice, to love mercy, and to demean ourselves with that charity, humility, and pacific temper of mind, which were the characteristics of the Divine Author of our blessed religion, and without an humble imitation of whose example in these things, we can never hope to be a happy nation.*[4]

I don't have time to mention the plethora of evidence that proves the United States' Christian roots, but we were founded upon the Bible as a Christian nation. While Governor Rick Perry dropped out of the 2012 republican presidential race, what he did by calling for a day of prayer and fasting is consistent with our roots. Playing "Amazing Grace" several times on the ten-year anniversary of 9/11 was also consistent. "Amazing Grace" is a Christian song about God's love for His people as expressed through the sacrifice of His Son, Jesus Christ, who *saved* a wretch like you and I — as believers:

> *Amazing Grace, how sweet the sound, that saved a wretch like me. I once was lost, but now am found, was blind, but now I see.*

Can we wholeheartedly admit we have gotten to the place where we are more comforted by tradition than truth?

Really?

Even when the new normal is children shooting other children in school at the same time the Bible has been dismissed, the Ten Commandments removed, and prayer in the classroom has ceased?

Please. I beg you – think.

Who are we going to follow?

Satan has created confusion, fuss, doubt, and antagonism over the Bible and its content. Having successfully accomplished that task, he has then been able to turn what God intended for good — sex, in this case — into something that we intend for sport or feelings. But, Satan is a liar. And our feelings, although they do matter, are not the point. God is! And God is purposeful. Sex has a purpose of creation, but it is also meant for pleasure. Food has a purpose — fuel for our bodies — but is also meant for pleasure. So, while God is interested in our feelings, these feelings must be balanced with God's boundaries and purposes. Satan wants us to follow our feelings without regard to God or His purposes. When we do, we are following our foe — just like Adam and Eve:

> *You belong to your father, the devil, and you want to carry out your father's desires. He was a murderer from the beginning, not holding to the truth, for there is no truth in him. When he lies, he speaks his native language, for he is a liar and the father of lies (John 8:44).*

"Eve was deceived by the serpent's cunning" — she followed Satan.[5] As challenging as this might be to believe, when we are not following God through His Word, we are following Satan, like Eve, even if implicitly. The result is that Satan ruins the lives God gave us, even if we only find out to what extent upon our physical death. He is so subtle that we are often caught in our sin before we even know what hit us.

Jonah 2:8

We forfeit grace by turning our backs on God as we pursue a worldly life. Although Jonah may have had an ulterior reason for saying this, what he said is true nonetheless:

> *"Those who cling to worthless idols forfeit the grace that could be theirs" (Jonah 2:8).*

When we cling to worthless idols, we sacrifice grace or God's best. While many of us continue to think God is preventing us from having a life, God is always the one trying to protect and bless the life that He has given us. Our own ignorance and stubbornness prevent us from the best life. We let Satan convince us that what God intended for good isn't good enough. Steven Tyler told Matt Lauer in an interview on *Dateline* that drugs lead to death, jail, and insanity. He emphasized it was a one-way street to destruction, even though he liked the ride.[6] Sin is often fun, just before it destroys us. We don't need to "dance with the devil," as Tyler remarked to an American Idol contestant. We need to dance with God.

I hope you dance

Years ago, I heard someone at my church sing the song "I Hope You Dance," by Lee Ann Womack. The lyrics to that song reminded me of something I was told years earlier: "Most men die with their dreams still in them." I remember the fear I felt hearing that. At the time, I was settling for second best. I was getting comfortable with mediocrity. While almost breaking out in tears as I heard the song, I recommitted myself to the dreams I had deep in my heart. These were the ones that required patient endurance, despite how long they might take to achieve. These are the ones that require absolute trust in God.

For me, that meant moving into the inner city and living among the poor at the expense of my safety and comfort. It meant patiently waiting on God to bring me the woman of my dreams, rather than taking matters into my own hands. And it still applies. More recently, it meant participating in an event I once thought impossible, an Ironman triathlon — which I successfully completed three times with my wife. This is what many people are forfeiting by their pursuit of their own way when it is contrary to God's. God says:

> *"Listen, you foolish and senseless people, with eyes that do not see and ears that do not hear. Have you no respect for me? Why don't you tremble in my presence? I, the Lord, define the ocean's sandy shoreline as an everlasting boundary that the waters cannot cross. The waves may toss and roar, but they can never pass the boundaries I set. But my people have stubborn and rebellious hearts. They have turned away and abandoned me. They do not say from the heart, 'Let us live in awe of the Lord our God, for he gives us rain each spring and fall, assuring us of a harvest when the time is right.' Your wickedness has deprived you of these wonderful blessings. Your sin has*

robbed you of all these good things" (Jeremiah 5:21–25).

God intended things for good, and they are, as long as we keep God first. God is the source of our true joy. Satan manipulates us to think those good things are the source of our joy rather than God. The good things then are turned into destructive behavior as we turn to comfort over purpose.

I did a search on Barry Dickel, my former boss from Bahia Marina in Ocean City, Maryland. Barry's mom died a few days ago. As a result, at the top of the Google page, was the obituary. I read it. It said that a Barry Dickel and Erik Dickel (Barry's son) were previously deceased. I did a search on Mark Sampson, who I worked with at the Marina. He confirmed Barry and Erik had died; Barry of cancer, and Erik drank himself to death. Only Barry's wife, Carol, remains. My urgency just went up for the lost. I sent an email to Phil saying I wanted to buy those three houses he is selling next to our property at Hoskins Park. I am signing the contract as soon as I can. (Author's journal entry, April 11, 2005)

I want to live my life for a purpose — God's purpose.

Don't you?

> *⁹ I took you from the ends of the earth, from its farthest corners I called you. I said, 'You are my servant'; I have chosen you and have not rejected you.¹⁰ So do not fear, for I am with you; do not be dismayed, for I am your God. I will strengthen you and help you; I will uphold you with my righteous right hand.¹¹ "All who rage against you will surely be ashamed and disgraced; those who oppose you will be as nothing and perish. ¹² Though you search for your enemies, you will not find them. Those who wage war against you will be as nothing at all.¹³ For I am the Lord your God who takes hold of your right hand and says to you, Do not fear; I will help you (Isaiah 41:9-13).*

Footnotes

1 Wikipedia, Boiling frog. This theory is contested by contemporary research while previous experiments appeared to support its theory if the heating was suitably gradual.

2 http://www.joemygod.blogspot.com/2012/05/north-carolina-baptist-preacher-calls.html.

3 Wikipedia, Scopes Trial.

4 Ushistory.org, Historic Valley Forge, Washington's "Earnest Prayer."

5 2 Corinthians 11:3.

6 I heard this myself on Dateline.

— CHAPTER 11 —

COMPROMISE — IT'S EASIER!

"Reverend Wheeler?" the man from a local unknown and un-named organization asked me.

"Yes, this is Tom Wheeler," I replied.

"I have some good news for you! I represent an organization of men that supports local non-profits, and we have selected Hoskins Park as the organization we want to raise money for this year," he went on.

"That is great!" I responded with the expected enthusiasm. We are always out of money. We particularly needed it when I received his call.

"Our fund raiser is going to be at a Halloween party we are sponsoring," he added, excited to be able to help.

"Halloween?" I replied, a bit surprised.

"Yeah, Halloween," he said again.

"Tell me more about it," I said.

"We are having a costume Halloween party, and the proceeds are going to benefit you," he said. The excitement now turned to a dampened curiosity.

"Well," I said, knowing I needed to say this as gracefully as possible. "As much as I appreciate you wanting to support us, I am going to have to decline your offer. Nothing personal, but we won't be able to accept your offer since Halloween is not a holiday we celebrate." I spoke with sadness, because we needed the money so much.

"What do you mean?" he asked. "We want to help you financially and you are saying no, because it's Halloween? What's wrong with Halloween? Are you judging all of us because we don't boycott a holiday you don't believe in?" He was offended.

"I am really sorry," I replied. "I am not judging you or anyone, but Halloween is not a celebration we honor at Hoskins Park, even though we appreciate your desire to help. I hope you can respect our decision whether you understand it or not." He hung up without a response. He didn't understand the reality of Satan and what happens in the inner city on Halloween.

> They were just trying to intimidate us, imagining that they could discourage us and stop the work. So I continued the work with even greater determination (Nehemiah 6:9, NLT).

Take the easy way out

Another tactic of the devil is to tempt us from our purpose by promoting the easy way out. A good example of this tactic is found in a story about someone unknown to most of us, Lyn Brooks of Baltimore, Maryland. She competed in the 1998 Kona Ironman Triathlon.[1] This event includes a 2.4-mile ocean swim, 112-mile bike ride, and a 26.2-mile run. Lyn was featured on an NBC program where she shared how that year, during the final marathon leg of the race, she was so tired she left the race, entered an aid tent because her body was aching, and she wanted to quit. In the tent was a man relaxing, drinking an ice-cold beer. Apparently, reading her thoughts, he said, "All you have to do is drop out of the race like me." She said, "Suddenly, I realized he represented the devil." She left the aid tent and reentered the race. Reflecting on the moment, her eyes filled with tears. "It was the hardest, and most glorious, day of my life."[2]

Satan's tactic?

Just quit and be done with the pain.

We live to regret choices like that. Comfort is not what we really want deep down (although we all like it in balance). We want to know that our lives have meaning or purpose. That means we have to sacrifice comfort, at least the hedonistic kind:

*That lesson isn't taught enough, and too many people
never realize that sacrifice is a requirement of life. You
either sacrifice today to reach tomorrow's goals, or you
give up your dreams in favor of the fleeting comfort that's
distracting you. The pleasant reality, for those who choose
the former, is that comfort is abundant when long-term
goals are achieved.*[3]

The comfort we so desire is fulfilling the purpose God has for us on
earth. This comes at the expense of the daily comforts of life without
compromising our God-given character.

Don't compromise

Years ago, I watched the show *Survivor* when Matt and "Boston" Rob
played. Matt was a Christian struggling with his faith, as he competed for
the million-dollar prize. While he wanted to win the money, his priorities
were divided because of his faith. I didn't watch enough episodes to
see how true he was to his convictions, but — based upon what I did
see — he appeared to choose God over money. He wouldn't sacrifice
his character to win. Rob, on the other hand, had one goal — to win
the million dollars. He had learned, from previous experience as a
contestant, how to play the game, and he put all morality, ethics, and
honor on the line as he manipulated his way to victory. All he had to do
was convince a few of the participants to sincerely believe that he had
their best interests in mind in order to have a shot at winning, which is
what he did. At the end of the show, even before the game deciding
jury voted, it was obvious he had won. He was the most convincing liar.
It was brilliant strategy, but it cost him his character. To be fair, many of
the contestants let the million dollars dictate their morality and honor.
Rob was just better at it than the others. But that is compromise, and
great people don't compromise their character for the easy way out. It
is actually their courage to stay the course that shows the depth of their
character, even to the point of death. Since truth is now up for debate,
we are a compromised culture. We need to return to the nation of people
that believes in Christianity, despite the consequences of doing so:

*We have come to share in Christ if we hold firmly till the
end the confidence we had at first (Hebrews 3:14).*

Make sin to be of no consequence

God is not happy about our culture's condoning of immoral behavior. Here is a scripture I have never heard in church, but it is clearly an angry God speaking to this issue:

> *"I've got something to say. Is anybody listening? I've a warning to post. Will anyone notice? It's hopeless! Their ears are stuffed with wax — deaf as a post, blind as a bat. It's hopeless! They've tuned out God. They don't want to hear from me. But I'm bursting with the wrath of God. I can't hold it in much longer. 'So dump it on the children in the streets. Let it loose on the gangs of youth. For no one's exempt: Husbands and wives will be taken, the old and those ready to die; their homes will be given away—all they own, even their loved ones—When I give the signal against all who live in this country." God's Decree. "Everyone's after the dishonest dollar, little people and big people alike. Prophets and priests and everyone in between twist words and doctor truth. My people are broken—shattered!— and they put on Band-Aids, Saying, 'It's not so bad. You'll be just fine.' But things are not 'just fine'! Do you suppose they are embarrassed over this outrage? No, they have no shame. They don't even know how to blush. There's no hope for them. They've hit bottom and there's no getting up. As far as I'm concerned, they're finished." God has spoken (Jeremiah 6:10-15, The Message).*

Sin has, as its consequences, a spiritual death — separation between God and us.[4] It also ruins our lives. Tiger Woods, Jesse James, and Arnold Schwarzenegger may not have done anything illegal by their adultery, but they all lost their most precious friend — their spouse. Their households became divided. Satan's tactic is for us to think it really doesn't matter what we do as long as it is legal, as long as we are comfortable, as long as we all just get along. That is the easy way out. It demands compromise. That method destroys truth, rather than unifying diversity through the truth.

One day, we will all find out the significance of our decisions.

Don't compromise.

Footnotes

1   Ironman Triathlon World Championship – Kona, Hawaii, USA, Results (swim 1:13:19).

2   http://www.bikesportmichigan.com/editorials/0000089.shtml.

3   Running Times, After the Last PR – A lifelong runner reflects on the virtues of living a runner's life, Dave Griffin, pg. 59.

4   Isaiah 59:2, Ephesians 2:1-3.

— CHAPTER 12 —

USE OUR PAST TO RUIN OUR FUTURE

W hen George finally gave up crack cocaine and committed to remain sexually pure, he got a temporary job. He had no idea this temporary job would take him next door to the house where he used to get high and be sexually active. After arriving at this house, shocking enough for him, the fellow who hired him left him alone. Outside of the window was a prostitute trying to make conversation with him. Then, while raking leaves out back, he found a bottle of crack cocaine. A voice in his head told him the girl could be his, but even if he didn't care, what would the harm be to just talk to her? And why not do some crack? Others get away with it at Hoskins Park, why not you? George flushed the drugs down the toilet. He ignored the prostitute without giving in to the tactics of the enemy. God was pleased with His son George.

> *Therefore, there is now no condemnation for those who are in Christ Jesus (Romans 8:1).*

Remind us of our past

Another tactic of Satan is to use our past to condemn our future. We deal with this often in the ministry, since most of our participants have felony records. This becomes a matter of faith:

> *Jesus looked at them and said, "With man this is impossible, but with God all things are possible" (Matthew 19:26).*

God will not let our past ruin our future.

But will we?

A good example of this is found in the character we know as Rocky.[1] In the original movie of the same name, Rocky Balboa (Sylvester Stallone) is a poor loan shark who gets a lucky break at the boxing heavyweight championship. He nearly wins because his challenger, Apollo Creed (Carl Weathers), underestimated him. There is a rematch in *Rocky II,* and Rocky beats Apollo by the skin of his teeth. The movie *Rocky III* begins with Rocky as a popular celebrity who had made it to the top. In past *Rocky* movies, he was a raw champion, dependent on his strength and ability to take a lot of hard punches from his opponents. Then he trimmed down, got cleaned up, and flaunted all the money he had made. As the movie goes, along comes another boxer called Clubber Lang (Mr. T.), destroying his opponents, and he becomes the number one contender to the heavyweight title.

You can't win, Rock!

Clubber was raw, strong, determined. He focused solely on the title. Meanwhile, Rocky's manager Mickey (Burgess Meredith) has been protecting Rocky from fighting Clubber because he didn't think Rocky could beat him. In fact, Mickey never mentioned him to Rocky. Finally, Clubber provoked Rocky in a public outing, and Rocky said he would see him in the ring.

They fought, and Rocky was badly defeated, just as Mickey warned before they agreed to the fight. Sadly, Mickey dies the same night. Rocky was at his lowest point when former opponent Apollo Creed mysteriously appeared at Rocky's gym. He revealed how Rocky could beat Clubber, and Rocky agrees to a rematch. But, while training, Rocky relived the severe knockout blow from his fight with Clubber, along with Mickey's death, and he was unable to train properly. In his mind, he kept hearing Mickey say, "You can't win, Rock." He believed *that* voice. Rocky's wife, Adrian (Talia Shire), confronted Rocky and got him to admit his fear of losing what he had: the cars, the house, the money. She convinced him that — win or lose — he needed to do his best without regard to those other things. That inspired him to train as Apollo suggested. Then, in Hollywood fashion, Rocky beat Clubber Lang in the rematch.

The enemy – Clubber Lang

Metaphorically, Clubber Lang represents Satan and we represent Rocky. For a season, our lives seem to work out according to our plan, just like Rocky. Once Rocky won the title, he settled into his new life and got comfortable just like many of us do. Then, along comes Clubber, who gave Rocky a beating he never expected and would never forget. That is what Satan does with us.

But, in our case, Clubber is disguised. Maybe he is disguised as an angry twenty-two-year-old with a gun and vendetta against politicians. Or maybe, he is disguised as a friend who offers us a drug to help us cope with life, or one more drink for the road. Perhaps, a new friend makes a subtle suggestion that we do something that deep down we know is wrong, like have an affair or sexually promiscuous relationship. Sometimes, he comes disguised as an abusive parent or spouse. Worse, perhaps he "masquerades as an angel of light" (2 Corinthians 11:14). Regardless of our ability to understand how or where or by whom Satan hits us, the carnage from his attacks can be identified. We may see his handiwork through:

- a divorce
- a lost job
- an addiction
- a health problem
- a wayward child
- a foreclosure
- a lost loved one
- bankruptcy
- or a set of other life changing circumstances.

Clearly, he won *that round*. Then along comes Apollo Creed.

Receive help

While we know Apollo as an acquaintance, we don't know him well — up close and personal. But he seems to know us. He tells us we can beat our adversary in a rematch. He tells us we can win our title back, if we do what he says. While Apollo is a poor representative of God in this metaphor, God knows how beat-up we are in life. He knows we have entered the ring alone with Satan one too many times. But He continues to remind us that He wants to train us — His way. He tells us He can use our past to benefit our future:

> And we know that in all things God works for the good of those who love him, who have been called according to his purpose (Romans 8:28).

We just need to receive His help and keep our eyes looking forward in life, rather than in the rear-view mirror.

You aren't what you did way back when; you are what you do now, today.

Rocky's wife, Adrian, might represent a good friend who we trust to confront us when we get discouraged, afraid, or off-track. A person like this can remind us that we can win again. Once Rocky committed to the rematch, believed he could win, and allowed Apollo to train him, he won back the title. Once we commit to a rematch with our God-given life, believe we can win, and allow God to train us His way, we will rise from the ashes and soar like eagles:

> But those who trust in the LORD will find new strength. They will soar high on wings like eagles. They will run and not grow weary. They will walk and not faint (Isaiah 40:31, NLT).

Entice our flesh

But Satan will not let us go without a fight. He will use any means necessary to get us back into the ring alone, without God. An old favorite tactic of Satan is to use our past to hurt our present. That is likely why people do not admit past mistakes — because someone will usually put it back in their face at some point in their future. We are a judgmental and unforgiving people — many Christians included. Once we are reminded of what we did in the past, Satan then dangles the perfect carrot before our eyes, at the perfect time, trying to lure us away from God. This is irrespective of whether we are successfully overcoming our past or not. Satan knows our weak spots, and he will put multiple temptations in front of us to keep us from living the best life possible. Satan uses temptation to hook us, like we use a lure to catch fish. A lure is an imitation. But, to a fish, it is pleasing to the eye. It looks like the real thing. The fish takes the bait, thinking it will satisfy the need, and typically finds out too late that the lure just made things worse.

Sin may look pleasing to the eye, even taste and feel good, but it ultimately kills us. The Bible says we need to resist Satan's lures and keep our focus on God and His plan for our lives.

Is there something in your past that is getting in the way of your future?

Are you still playing that old tape in your mind?

Let it go.

Yesterday is gone.

You've got today.

Let God be your new coach.

A way out

While my aforementioned friend George was being tempted, he felt like he was physically pushed. Coinciding with that feeling was a clear reminder of the results of his past drug use. He felt like God did that to keep him from going back to his old ways — God provided a way out:

> God is faithful; he will not let you be tempted beyond what you can bear. But when you are tempted, he will also provide a way out so that you can endure it (1 Corinthians 10:13).

While the enemy tempts us to follow our past, God gives us a way out for the sake of our future. We just need to constantly choose God's way over Satan's. That means never getting in the ring with Satan alone, even when he reminds us of our past mistakes.

The devil

I would be remiss if I did not clarify Satan's need to report to God before he can impact a person's life. We are reminded that before Satan could attack Job, he first spoke with God:

> "You have blessed the work of his hands, so that his flocks and herds are spread throughout the land. But now stretch

out your hand and strike everything he has, and he will
surely curse you to your face." The LORD said to Satan,
"Very well, then, everything he has is in your power, but on
the man himself do not lay a finger." Then Satan went out
from the presence of the LORD (Job 1:11–12).

The same is true with Simon Peter. Jesus told Peter that Satan had asked if he could challenge his faith:

"Simon, Simon, Satan has asked to sift you as wheat" (Luke
22:31).

God uses Satan as an instrument to turn us back to Him, our Creator. Remember, our ways are not His and vice versa. Those, who write off God because of what they perceive He allowed or even initiated, do not understand the issue that is at stake — our eternity. Satan is a thief who wants to ruin us; God is our rescuer who has our best interests in mind:

[Satan] comes only to steal and kill and destroy; [God has]
come that they may have life, and have it to the full (John
10:10).

As long as we draw near to God, the devil will flee:

Submit yourselves, then, to God. Resist the devil, and he
will flee from you (James 4:7).

God is in us, as believers, and greater is He that is in me,
than he that is in the world (1 John 4:4).

But, is it still our choice?

So, how do we fight this battle? How can we move from pursuing a victory in our own strength to letting God and His people guide us to victory? Let's find out.

Footnotes

1   Stallone, Sylvester, perf. Rocky. Dir. John G. Avildsen. United Artists, 1976.

— CHAPTER 13 —

IN THE DESERT AND THIRSTY

Some wandered in the wilderness, lost and homeless.
Hungry and thirsty, they nearly died. "Lord, help!" they cried
in their trouble, and he rescued them from their distress
(Psalm 107:4-6).

There are over 750,000 homeless people on any given night in the United States of America. About 8,000 of those are in Charlotte, North Carolina.[1] While homelessness does not always equate to its preconceived connotations, it does represent a good percentage of those who are on the bottom. There are also approximately 3.6 million addicts in the US — substance abuse addicts only; many more of us are addicted to something other than substance abuse. There are millions who are judged, shamed, displaced, discriminated against, abused, defamed, or who have just been beaten down by life. On any given night, Hoskins Park Ministries takes care of over sixty previously homeless men in Charlotte, North Carolina. These are men who are on the bottom and who have finally figured out the answer to their problems start by looking up. People needing a second wind and finding one — in God.

If you listen to these commands of the Lord your God
that I am giving you today, and if you carefully obey them,
the Lord will make you the head and not the tail, and
you will always be on the top and never on the bottom
(Deuteronomy 28:13 - NLT).

While nearing my home late tonight having returned from another visit to see my dad in the hospital, a black Blazer flew past me at probably ninety mph followed by three or four police cars, sirens blaring. The Blazer crashed ahead near my house and I saw the driver fleeing from the police. I am now inside my house with helicopters overhead searching the area as I unpack. On the news, they say he is a murder suspect. Welcome home! (Author's journal entry, May 11, 2004)

God is making his appeal through us. We speak for Christ when we plead, "Come back to God!" (2 Corinthians 5:20, NLT)

Desperate!

While we have an enemy whose purpose is to destroy us, using the aforementioned tactics, we have a God whose desire is to rescue us. We just have to ask for His help. That reminds me of my fraternity initiation years ago and how desperate I was to get out of what is referred to as "Hell" week. I, along with the other pledges, was put through the typical hardships of constant, hard, meaningless work, along with sleep deprivation, often part of an initiation process. During the last phase, we had to endure some sort of traditional ritual. No longer did we have to work. Even worse, we had to endure boredom. We were required to stare at candles without flinching while listening to "Bolero."[2] If you dozed off while staring at your respective candle, there was an always-watching fraternity brother who would snap his fingers in your ears to awaken you. While gazing at my candle, I noticed that the brothers in the room seemed concerned for our safety. So, although I was fine, I decided to see what would happen if I acted like I was "flipping out." I started shaking and twitching while continuing to look at the candle. The next thing I knew, I was out of that room. I thought I was the coolest person to be able to get one over on these smart, older, fraternity brothers! But it wasn't over.

Help!

Now blindfolded, I was led to another part of the house with just enough candlelight to know it wasn't pitch-dark. In addition, all the stereo speakers in the house were cranked up as loud as they could go on the static channels of the radio. For hours upon hours, I baby stepped around in the dark listening to static until I finally could not take it anymore. At that point, I physically reached out my hand in the darkness, pleading for someone to take it, and someone did. The initiation was over. Although I do not think I was in an "initiation process" with God, because His ways are not our ways, I had that same type of desperation when I extended my hand and heart out to Him. He may have always been with me, just like in the initiation process where a brother was always present. But, until I cried out to Him, He let me do my own thing. I believe any initiation process that I had with God was created by my own choices in life. God is who I wanted all along, but until I was desperate, I ignored my need for Him or my desire to know who He was:

> I lift up my eyes to the hills — where does my help come from? My help comes from the Lord, the Maker of heaven and earth (Psalm 121:1–2).

The enemy's purpose was to destroy me.

All the while there was a God trying to rescue me.

I just had to believe — in Him.

You just have to believe, too.

Alive[3]

Another example of the desperation for a second wind is the true story of an airplane crash in 1972. The Uruguay rugby team was flying to Chile to play in a game when their plane crashed in the Andes. For seventy-two days, survivors struggled to stay alive despite incredibly difficult odds. Miraculously, however, sixteen of the original forty-five were rescued. What is interesting about this story, besides the fact that they had to cannibalize the flesh of the dead in order to survive, was the drastic contrast between the start of the movie and its end. At the beginning of the journey, the team is confidently tossing the football around the cabin, laughing and joking while the captain of the plane periodically asked everyone to stay seated for safety reasons, to no avail. Then something changed. The plane hits an air pocket and takes an immediate and dramatic drop in altitude, catching them all off guard.

The laughter and jokes stop for a moment as a little fear creeps into the minds of all those aboard as they remember they are in an airplane, and airplanes have been known to crash. At this point, some listen and take their seats, while others write off the drop as an anomaly and continue as they were. It happens again. This time, most of the kids take their seats, knowing something is wrong. A few remain optimistic.

Finding God

Within moments of the initial drop, the airplane hits a peak of the Andes and splits in two. The teammates in the front portion of the plane watch the lower half of the plane and those seated in the rows from the wing to the tail disappear into the freezing cold atmosphere of the Andes. The folks in the front of the plane are now clinging to their seats as the airplane rockets down to the snowy ground at Mach speed. The plane miraculously lands in the snow. Fun and confidence turned into fear, then fear became shock. Days later, on the small radio the survivors hear that the search for their rescue is called off by the local authorities. Their shock turns into despair. More time goes by. Then the despair turns into resilience as the survivors attempt their own rescue plan. By the end of the movie, there is very little laughter, but great joy as sixteen are miraculously rescued. They had survived an airplane crash, starvation, an avalanche, and freezing temperatures. Furthermore, where there previously was no discussion of God at the beginning of the flight when these strong, young athletes were headed to do what they did best, by the end of the movie, many of those who had survived the ordeal seemed to either know God or have a totally different outlook of Him. Everything that had blocked them from hearing God, or even giving Him the consideration He deserved in their comfortable lives before the accident — including the busyness of daily life — was taken away. They had nothing left but God. While living comfortably, we may ignore the realities of life, death, disaster, God, and pain (ours or others), but we might be doing so at the expense of knowing God, of living life as He intended.

Present-day reality

Japan witnessed the worst earthquake in its history in 2011. It hit a couple hundred miles off shore, and sent shock waves throughout the country. Worse, the resulting tsunami wave hit the island so fast (some reports say the waves were traveling at 500 mph) that ships and buildings were sent floating downstream upside down like cars. Thousands of people died, hundreds of thousands were left homeless, and millions lost power. And a nuclear meltdown haunted them, even as they began to dig themselves out of the rubble. China dealt with flooding that displaced five million people in 2011.[4] At the same time, the Libyan dictator, Muammar Gaddafi, began killing civilians unhappy with his oppressive style of governing, causing the US to take military action against yet another country. That is despite the fact we, the US, were bankrupt, for all practical purposes. Syrian President Bashar Assad is doing likewise, killing rebels in order to maintain power while the world tries to figure out what to do. America has been hit with incredible numbers of tornadoes, flooding, droughts, forest fires, and other natural disasters that might cause us all to pause. And then, there is the reality of our own lives.

Has your life *really* worked out as you expected it to?

Really?

We need to be rescued

So, while we might take the bait and think this discussion of a war is hard to believe or even silly, perhaps we are not looking carefully enough at the facts that we deal with every day. You and I live in a hard world. We all deal with its harsh reality, even if we do so with an optimistic attitude. We are at war and the devil is real. He is tactical. We need to be rescued. Our part is to cry out to God. He promises to rescue us, despite what we may have done in our lives:

> He turned to me and heard my cry. He lifted me out of the slimy pit, out of the mud and mire; he set my feet on a rock and gave me a firm place to stand. He put a new song in my mouth, a hymn of praise to our God (Psalm 40:1–3).

A second wind works. Finding victory works. Receiving a rescue works.

I know, because God rescued me.

So, how about you?

Do you need to be rescued? Are you willing to be rescued?

Footnotes

1 http://charlotteareanews.blogspot.com/2009/11/way-home-hosts-fifth-annual-hope-for.html.

2 http://www.last.fm/music/Maurice+Ravel/_/Bolero.

3 Alive. Dir. Frank Marshall. Paramount Pictures, 1993.

4 CNN, 6:42 pm, EST. Live report.

— PART THREE —

WHERE IS MY HELP?

US Air Force Capt. Scott O'Grady
was shot down over Bosnia in 1995
and found himself behind enemy
lines. When he was finally rescued
they asked him how he managed to
survive. His answer was enlightening
as he said:

"God, period, dot."

— CHAPTER 14 —

GOD IS IN CONTROL

M y elderly friend, Mrs. James, woke me up at 6:30 a.m., wondering how my back and throat were doing. Having taken a couple Vioxx (nonsteroidal anti-inflammatory drug — NSAID), I told her I felt great as I hung up, drifting back to sleep so that I wouldn't be telling her a story. Then Luci (my rescued street dog) stuck her nose in my face, her usual whining forcing me to get up and let her out on a leash or suffer the consequences. When I got out of the shower, I looked outside to see how Luci was doing; she was tearing my newspaper up in the front yard. It was her newest trick, slashing it from side to side as fast and hard as possible, as if to completely shred it. I looked across the street and saw my neighbor pacing in his yard with a rifle in his hand. I wasn't sure if I should open the door and tell Luci to stop shredding the paper or ask my neighbor what he was doing with that gun. I opened the door and asked Luci to stop, grabbed my paper, ignored the gun in my neighbors hand, waved, and came inside thinking I was either crazy or everyone else was. *(Author's journal entry, March, 2004)*

"The shelter has accepted your resignation letter," Bill told me after he had turned in a letter I wrote that I had not wanted submitted unless necessary.

"Bill," I said, "I didn't give you that letter to resign, I gave it to you so they could see that I would resign if that is what they really wanted, knowing I had complied with their demands."

"Well, they accepted it," said Bill.

That was my last day of employment at the Uptown Men's Shelter after approximately one year. Because my church had affirmed my call to work at the shelter and because the staff that had known me had been replaced, they were unable to continue their financial support. I was now without a job, and I lived in the inner city of Charlotte without any means of support. The result? Hoskins Park Ministries was birthed November 19, 2002, under an umbrella company, the National Heritage Foundation. God then brought one man to help with its finances. It has been growing ever since.

> *The LORD Almighty has sworn, "Surely, as I have planned, so it will be, and as I have purposed, so it will stand" (Isaiah 14:24).*

Who is God?

Statistics indicate that over 90 percent of us say we believe in God. But most of us don't know who this God really is. Many people think of God as a mean, control freak. Others consider God to be some mysterious force or entity that set the world in motion and then disappeared. He may show Himself from time to time, but otherwise, He is mysteriously absent. Still, others think God is everywhere, in everything, inside of all of us. A final group considers God as a God of love without regard to His holiness. In other words, anything goes. While it may be true that most people do chose one of these four alternatives,[1] none of them is completely Biblical. God is not a mean control freak, although He is in control. Nor is He a powerless nothing, although He does allow us free will. Although God is omnipresent, He is not in everything either. And while it is true that God loves us, He does so while being true to His other characteristics as well, including His holiness. The truth is God is a perfectly loving heavenly Father. That is why the Lord's Prayer begins with "Our Father, who art in heaven." As a Father He wants to have an intimate relationship with all of us. But again, that is not how most people think of Him.

God is completely in control

While God maintains control of His universe, He is not a despot who dictates what we wear, eat, think and do, as was depicted in the movie *The Truman Show*.[2] In this movie, the main character, Truman (Jim Carrey), is born into a 24/7 live television studio setting. Without his knowledge, he is an actor in a manmade show directed by a fellow whose name is Christof. Christof (Ed Harris) is managing every detail of Truman's life from the day he is born to the day he is married and all details in between. All of it is fiction, including his wife (also playing a role). The only person who doesn't know what is going on is Truman. That is, until Truman figures out something is wrong — and succeeds in breaking out. The movie ends with Truman confronting Christof and breaking away from the control that he had imposed on his life. That is the kind of dictator many consider God, perhaps even the producer of the movie. They believe God is controlling or trying to control our lives, so we never really have a life. But again, that is not the God of the Holy Bible.

Not a dictator

This misunderstanding is implied in a parable about a master and his servant, often referred to as the Parable of the Talents.[3] In this story, the master goes on a journey and entrusts his servants with his wealth. How they deal with the talents is a statement of faith about their master. The first servant receives five bags of gold from his master, invests them, and makes five more. The second servant did the same with two bags of gold — he doubled his share to four. The third servant took his one bag of gold and buried it. When the master returned, he praised the two servants who doubled his investment, while rebuking the servant who buried his gold because of his excuses. It was all about how they understood their master's character. Rather than knowing his master to be a trusting man who gave him one of his talents to look after, like the first two servants, the third servant assumed the master to be "a hard man" who was unethical. The parable implies that the third servant was "just talking," rather than understanding his responsibility for his master's talent. It was just an excuse for the servant to do as he pleased. This might be better understood as an employee/employer relationship as we understand it today, keeping it in context, or a parent/child relationship. The big point is the servant (employee or child) was judging the master (employer or parent) unfairly, not the reverse. We need to get a right view of God — from the Bible — not from opinions.

God is the one rescuing us.

God is not the one harming us.

God is not pushing us to do things for Him that are not also best for us.

Footnotes

1 Neue magazine, June/July 2011, The Four Views of God, pg. 16.

2 Carrey, Jim, perf. The Truman Show. Dir. Peter Weir, Paramount Pictures, 1998.

3 Matthew 25:14-30.

— CHAPTER 15 —

CONTROL AND OUR INTERESTS

I t was probably the thousandth time I had to ask Seth to do something that he would not or did not do. This time, I verbally began to push him. As I did, he began pacing back and forth in the small kitchen of the house where we both lived, visibly upset. I could feel my anger rising as my patience ran out. The increasing volume of my voice was only making matters worse. Frustrated, but knowing nothing was working, I left the kitchen and went to my room. I got on my knees and begged God to help me with Seth. What I did not know was Seth had followed me and was watching me. After that incident, things were different. I had no idea why. Seth watched me walk away from him that evening and go to God on his behalf, rather than kick him out of my home. Although that moment was one of the most challenging moments of my ministry to that point, I finally started to understand it was not that I was helping Seth as much as Seth was teaching me how to love God by loving him. God had both Seth's and my best interests in mind through that trial. Seth did what I asked from then on, at least to the point he was able. *(Author's journal entry, December 14, 2002)*

Jonathan threatened suicide, so we took him to mental health about 10 p.m. tonight. He is nineteen, but addicted to alcohol and hanging out with the wrong people, other drug addicts. He cannot control the drinking, but he can control his friends. We are exploring other options for him. We also want to talk to his parole officer. On another note, I talked with Lester who has been out drinking lately. We are advising him to go the Charlotte Rescue Mission or another Christian drug/alcohol treatment facility. Things are good otherwise. I am broke though. But God is in control. *(Author's journal entry, November 21, 2004)*

"Return to me, and I will return to you" (Malachi 3:7).

Powerless nothing?

God is not a powerless nothing.

I would imagine most of the people who believe in God think He is mysteriously absent from the details of their lives or disinterested. Every now and again He might wake up and see the immorality on the earth and do something about it. He may rescue us from a potential accident or solve a health problem, but most of the time, we are on our own. I imagine most envision God just napping or taking notes. I think that belief system justifies itself by the suffering seen in the world, like the tsunamis that hit Indonesia and Japan, or because of the suffering in our own lives. Many who share this view, think if God were active and interested, He would stop those things from happening. That thought crosses my mind from time to time when I deal with the harsh reality of life. A tactic of Satan is us blaming God for the abuses in the world.

We have not been abandoned

If you think about it, how could God possibly be sleeping at the wheel? Does any car drive itself without some form of intelligence driving it? Has anything been built without someone building it? Do you get in shape by going to the gym and watching others exercise? There is not one example or person I know of where one is able to build, develop, or control something without intimate participation. Why would we think it possible in the universe? So, while we still might assume that we have been left alone to fend for ourselves, that assumption might be one of the most unintelligent made. God is in control.

The miraculousness of creation

Much of the proof is in creation, something we can remember every day of our lives. Besides the fact that you and I are alive, we are currently spinning at roughly 1,000 mph on planet earth as it rockets through space at 67,000 mph in the sun's orbit.[1] Although scientists call what keeps us on the planet during this roller coaster ride through space "gravity," they still do not understand how it works, though they can describe it.[2] Additionally, the universe is so large that it takes light 100,000 years going 656,215,200 mph to traverse our Milky Way galaxy, and our galaxy is just one of billions in the universe.[3] To say the universe is really big, just doesn't quite do it justice. We cannot fully explain how a huge ball of fire, the sun, lights and heats the earth at some 27 million degrees Fahrenheit at its core, without burning out.[4] Nor can we explain the birth of a child from its mother's womb.

Some things just need to be left to God. Faith is required from all of us. And the Bible agrees. If we really think about life, deep down, we all know there is a God who is in control:

> For since the creation of the world God's invisible qualities—his eternal power and divine nature—have been clearly seen, being understood from what has been made, so that men are without excuse (Romans 1:20).

From dust to us

We, too, are part of His divine creation; God made us from dust:

> The LORD God formed the man from the dust of the ground and breathed into his nostrils the breath of life, and the man became a living being (Genesis 2:7).

Factually speaking, our body composition is made up of dust. Dust is made up of atoms, and our physical bodies are just a bunch of atoms stuck together.[5] Only when compacted do atoms become visible matter. For instance, over one billion atoms can fit on the top of a pin. While we cannot see an individual atom, they are still mass, just invisible to the human eye. Air is made up of atoms too, which is why you and I can feel the air, particularly when it blows.[6] Bottom line — God made you and I using dust, lots of dust, just like the Bible says.

How else did you and I get here?

We certainly didn't think ourselves into existence.

Did we?

God knows us

The Bible also says that God knew us before we were physically born. Then He knit each of us together in our mother's womb, ordaining all of our days before one of them came to pass:

> "Before I formed you in the womb I knew you, before you were born I set you apart" (Jeremiah 1:5).

That is why most Christians believe abortion is wrong. We aren't thinking of life from just a physical perspective; we are thinking of life from a godly one. Specific verses from Psalm 139 underscore my point:

> O LORD, you have searched me and you know me. You know when I sit and when I rise; you perceive my thoughts from afar. You discern my going out and my lying down; you are familiar with all my ways. For you created my inmost being; you knit me together in my mother's womb. I praise you because I am fearfully and wonderfully made; your works are wonderful, I know that full well. My frame was not hidden from you when I was made in the secret place. When I was woven together in the depths of the earth, your eyes saw my unformed body. All the days ordained for me were written in your book before one of them came to be (Psalm 139:1–3, 13–16).

How could God possibly know us before birth, knit us together in our mother's womb, and ordain our life before we existed, if He was a powerless nothing? He could not. This is but one of thousands of examples of God's control as found in the Bible. In fact, the Bible starts off making it clear that He is in charge, as it says, "In the beginning God." It goes on to give God credit for all of creation. Perhaps, that is why the word *history* is made up of two words, *his* and *story* — or His story. The words "The Lord says" are used 3,800 times throughout the Bible as well. Therefore, we know God is actively involved in creation. He is also intimately involved in the lives of His people.

God is intimately involved

Take Noah. It says God "said to Noah" what He was going to do to the people, why He was going to do it, and what He wanted Noah to do for Him: "and Noah did all that the Lord commanded him" (Genesis

7:5). Another example of God being in relationship with His people is Abraham, the father of Judaism, Christianity, and Islam. The Bible says:

> The Lord had said to Abram, "Leave your country, your people and your father's household and go to the land I will show you" (Genesis 12:1).

Eventually, God renamed Abram *Abraham* — meaning "father of many nations" (Genesis 17:4). Abraham had a son when he was one hundred years old and when his wife Sarai was ninety. Abraham became the father of many nations. All through the Book of Genesis, God is intimately involved and in control. Then we come to the next book in the Bible, Exodus, and the story of Moses. Most people know that God met Moses at the burning bush. Most of us also know that God sent Moses to rescue His people from oppressive slavery under the rule of Egypt's Pharaoh. Again, God was involved. The next book in the Bible is the Book of Leviticus, an instruction book or book of law, given by God to His people about how to live a godly life. The rest of the Old Testament continues to show God interacting historically with people and events in this same manner, under His control, using us, and for our good. In fact, God says we are like clay in the hand of the potter:

> "Like clay in the hand of the potter, so are you in my hand, O house of Israel. If at any time I announce that a nation or kingdom is to be uprooted, torn down and destroyed, and if that nation I warned repents of its evil, then I will relent and not inflict on it the disaster I had planned. And if at another time I announce that a nation or kingdom is to be built up and planted, and if it does evil in my sight and does not obey me, then I will reconsider the good I had intended to do for it" (Jeremiah 18:5–10).

These verses continue reminding us that God is more in control than most people think. The second half of the Bible, called the New Testament, is when God entered history as Jesus, giving us all the ability to have a personal relationship with God Himself.

My experiences

Incidents in my own life have helped convince me of God's control and involvement. Perhaps these will remind you of stories that you have experienced in your own life with God's fingerprints on them.

This story is about a good friend of mine from college whom I will call Ruth for the sake of the story. There was a song that I associated with Ruth. One day I was riding a stationary bike at the YMCA and I happened to look up at the silent television screen high up on the wall. It was asking what the number one song was back in the '80s. It gave three potential choices, one being the song that reminded me of Ruth. I laughed, said it was probably that song, and it was. So, I plugged in my headphones and listened to the song as I thought about my friend, who I had not seen or heard from in over ten years. When I got home, there was a message on my answering machine — from Ruth. She wanted to see me.

Born again

I agreed to meet her, and we ultimately ended up at a coffee shop together, without her husband. She explained to me that days before she had been praying and heard a voice in her head tell her to "find Tom Wheeler." That was all she heard. Her brother lived in the Charlotte area, and she knew that I did also, so she came to visit her brother. I asked her what was driving her need to see me, and she told me she and her husband were having marital trouble. The advice she was getting from everyone was to divorce him, while she remained reluctant. Then she prayed and my name came to mind. As soon as I understood her issue, I asked her if she had ever accepted Jesus Christ as her Lord and Savior. She said no. I shared the gospel with her. I then asked her if she wanted to invite Him into her heart and live for Him for the rest of her life. She said yes. So we prayed, and she asked Jesus to come into her heart. The Bible says:

> *Everyone who calls on the name of the Lord will be saved (Romans 10:13).*

Having become a born-again Christian changed everything. Once we trust in the God of the Holy Bible, we need to honor what the Bible says. The Bible is clear about the issues of divorce. It says that God hates divorce:

> *So guard yourself in your spirit, and do not break faith with the wife of your youth. "I hate divorce," says the LORD God*

of Israel (Malachi 2:15–16).

The only thing I have ever heard from her was that she stayed married and that our time together changed her life. That was it.

Now we all have to decide what really happened.

Coincidence? Many people will think so.

Telepathy? That was my dad's explanation.

God? That is my explanation.

My Creator had a plan. A plan for Ruth's life — personally and eternally. A plan to give her a second wind. And a plan to remind me of mine.

Zoom, zoom

This next event occurred on August 13, 2002, while I was driving home from Raleigh, North Carolina. I saw one of those big, black billboards that says (in large white letters), "We need to talk —God." Have you seen them? Well, you can't mistake them if you have.

I said to myself, "OK God, let's talk!" I started to complain about my life. It was the "What about me?" complaint. How I wanted to be married, have a family, etc., and here I am still single while doing what I believe the Lord has called me to do. I was going on and on and on … complaining. At that exact same moment, a car sped by me going about 90 mph. In the rear windshield of the car was "Luke 9:23" in very large print. You couldn't miss it, as it took up the entire back windshield. The timing was perfect with my thoughts and complaints to God. I stopped the car to read the scripture, since I had not memorized that verse from Luke: "If anyone would come after me, he must deny himself and take up his cross daily and follow me."

I laughed and said, "OK God, I get it." It meant I had to accept my life as it was, regardless of my complaints. So I did. Eventually God brought that special person into my life and we were married, but in His time, not mine. There are countless stories like that from my life. God's fingerprints are all over them.

That is true of all of us.

Whether we realize it or not.

Whether God ever gets the credit.

God is at work, showing His intimate involvement in our lives.

Soul surfer

The young life of thirteen year-old surfing star Bethany Hamilton is a good example of God's intimate involvement in the lives of His people today. A shark attacked her and took her entire left arm while she surfed in Hawaii. According to reports, she lost 60 percent of her blood before she got to the hospital and was not expected to live. Miraculously, she did. Here is what she says of this experience:

> *It was Jesus Christ who gave me peace when I was attacked by the shark. They had to get me to the beach, which took 20 minutes of paddling. "The peace of God, which transcends all understanding, will guard your hearts and your minds in Christ Jesus" (Philippians 4:6–8).*[7]

That is from a 13-year-old. According to the story, Bethany's youth leader, Sarah Hill, gave her this verse the same day as the attack:

> *"For I know the plans I have for you," declares the LORD, "plans to prosper you and not to harm you, plans to give you hope and a future" (Jeremiah 29:11).*[8]

That morning, through that scripture, God reminded Bethany that He had a plan for her life. Some will still question why God allowed this to happen to her in the first place, if He really is in control. But this is what Bethany and her mom were praying before this event happened and their conclusions:

> *When the attack happened, Cheri and Bethany had been praying for God to give Bethany a platform to show His love to the surfing world and beyond. After the attack, our family tried to process the event and how all of our lives were changed in an instant. I definitely struggled with the big questions: Why? What is your purpose in this God? He slowly started speaking to my heart about how Bethany would overcome and reach more souls for Him, and continue the work that He started in our family. The movie Soul Surfer is part of that work, along with everything else*

God has in store for the future![9]

It is now a Hollywood film delivering this message. Bethany became a professional surfer and delivers the message of God's salvation from her platform. Coincidence? It would take someone with a lot of faith in chance to believe that was not God.

Would you be willing to give up your arm to fulfill God's plan in your life?

There are others, like Patrick Swayze, who have similar experiences, but never credit God.

Out of Oxygen At 13,000 Feet

According to Patrick Swayze's autobiography, he thought he was in control of his life. But he wrote about an incident where he had hypoxia (oxygen deprivation), while flying his airplane, and survived. He considered his survival a miracle — but without the mention of God. During one of his frequent trips, he was flying his twin engine Cessna at 13,000 feet on autopilot. Because of a flaw in the pressurization of the airplane and his smoking habit, he lost consciousness, awakening miraculously in time to land safely on a road that was under construction in Prescott Valley, AZ. Besides the fact that he lived to tell about that story, nobody can figure out how the plane was knocked off autopilot. If it had not descended, Patrick would not have had the oxygen he needed to regain consciousness at the last second. That just doesn't happen. Furthermore, according to air traffic controllers, he almost hit the ground eleven times before regaining consciousness and landing safely. Robert Crispin of the National Transportation Safety Board (NTSB) said, "This is the first time I've ever gotten to talk to a pilot who's suffered hypoxia." This is one of many incidents where Patrick Swayze "cheated death."[10]

What do you think?

Circumstantial?

Spiritual perspective

I know. We all do it sometimes. We often view our circumstances as circumstantial. But if we look at them from a spiritual perspective, we might see God's fingerprints on them:

"When evening comes, you say, 'It will be fair weather, for

the sky is red.' And in the morning, 'Today it will be stormy, for the sky is red and overcast.' You know how to interpret the appearance of the sky, but you cannot interpret the signs of the times" (Matthew 16:2–3).

Sailors understand this similarly today: "Red at night, sailors delight. Red in the morning, sailors take warning." Jesus was hard on the religious leaders of His day when they could not recognize who He was. Shouldn't it have been obvious by the miracles He performed? By how the Scriptures identified Him as the Messiah?

Perhaps it is true of us as well. While we live in the miraculous, we accept it as normal. We are used to life as we see it. But in the midst of our daily lives, God is doing miraculous things; we just need to open our eyes to them. We must remember what it is like to witness the birth of a child. Very little is normal about our lives, if we slow down enough to truly think about it.

God is active.

He maintains control.

He has our best interests in mind.

And He does so while allowing each of us our free will.

Footnotes

1 http://mani4astro.blogspot.com/2010/07/know-astronomy-facts.html

2 http://www.nasa.gov/centers/kennedy/about/information/science_faq.html

3 http://www.physics.org/facts/sand-galaxies.asp. NASA, Kennedy Space Center, Frequently Asked Questions. Speed of light is 186,282 miles per second or 656,215,200 mph. Light would take 100,000 years to travel from one side of the Milky Way to another (our galaxy) going 656,215,200 mph. Therefore, it takes 100,000 light years to traverse our Galaxy. Wikipedia, Milky Way. NASA, How Big Is Our Universe.

4 Wikipedia, Sun.

5 Roughly 7x1027 atoms, that is a 7 with 27 zeros behind it. Physics Central, How much of the human body is made up of stardust? http://www.physicscentral.org/explore/poster-stardust.cfm.

6 How Stuff works? How Atoms Work. Craig Freudenrich, Ph.D. http://www.howstuffworks.com/atom.htm/printable.

7 http://www.soulsurferwave.com/meetthehamiltons

8 Ibid.

9 Ibid.

10 The Time of My Life, Patrick Swayze and Lisa Niemi (ATRIA, Simon & Schuster, New York, NY, 2010), pg.'s 212-213 & 215-217.

— CHAPTER 16 —

CONTROL AND FREE WILL

"I did something I need to tell you about," one of my residents said to me late one evening.

"What's that?" I asked.

"Well, I accidentally went to the bathroom in your chair. I couldn't help it," he said without looking at me.

"Excuse me, what did you say?" I asked, caught off-guard.

"I urinated in your chair!" He said with more emotion and visibly irritated by my need to hear his message for the second time.

"Which chair?" I asked.

"That one," he said, pointing to my favorite recliner chair.

"Did you clean it up?" I asked.

"No!" he said, getting angry.

"Why not?" I asked.

"Now you are making me feel ashamed! People always do that to me! Why can't people just leave me alone?" he shouted.

"I am not trying to make you feel ashamed of what you did," I replied, "but if someone spilled their chocolate sundae in my nice chair, I would expect him to clean it up! Now, the fact that you went to the bathroom in it is not that important to me, but the fact you didn't clean it up, is! Now, please go and clean up that chair!"

He cleaned my chair. I had to laugh — again. *God,* I was thinking, *it's really your chair anyway. I guess you probably don't mind that someone went to the bathroom in your chair! Neither will I, although it's no longer my favorite chair. (Author's journal, September 15, 2002)*

"What do you want me to do for you?" (Matthew 20:32)

Bruce and free will

In the midst of His control, God must continue to give us a choice, or He is not honoring our own independence as His loving children. Most of us are old enough to know that love has to be a choice, a free choice, with no strings attached. When God told Bruce in the movie *Bruce Almighty* that he could run the universe his way for a while, the only stipulation was he could not take away free will, each person's ability to make choices. Having lost his girlfriend, Grace, while selfishly indulging with his newly given power, he realized he wanted her back. But he couldn't control Grace, even with his powers. So he asks God this profound question, which is something we should all consider:

> **Bruce:** *How do you make so many people love you without affecting free will?*

> **God:** *Heh, welcome to my world, son. If you come up with an answer to that one, let me know.*

The answer is, you don't. God maintains boundaries on the universe but without forcing His will on our lives. That does not mean He will not manipulate circumstances to get our attention though. God loves us enough to teach us His ways before letting us go completely on our own. Consider Jonah.

Jonah

Most of us recall the Biblical story of Jonah and the whale. Perhaps the only detail most remember is that Jonah was swallowed by a whale and then lived to talk about it. But, there is a lot more depth to this story than that one point. Jonah was given a direct order by God to go preach to a group of people called the Ninevites (Jonah 1:2). Instead, Jonah fled from the Lord and jumped aboard a boat headed for Tarshish, which was the opposite direction from Nineveh (1:3). The Bible says the Lord then stirred up the wind and seas so that all those aboard began calling on their own "god" to save them, while Jonah went to sleep (1:4–5). Stunned that Jonah could sleep through such a storm, the other passengers woke him up, only to learn he was fleeing from God, and, therefore, responsible for the storm (1:9–10). The Lord continued to increase the magnitude of the waves until the men on the boat finally threw Jonah overboard — which immediately calmed the seas (1:12, 15). God commanded a whale to bottom fish for Jonah, who then repented of his rebellion. Then, the Lord commanded the fish to spit him out onto dry land (Jonah 2) and repeated His request of Jonah:

> "Go to the great city of Nineveh and proclaim to it the message I give you" (Jonah 3:2).

This time Jonah obeyed, albeit reluctantly. Jonah did not like the sinful Ninevites, and he did not want God to forgive them of their sins because of His grace and mercy.

The free will to run

What point can we glean from this rich story?

Jonah had the free will to run from God, which he did, but God's will was still done.

Ultimately, the Ninevites heard the message and repented of their evil ways, and God spared them from the destruction He had planned for them. The fact that God manipulated Jonah's circumstances until He got his attention is due to God's grace and mercy rather than His control. If God can cause a storm and command a fish, He sure didn't need Jonah to do anything at all. He could have used someone else. He was teaching Jonah a lesson that His servant needed to learn; God has a right to be gracious and compassionate, slow to anger and abounding in love, one who relents from sending calamity, if He chooses (Jonah 4:2). He has the right to give people, like the Ninevites, a second wind — just as He gave Jonah a second wind, whether or not Jonah ever understood that correlation.

God was revealing His true character to Jonah for Jonah's good. That was the point. So, while the level of control God uses on our lives might just be up to each of us individually, we still maintain our ability to choose — and God's will still gets done. Of course, God hopes that all of us choose Him and allow Him to fulfill the plan He has for our lives.

But it's still a choice.

Will I choose Him?

Will you?

— CHAPTER 17 —

GOD'S PLAN

boarded the Southwest airplane in Raleigh, North Carolina, and chose an open seat. Moments later, the attractive woman I had noticed in the airport asked if she could sit next to me, an unusual request, unless God was up to something. During the flight, I finished reading the book *Left Behind* and a conversation stirred, which eventually revealed her father's illness. I ended up giving her the book *Left Behind,* and she gave me her father's address, as I had promised to send him a Bible. Shocked, upon my return from Rhode Island (before cell phones were ubiquitous), I had a message on my answering machine from the boyfriend of the strange girl I had met on the plane. Somehow, he had found my number, called me, and explained how he had prayed for God to put someone next to her on that flight who would share Jesus as Lord, Savior, Daddy, King and Friend, rather than just a religious figure — which is what I had done on that flight. Months later, this same couple got engaged and she ended up moving from her home in Long Island, New York, to Charlotte, North Carolina. At that time, I worked as the Assistant Director of Discipleship at my church, Forest Hill. As part of my responsibilities, I taught the membership class called "Connection." David Chadwick, the senior pastor of Forest Hill, did introductions with all of the prospective new members. This class was no different. When he got to one unfamiliar woman, he asked the standard question, "What brought you to Forest Hill Church?" Her reply, "Tom Wheeler. I met him on an airplane years ago." She explained the journey that amazed us all, including me as I pondered how my only part was to get on an airplane — in another city — and share my faith with the passenger next to me.

"For I know the plans I have for you," declares the LORD, "plans to prosper you and not to harm you, plans to give you hope and a future" (Jeremiah 29:11).

A plan for our lives

God had a plan for Bethany Hamilton and Patrick Swayze, just like He did for Jonah and the Ninevites.

God has a plan for passengers on a plane.

God has a plan for each of us.

He is not random or haphazard. I remember watching a NFL football game, wondering how many of the players on the field thought they were fulfilling their purpose by making money and entertaining audiences like me. In my mind, I compared them to those who thought their careers simply gave them a platform to do something even greater, like Bethany Hamilton. I think it is the same with other jobs, careers, or vocations as well. We might see them as a means to a selfish end, while God sees them as a means to a spiritual one. The apostle Paul compares our physical body to the spiritual body of believers. He says that we all play a role:

> *Just as each of us has one body with many members, and these members do not all have the same function, so in Christ we, though many, form one body, and each member belongs to all the others. We have different gifts, according to the grace given us (Romans 12:4–6).*

We have all been given a purpose, and we were all meant to have a role in the body of Christ. In that regard, we are all significant. As all boats leave a wake in their path as they travel, we too leave a trail in ours as we live our lives.

Your wake

I remember when my mom, dad, and I were traveling in their 45-foot Bayliner boat. I noticed an all too familiar freighter off in the distance of the Delaware Bay. This one had a lot of white water in its wake, which is the water that follows any boat because of the vessel's weight against the water. Mariners call the water on top of a wave "white caps," which is what I saw following this large freighter. Those white caps were a long way away from our boat, but it was unusual I could see them in the distance. While freighters like this one often traverse those waters, their wakes are typically manageable for us, even though they are larger than most. But, this wake appeared different. When the wake was close enough for us to see it in more detail, it was not normal at all; in fact, it was probably the largest wake I had ever seen. I quickly cut the engines back so we would not hit it at cruising speed, which was about 20 mph. We hit hard, but no damage was done to our boat or any of our belongings. The big ship was speeding in the Delaware Bay, endangering all small vessels in its vicinity.

Our lives are similar. We all leave a path or wake behind us as we live. How we live determines the size of our wake and its impact on those around us.

Every life is significant

To the extent we are focused on our God given calling might be indicative of the size, impact, or safety of our wake. Consider Barack Obama, Ronald Reagan, Michael Jordan, Martin Luther King Jr., Billy Graham, Steve Jobs, or any other person who you know that has had a popular influence on people. They are people just like you and I, who appear to have been laser-focused on their vocation (whether you like them or not). There are others who we might know of as well, like Osama Bin Laden, former leader of the Taliban terrorist organization and the mastermind behind 9/11. Or Saddam Hussein, the former president of Iraq, or Mahmoud Ahmadinejad, the president of Iran who denied the Holocaust and suggested his desire to eliminate Israel from the face of the earth.[1] I was thinking about the unknown person who was responsible for the 1982 Tylenol poisoning in Chicago. Nobody was ever convicted for this crime that killed seven people who took Extra-Strength Tylenol laced with potassium cyanide.[2] Because of that one person's crime, reforms were made in federal law, and tamper-resistant packaging was introduced. All of these people had (or have) a significant "wake" or impact on our world. To the extent they are focused on their God-given purpose, however, may be the difference between someone intentionally speeding in the confines of the bay, sinking the hapless vessels around them, or whether they are vessels safe to follow. The better question, therefore, might not be whether we have a purpose or not, but rather are we using our gifts to serve God or to serve something or someone else.

We all have a wake.

Individual calling

Take Billy Graham, since I already mentioned him. His purpose has been to preach the good news to the world. He believes God called him to this task.[3] He has preached the gospel to millions of people who have developed a personal relationship with God through Jesus Christ. Billy Graham's wake is large, and it is worthy to follow. David Chadwick's mission is to be a friend to seekers. He is one of the greatest evangelists and "friends to seekers" I know. He told me he heard either a strong, silent voice or an actual voice telling him to share God's love to a hurting world. He, too, has led countless people to a personal relationship with Jesus Christ, myself included. His wake is large and safe to follow as well. Mother Teresa was clearly called to the poorest of the poor. In fact, when asked why she didn't focus on the political problems that cause poverty, she said:

> *My job is to help them where they are, someone else is to do the political job.*[4]

God used Mother Teresa to build one of the largest organizations in the world, one person at a time, starting with twelve members in Calcutta, India, back in 1950. In 2010, the Missionaries of Charity consisted of over 4,500 sisters, over one million co-workers, and over a billion dollars in financial support, and they were active in 133 countries working on every continent in the world.[5] We all know her wake was huge — and worthy to follow.

It cost her denying herself and her own plans.

My call

My own personal calling is to share the love of Christ with the least and lost. Every time I read or heard the following scripture from the story of the sheep and the goats, I felt God was speaking to me:

> *"The King will reply, 'Truly I tell you, whatever you did for one of the least of these brothers and sisters of mine, you did for me'" (Matthew 25:40).*

The story implies that whatever we do for the poor, who many consider the least, we do for God. I was also compelled to help the homeless I saw on the street corner — I had to do something because my heart was burdened for them. More specifically, I believe my calling is to come alongside Christian inner-city leaders to help them accomplish their God-given assignments. The Bible implores us, as Christians, to disciple men rather than convert people to Christianity.

I am called to help the leaders who help the poor in a discipleship relationship (Matthew 28:19) because I support them and their cause. I see how they struggle because they often receive more advice than support.

Although discovering my specific calling was a fairly arduous process for me, I am certain God is guiding my life to fulfill the plan He created me to fulfill. And I also know He is going to complete that plan in my life:

> The LORD will fulfill his purpose for me; your love, O LORD, endures forever — do not abandon the works of your hands (Psalm 138:8).

But it came at a cost.

I couldn't go on living the way I used to and fulfill God's plan for my life.

Your call

God has a plan for our lives.

He is faithful to complete that plan.

That includes you, even if you have caused a wreck of your life or in the lives of others. God is able — you just need to trust Him:

> The LORD Almighty has sworn, "Surely, as I have planned, so it will be, and as I have purposed, so it will stand" (Isaiah 14:24).

Are you willing to exchange your plans for God's?

Another choice. We are a culmination of our choices.

What choice will you make?

Generic calling versus a specific one

Having said that, while some may continue to seek a specific calling or purpose for their lives, we must not do so at the expense of our generic calling. For instance, generically, the Bible says:

> *"'Love the Lord your God with all your heart and with all your soul and with all your mind.' This is the first and greatest commandment. And the second is like it: 'Love your neighbor as yourself'" (Matthew 22:37–39).*

We are all called to love God first, then our neighbor as ourselves — our neighbor being any person we come across in life. That is a generic calling. It is also much easier *said than done* since many of us have neighbors who are not easy to love!

What about Bob?

"What can I do for you?" I asked the man near the front door of the shelter.

"I'd like something to eat," he replied matter-of-factly. I was the on-duty supervisor and always tried to help those who came to the shelter — even the ones we couldn't admit — which was the case with this man. I got him a sandwich.

"I don't want a sandwich," he said, as I handed him a brown paper bag. "I want a hot meal."

Having worked at the shelter for some time now, I was familiar with my need to have a lot of patience. I chuckled a bit under my breath. "OK. I'll see what I can do," I said, with my own straight face. I returned a few minutes later with a hot meal.

"I'd like something to drink," he said, without thanking me for the hot meal. Again, I walked away and returned with a cold glass of water.

"I'd like a soda," he said, never thanking me for anything. He refused the water, while staring at me with his big sombrero that was several times the size of his head. I returned with a cold soda, and I asked him a question: "Have you ever seen the movie *What About Bob?*" He did not answer as he ate his hot meal looking at me funny, sombrero hat still in place. "Well, in the movie, Bob, played by Bill Murray, is driving his doctor, Leo Marvin, played by Richard Dreyfus, crazy. In one scene, Bob cries out to Dr. Marvin, pleading for help time and time again: 'Please Dr. Marvin, give me, give me, give me, I need, I need, I need!' until Dr. Marvin complies to Bob's persistent whining." I cracked up while telling the story because that scene is so funny to me. "And you, strange sombrero man, remind me of Bob," I added. Sombrero man stopped eating, looked me in the eye as seriously as he could, smiled, and said, "I *am* Bob!"

Loving the Bobs of the world is not always easy. But, we can love them. We can learn from them.

Perhaps, we all have a bit of Bob in us.

Widows, orhans, the poor and the world

We are also called to take care of widows, orphans, and the poor, and we are to keep ourselves from being corrupted by the world:

> *Religion that God our Father accepts as pure and faultless is this: to look after orphans and widows in their distress and to keep oneself from being polluted by the world (James 1:27).*

> *All they asked was that we should continue to remember the poor, the very thing I was eager to do (Galatians 2:10).*

And remember, there is nothing God cannot do with one God-fearing and God-believing person, including you. God has a plan for your life.

Seek it.

It's your Promised Land. It's your second wind.

Footnotes

1 He denies having said or implied that, to the distaste of Benjamin Netanyahu, the Israel Prime Minister.

2 Wikipedia, Chicago Tylenol murders.

3 Charlotte Observer, March 10, 2003, the Billy Graham column.

4 Chawla, Navin. Mother Teresa: The Authorized Biography, Diane Pub Co. (March 1992).

5 Wikipedia, Missionaries of Charity.

— CHAPTER 18 —

GOD'S WISDOM

Last night, I cooked some chicken for Al, since I took him to the labor pool at 5 a.m. and knew he'd be hungry, having worked all day — something he hadn't done since moving into my house. I left it on the counter for all of them around dinner time and told Montel to make sure Al got some of it as soon as he got in from work. "Pastor, what did you do with the chicken you said you left for us to eat?" Montel asked about 7 p.m.

"I left it right here on the counter, like I told you before I left." I replied.

"Well, where did it go?" he continued.

"I don't know, since I just walked in the door. Anyway, I left it with you! You tell me what happened to it. Didn't you eat any of it?" I asked, a bit frustrated.

"I never saw it," he replied.

"You never saw it, hmmm. Go get the others in the house." I said, trying to figure out how to deal with another bizarre situation. Todd, Montel, and Al are now standing before me. "OK, who ate the chicken I left here on the counter? Did you eat it?" I asked each one, one at a time.

"No."

"No."

"No." They said in unison. I looked into the trash and saw the crumbled foil I had wrapped the chicken with. Now laughing a bit, because I knew I was at one of those moments, I said, "Well, here is the foil. Someone must have eaten it! Do you all mean to tell me that none of you ate this chicken, which is now gone, and yet the foil it was wrapped in is balled up in the trash?" They all shook their heads — none of them ate the chicken, and yet it was all gone — which then had me shaking my head. *(Author's journal entry, June 16, 2002)*

> *The fear of the LORD is the beginning of wisdom (Proverbs 9:10).*

God is omniscient

The next amazing, sometimes scary, sometimes reassuring, truth is that God knows what is going on with you and me, right now. This has been implied, but it is worth repeating. God is omniscient, meaning all-knowing. He not only knows what is going on today, but He knows the future. That was the point of Psalm 139 and is the idea behind many other Scripture passages.[1] Consider what God said about King Sennacherib of Assyria when he was mocking God while threatening King Hezekiah of Judah, early in Judah's history:[2]

> *"But I know where you are and when you come and go and how you rage against me. Because you rage against me and because your insolence has reached my ears, I will put my hook in your nose and my bit in your mouth, and I will make you return by the way you came." (2 Kings 19:27–28).*

God was aware of what King Sennacherib was saying, and He responded. He also delivered on His promise. This is a consistent theme throughout the Bible, and it is a consistent theme today. His eyes are everywhere, watching everything.[3]

For our good.

> *Whenever our hearts condemn us, God is greater than our heart, and he knows everything (1 John 3:20, ESV).*

Daniel

Many of the men who come to Hoskins Park Ministries abuse drugs or alcohol. They arrive at our doorstep as broken men, some without hope. We teach them the truths of the gospel. Then, we watch God move in their lives in order that they might surrender their destructive ways to Him. It is a process for all of them, like all of us, and Daniel was no exception. After Daniel had been with us for several weeks, drug free, he woke up early one morning with a strong urge to use drugs again. He began dressing in the dark, waking up his roommate, who questioned him about his motives. He responded, "A man has to do what a man has to do," indicating he was going to get high. Despite the beckoning of his roommate not to do so, he headed downstairs with only his shoes left to put on. Then, he heard the train blow its loud and notorious horn. Hoskins Park Ministries is located on one side of railroad tracks, and a popular crack house was located on the other side of the tracks (it subsequently burned down). Daniel knew where to get drugs — quick — on the other side of the tracks. The only thing that could possibly stop him from getting his addiction met that night was that train. He put his shoes on as fast as possible and headed out the door. Typically, he would have had ample time to beat the train. Not this night. The slow moving train that had suddenly appeared was already passing by the house. There was nothing Daniel could do, but wait. Then, the train stopped. For the next fifteen minutes, while Daniel waited, the train went back and forth without any way for him to safely cross over the tracks. Finally, he decided the Lord was being true to His Word by giving him a way out, and he returned to his bed, drug free. Daniel didn't use drugs that night and has not since. He believes, as do I, that while Satan was tempting him back to drugs, God moved a train into his path to help Daniel stay clean. God watches all of us all the time:

> And the LORD said, "That's right, and it means that I am watching, and I will certainly carry out all my plans" (Jeremiah 1:12, NLT).

He is aware of everything!

Because God is watching, we do not get away with anything ever although we might for a period of time. What people do in the darkness is eventually revealed. The Bible says:

For all that is secret will eventually be brought into the open, and everything that is concealed will be brought to light and made known to all (Luke 8:17, NLT).

And yes, it is that simple. At least it is for those who trust God and believe the Bible. Just like most of us can feel a pinprick on any part of our body, perhaps God feels the pin pricks of our souls on His body. He is not numb to any of us:

He is aware of everything going on.

He feels our pain.

He knows where we put our faith by watching how we live our lives.

Daniel ultimately showed whom he trusted by crediting the Lord with his circumstances. He understood the war we are fighting and chose sides — God's side. God truly is everywhere:

"Can anyone hide from me in a secret place? Am I not everywhere in all the heavens and earth?" says the LORD (Jeremiah 23:24, NLT).

God is not in everything

Although God is omnipresent, He is not in everything as some suggest. This is an interaction God has with the prophet Elijah about this particular issue:

The LORD said, "Go out and stand on the mountain in the presence of the LORD, for the LORD is about to pass by." Then a great and powerful wind tore the mountains apart and shattered the rocks before the LORD, but the LORD was not in the wind. After the wind there was an earthquake, but the LORD was not in the earthquake. After the earthquake came a fire, but the LORD was not in the fire. And after the fire came a gentle whisper (1 Kings 19:11–12).

God created all that we know to be true, but God is separate from creation. He is involved in it, but He is not "creation" itself. In fact, creation groans for God to liberate it from its bondage just as we do:

We know that the whole creation has been groaning as in the pains of childbirth right up to the present time (Romans 8:22).

God is not the creation. He is the Creator.

Let's remember that - God is aware!

So, what is going on in your life right now? God knows about it.

He knows everything — doesn't he also know what you are doing? (Psalm 94:10, NLT)

That includes knowing you.

He is aware of your circumstances.

He is with you.

And He cares.

Just believe.

Footnotes

1   1 Samuel 23:9-13; 2 Kings 13:19; Psalm 81:14-15; Isaiah 48:18.

2   Life Application Study Bible, New International Version, (Tyndale House Publishers, Wheaton, Ill., 1991), pg. 655.

3   Job 24:23; Psalms 33:13-15, 139:13-16; Proverbs 15:3; Jeremiah 16:17; Hebrews 4:13.

— CHAPTER 19 —

GOD'S HOLINESS

In 2000, I donated clothes to the Uptown Men's Shelter — my best clothes. I felt the Lord challenge me to give up things I really loved, not things I didn't need. He wanted my best. When I checked myself into the shelter later that same year as a homeless person, I entered with only the clothes on my back. I forgot about my earlier donation, nor did I have any idea what they did with it after I donated the clothes. Sunday morning, while everyone was getting ready to go to church, I needed some decent clothes. I was taken to the shelter's clothing closet. To my surprise, I found the very clothes I had donated on the rack. I was able to wear my clothes - to church – while homeless and living in the shelter. Amazing. God knows the past, present, and the future.

> But just as he who called you is holy, so be holy in all you
> do; for it is written: "Be holy, because I am holy" (1 Peter
> 1:15–16).

God is holy

The best definition I know for holy is "perfection." God is perfect in every aspect of everything. That is His nature:

> As for God, his way is perfect (Psalm 18:30).

That means He is morally perfect, He is loving, merciful, without spot or blemish, truthful, faithful, excellent in all things, ethical, and He cannot look upon sin. Testimony to His perfection is the fact that we are all living and breathing, as I said about the miracle of creation. We are all made up of about a trillion cells, with our DNA code stamped on each cell. If spelled out, our DNA code would take up one thousand 1000 page telephone books — on every cell.[1] We are all walking miracles, no matter what might be wrong with our bodies today.[2] Moreover, science agrees. The second law of thermodynamics says that the natural order of all change is to create a greater degree of disorder and randomness rather than cohesion and order.[3] In other words, if life were random, it would be total and absolute chaos. Although some might agree with the Darwinian theory that life evolved "naturally" by a survival of the fittest process, this contradicts this law of physics.[4] Things do not naturally evolve in an orderly way. Think of it this way: If you were to let your kids run your household unchecked, how long would your house remain standing? Or, when riots break out on the streets of cities like London, left unchecked, what happens to the city? Anarchy happens when boundaries are not implemented on creation. God's holiness refers to His perfection, and His perfection is proven by the fact that you and I are alive today in a universe that has boundaries, God-made boundaries. And because God is holy, His own perfect nature *demands justice*.

Justice

Few of us will ever forget that on September 11, 2001, hijacked airplanes hit the Twin Towers of the World Trade Center buildings. One also hit the Pentagon, and we know another hijacked jet was crashed into the ground before hitting its target. In the wake of the terrorist crisis, many were demanding justice — "Dead or alive," then President George W. Bush said about Osama bin Laden, the confirmed leader of the terrorist sect, responsible.[5] And President Obama saw that justice was done when he authorized a successful military operation to kill Osama bin Laden. Life without justice is anarchy or chaos. Justice is required to keep order. Someone or something must pay for any injustice or wrong that is done in order to maintain justice. So it is with God. The Bible says that God is just.[6] Therefore, justice requires that the penalty for our sin, our flaws, be paid. God loves us more than we can imagine, but He must deal with the problem of our sin, *or He is defying His own perfect nature*. While many of us admit we are sinners, we still don't understand what this means in God's terms.

Who we are

We compare ourselves to murderers, terrorists, or whoever is beneath us (morally), and we think we are all right compared to them, irrespective of God's perfection. Don't we? But, the bad news is that we need to compare ourselves against God, and none of us are "good enough" to please Him on our own. The Bible says there is no one righteous, not even one, and all have sinned and fall short of the glory of God.[7]

In comparison to the true measurement of God, it doesn't really matter how much better we stack up to someone else; we still don't reach God's standard. Although most of us enjoy finger-pointing at the more seriously flawed people in the world, the bottom line is that *we are all flawed*.

Let's remember that: *We are all flawed*.

Are you a good person?

Again, you might think you are a good person in comparison to others, but who isn't a good person when compared to someone else? This is one of the major stumbling blocks to Christianity. In order to even accept Jesus' message, you have to come to grips with the reality of your sin — not everyone else's sin, just your sin in the context of God's perfection. It really is interesting to me that statistics say seventy-seven percent of "non-religious" people believe they are headed to heaven, while few believe they are headed towards hell because they are "good people."[8] But the Bible even calls our good works "filthy rags," because, in comparison to God, all of our works or efforts to please Him fall short of His glory:

And all our righteous acts are like filthy rags (Isaiah 64:6).

Even though many of us do good things, God must deal with our shortcomings (our sin) and these shortcomings separate us from God:

Your [sins] have made a separation between you and your God, and your sins have hidden his face from you (Isaiah 59:2, ESV).

God cannot look upon our sin because of His holiness. Thus, the question becomes how do we account for our sins against a holy God? The short answer is, we can't. We can never do enough to compensate for our sin because God is perfect and we are not. We cannot repay Him for something He gave us. Can a thief repay the one he stole from with the goods he stole? Of course, he can't. We may not be thieves, but the same issue applies.

Germs to our body versus sin to God's (body)

Consider it this way. What if sins (our faults) are to God what germs are to our body? If a germ enters our body, our body reacts naturally to kill or destroy that germ because it is inconsistent with healthy life. Our bodies do not debate whether one germ is better or worse than another (although some are); all germs can eventually kill us if our bodies do not kill them first. Years ago, the common cold killed people. Germs are germs; they are inconsistent with good health. Our nature is to destroy that which will hurt our survival.

What if that is the way it is with God and sin? If sin is to God what germs are to us, then God has to kill the sin in order to remain God. He cannot deal with it *because of His nature*. Now, we might say, "Of course He can, He is God!" But that appears to be redefining God's character. God is perfect, holy, and we are not. He cannot be in the presence of our sin, but He loves us. Therefore, God had a divine problem. How does He maintain His holiness while also continuing to love His sinful creation?

Footnotes

1   http://www.healthieryou.com/complete.html.

2   Furthermore, when we think that disease or any problems on earth are a result of God being imperfect, we discount the fact that love demands a choice and many of us choose sin. We choose, ourselves, to put awful food in our bodies. And sin passes on from generation to generation. We call that genetics.

3   Henry M. Morris, The Twilight of Evolution (Baker Books, Grand Rapids, 1963), pg. 43-44. From James F. Crow: "Genetic Effects of Radiation," Bulletin of the Atomic Scientists, Vol. 14, January, 1958, pp. 19-20. "Thermodynamics is a physical theory of great generality impinging on practically every phase of human experience. It may be called the description of the behavior of matter in equilibrium and of its changes from one equilibrium state to another. Thermodynamics operates with two master concepts or constructs and two great principles. The concepts are energy and entropy, and the principles are the so-called first and second laws of thermodynamics..." pg. 34.

4   Charles Darwin's 'Origin of the Species' says that life randomly evolved over millions of years.

5   The Telegraph, Bin Laden is wanted: dead or alive, says Bush, November 21, 2010.

6   John 5:30 - my judgment is just. See also Romans 3:22-26. Christ paid for our sin.

7   Romans 3:10, 3:23, Psalm 53:1&3. See also Jeremiah 17:17 about the deceitfulness of the heart.

8   Poll: Elbow Room No Problem in Heaven, abc NEWS, December 20, 2005, http://abcnews.go.com/US/Beliefs/story?id=1422658.

— CHAPTER 20 —

GOD'S LOVE

"Uh oh!" I said, upon returning from a visit with my mom and dad in Virginia. "Why are you both in my house close to midnight? What did Todd do?" I asked Johnny and Doug, since I figured it was about Todd.

"Well, you better check your things." Johnny replied. "We know Todd took your DVD player, your new tools from the shed, who knows what else, and sold them for crack cocaine. He also invited in someone off the street — we think it was his crack dealer." Shaking my head, I sat down took a deep breath and asked them where Todd was now.

"He's gone." We prayed for Todd, and they left. Days later, Todd returned.

"Well, I don't know if it matters, but I'm really sorry for selling your things. I feel worse about your silver coins, since I know how special those were to you." Todd said while shaking his head in disgust, since he had sold my most valuable possessions. "At least, I had the presence of mind not to sell my guitar."

I looked at him funny and said, "You sold all my stuff, but are finding satisfaction in the fact that you did not sell something of yours because it was special to you?" No words.

At Hoskins Park, I have learned that our success is not dependent upon what our men do in response to our care. Our success is based upon how well we love the people God brings us. God is responsible for the results. We love the Peters of the world, the Todds, the Pauls, the Bobs, and we love those disguised as Judas, even if they, too, put us on the cross. As Mother Teresa is known to have said, we are not called to be successful, we are called to be faithful.

> *God is love. Whoever lives in love lives in God, and God in him (1 John 4:16).*

Definition of love

Many of us believe God to be a God of love, which He is according to the Bible: "God is love."[1] But often, we may not understand the true definition of love. I didn't. In fact, I mistakenly defined love as lust for most of my life. As long as I had the right feelings for another person, I considered myself to be "in love." Love was a feeling, and that feeling was what I most wanted in life. Furthermore, the physical manifestation of those feelings, or sex, was the ultimate expression of love. Love without sex actually seemed infantile to me. Once those feelings subsided, so did the love. I learned this from our culture, rooted in Hollywood and my peers. I felt this way until I began studying the Bible. It was then that I discovered that while lust plays a role in a romantic relationship, it is merely a role, not the relationship. Love is far deeper than feelings, and it is actually the antithesis of lust, since it is about giving rather than receiving. Moreover, while I never thought so many others had misunderstood love to the degree I had, the divorce rate seems to testify otherwise. Love is not a *quid pro quo*, as is clearly stated Biblically:

> *Love is patient, love is kind. It does not envy, it does not boast, it is not proud. It is not rude, it is not self-seeking, it is not easily angered, it keeps no record of wrongs. Love does not delight in evil but rejoices with the truth. It always protects, always trusts, always hopes, always perseveres. Love[2] never fails (1 Corinthians 13:4–8).*

Our understanding of love

Take patience, for instance. This definition of love says patience is required when most of us consider patience to be last on the list of virtues we want — and kindness goes right out the window when we don't get what we want on demand. I heard the recording of a woman at a Burger King drive-through who hysterically called 911 because she wasn't getting her Western Burger her way![3] While watching CNN, I saw a video of someone else throwing something through the window of a McDonald's drive-through, then attack the cashier because she couldn't get Chicken McNuggets for breakfast (they don't sell them until lunch time).[4] This is the world we live in. Instant gratification or else! Attributes of love like patience and kindness are no longer in style. If we are going to love the way the Bible says, we must be patient and kind in how we deal with others. Mother Teresa is known to have posted the following words (originally written by Kent M. Keith) on a sign on the wall of Shishu Bhavan, the children's home in Calcutta:

> *People are often unreliable, illogical, and self-centered; forgive them anyway. If you are successful, you will win some false friends and true enemies; succeed anyway. If you are honest and frank, people may cheat you; be honest and frank anyway. What you spend your years building, someone may destroy overnight; build it anyway. The good you do today, people will often forget tomorrow; do good anyway. Give the world the best you have and it may never be enough; give the world the best you've got anyway. You see, in the final analysis, it is between you and God. It never was between you and them anyway.[5]*

I don't know about you, but that seems hard to do, doesn't it? But that is the point. Remember Bob? Being patient and kind is much easier said than done, like most things. Thankfully, that is how God is to us. He patiently waits for us to turn to Him for our identity. When we stop clinging to the world and seeking our identity from it, He is waiting.

Love's focus is not on self

The rest of the definition of love is just as difficult. For instance, this definition does not seem to include feelings as part of love *at all*. But that doesn't make any sense. Our culture says, "If it feels good, do it and if it doesn't, don't." That's what I thought. In fact, years ago, if anyone had suggested anything otherwise, I would have walked away. That is why the last part of this definition of love was shocking to me — until I started to think about it. Love never fails because it is not about a response. Surprisingly, love does not have to be a two-way street, despite our desire for it to be that way. That is the bad news, at least for those who were expecting love to be more about lust. Love is about sacrifice, a concept that was foreign to me as a young adult, even though my own mother modeled it better than any person I have ever known. She exemplifies its definition. My mother rarely did things for her own selfish indulgence — she did things for those she loved. In fact, it cost her productivity. In order to love, many of us *task-oriented people* might have to slow down a bit.

Inner city

When I first moved in next door to Johnny in northwest Charlotte, North Carolina, he had nine previously homeless men living with him in his own house. I didn't have any experience with the homeless, but I was a Christian who read the Bible. Scripture says that whatever I do for the least, I did for God (Matthew 25:40). In fact, as I stated earlier, it was part of my calling to help the homeless. Although I was not addicted to drugs and had never been homeless, I believed my own life experiences and my understanding of the Bible gave me ample expertise to help in this area, despite whatever inadequacies I may have had. I've had my share of struggles in this world, and I understand addiction well; mine just weren't illegal drugs. Given that background, one of my first assumptions in working with Johnny was that we needed to kick guys out for doing drugs. I thought, *Come on, drugs are illegal, is there any need to discuss this issue further?* Having patience with someone continuing to use drugs didn't even cross my mind. I wanted to get this ministry in right order — right away. Maybe you know what I mean? Johnny, previously addicted to crack cocaine, formerly homeless, and formerly a drug dealer, felt differently. Johnny told me that he didn't believe in kicking someone out of his bed for the behavior that brought him to us in the first place. His method, one that had worked for him in his own life (a very important point), focused more on Jesus than drugs. It was about teaching the message of grace (unmerited favor, unconditional love), while letting God do the hard work of getting a homeless man to surrender (often at the expense of Johnny — and then me!). Johnny and I were at a stalemate. I wanted to clean up the ministry and make it look good; Johnny knew it took time to help one man, often at the expense of looking good.

Romans 2:4

For the next four years, I had to learn that God's kindness leads to repentance:

> Or do you show contempt for the riches of his kindness, tolerance and patience, not realizing that God's kindness leads you towards repentance? (Romans 2:4)

That was the kindness, tolerance, and patience God had shown me in my life, and that was the way He wanted me to love His poor, including Johnny: by sacrificing what I considered to be productivity for the sake of a person. And people take time and patience — all people. [6] The Bible says:

> Accept one another, then, just as Christ accepted you, in order to bring praise to God (Romans 15:7).

Four years after I moved in as Johnny's neighbor, we merged our respective ministries into one united organization. It took us that long to realize that if we could not model love between ourselves, dropping our self-serving to-do lists, we certainly couldn't teach love to others. Helping as many homeless people as possible is no longer our primary ambition either — it is to love one person at a time. This is hard teaching for many task-oriented people like me. It just doesn't work as we think it should. My change happened when I hypothesized that God is love and the definition of love is truly the definition found in Corinthians. The lesson got a little easier for me to understand and appreciate. If God were task-oriented about us, always pushing us to do things to the point of perfection, He might just return us to dust sooner than later! But He is not. He is the essence of love and, therefore, its definition. He comes alongside us in an effort to teach us.

God's character

If we substitute God for love in this definition, we get an understanding of His character. It reads something like this:

- God is patient,
- God is kind,
- God does not envy,

- God does not boast,

- God is not proud,

- God does not seek satisfaction for Himself,

- God seeks the satisfaction of others,

- God may get angry, but not at the first provocation, and His anger is justified as a righteous anger aimed at helping others,

- God doesn't keep a list of wrongs, waiting to dump every bad thing someone has done on them when provoked,

- God doesn't entertain evil, since evil is self-focused,

- God celebrates the truth,

- God always protects,

- God always trusts,

- God always hopes,

- God always perseveres.

This definition concludes by saying, "God never fails." That's the good news. Even better is that these words are not just words. They define Jesus.

The proof of God's love

God didn't just define Himself Biblically, using this definition of love — He did so by coming to earth as Jesus. Jesus is God's answer to the problem of our sin and His holiness. If you take away Jesus Christ, as we know Him Biblically, you have no real proof that God loves us at all. Christianity is not about what we do, save for the fact we need to accept Jesus as our Lord and Savior. It is about what God has done. We need only accept the gift by believing the message. The Bible says that God sent Jesus, His own Son, to die in our place as a payment for our sin. This is how God showed His love among us: He sent His one and only Son into the world as an atoning sacrifice for our sins. Christ died for our sins according to the Scriptures and was raised on the third day.[7]

There is no greater act of love than someone who gives up their life for another:

> Greater love has no one than this, that he lay down his life for his friends (John 15:13).

Jesus — the ultimate sacrifice, proving God's love for you, for me, for all of humanity.

The challenge

Let's not move on yet.

Slow down with me for a moment and consider this message further. Deeper.

Do you see this kind of sacrifice in our world today? Do you make this kind of sacrifice yourself? Or is it just a nice message? Words? More talk?

Many of our soldiers have given their lives to ensure our freedom. They have paid the ultimate price by dying for our sake. They do what they are told, at the risk of death. Do we value their sacrifice?

Many parents have sacrificed their way for their children. Do we understand the cost necessary to raise healthy children? I have heard it said that children spell love, T-I-M-E. Maybe, we all do.

Do I have the time to love? Do you? Do we?

Have we made the connection that, in order to follow Jesus, we must put others ahead of ourselves?

We must give up our selfish agenda. We can't have it all, despite our attempts to suggest otherwise.

Are we capable of sacrificing productivity, as it regards promotion, success stories, pride, numbers, wealth, statistics, or our own personal legacy, for the sake of something greater? For the sake of someone greater? For the sake of God's call on our lives? For the sake of discipleship?

Do we remember the rich man who walked away from Jesus because Jesus told him he was clinging to his money? Is that you? Is that me? Is that us?

Do we even know what the Bible is talking about when it says to "pick up our cross" and "die" daily (Luke 9:23)? More words?

Do we know that a servant serves other people rather than being served?

Is our focus still on worldly success rather than the godly kind? If someone we know is the weak link, do we realize we are only as strong as they are, or do we just replace them so we get stronger at their expense?

Do I really matter?

Do you really matter?

Does a homeless person really matter?

At what price? At what sacrifice?

We live in a very selfish world, a world focused on getting its own needs met at the expense of others.

This message is about doing the opposite because that is what Jesus did for you and me. Jesus was the ultimate sacrifice for mankind.

We should stand in awe. And then we should remember something else …

We are called to follow Him.

Footnotes

1   1 John 4:16.

2   It should be noted that there are three definitions of the English word "love" in the Greek language (as opposed to only one in the English language). The word used here, agape, is the deeper form of love that is not about feelings while other words, such as agapetos, might be more feelings based and are used in the NT. Some might consider this to question what I am saying, but most of us know that love cannot be "feelings" based in order to survive our fleeting feelings. When we get married, we make a vow – a commitment and that commitment gets us through our up and down feelings. So, while this is a good point, it does not change the message I am delivering.Zondervan NIV Exhaustive Concordance, Second edition, (ZondervanPublishingHouse, Grand Rapids, Michigan, 1999).

3   http://www.snopes.com/crime/cops/burger.asp. You can hear the audio file!

4   The Huffington Post, August 11, 2010, McDonald's McNugget Rage Video: Drive-Thru Assault, Window Smash Caught on Tape.

5   http://www.paradoxicalpeople.com/paradoxicalpeople/the_mother_teresa_ connection/.

6   1 Thessalonians 2:11 and 2:8.

7   1 John 4:9-10, John 3:16-17, 1 Corinthians 15:3-6. See also John 11:25, John 10:30, Romans 5:6-11, & Acts 10:39.

— CHAPTER 21 —

JESUS IS OUR SAVIOR

"This place is just like jail," one of the unruly residents complained to me about Hoskins Park Ministries. It was early in the history of the ministry, when comments like his irritated me to no end, since all we were trying to do was help them. I still believed I had to get these guys to surrender to me rather than letting God deal with them His way. Within two weeks, this same resident was arrested for theft. As I entered the jail, I had to chuckle at the irony of the event, particularly as my resident approached me in his new orange garb.

"Tom," he said, remembering his remark just days ago, "your house isn't like jail."

"Yeah, I know," I said, realizing how insufficient our opinions are at judging reality and God. *Thanks God. That was another lesson I could not teach, only you.*

> *"She will give birth to a son, and you are to give him the name Jesus, because he will save his people from their sins" (Matthew 1:21).*

I believe in God

Perhaps you believe there is a God, but are still not convinced you need to put your faith in Jesus? That is what most of the thousands of world religions believe, as well. It is wonderful to believe in God. But, it still does not account for the problem of our sin:

You believe that there is one God. Good! Even the demons believe that — and shudder (James 2:19).

Therefore, it won't get us to Heaven. God sent His own Son to earth to atone for our sins, because of His holiness. Many will continue to doubt Jesus' claim to deity, but this is despite a plethora of verses in the Bible, such as these:

I and the Father are one (John 10:30).

I am the resurrection and the life (John 11:25).

"Before Abraham was born, I am" (John 8:58).

Jesus answered, "I am the way and the truth and the life. No one comes to the Father except through me" (John 14:6).

The Father, Jesus refers to, is God Almighty. Jesus is saying He is one with His Father. In the second passage, Jesus is saying that He is our new, resurrected life. In the third passage, He is saying that He existed before Abraham — the father of Judaism, Islam, and Christianity — was even born. In the fourth passage, He tells us that He *is the truth, and nobody gets to God without going through Jesus.* So, while the truth of Jesus as our Lord will continue to be debated, it isn't a question, Biblically. Jesus is Lord.

As Savior

Jesus came to earth, lived perfectly, bore our sins, died with them, and was resurrected from the dead, so that whoever believes in Jesus as Savior will live with His Holy Spirit for eternity. That is how God resolved the divine dilemma He had regarding our sin, His holiness, and His love for His creation:

God made him who had no sin to be sin for us, so that in him we might become the righteousness of God (2 Corinthians 5:21).

He himself bore our sins in his body on the cross, so that we might die to sins and live for righteousness; by his wounds you have been healed (1 Peter 2:24).

As Savior, the Bible calls Jesus the bread of life:

Jesus said to them, "I tell you the truth, unless you eat the flesh of the Son of Man and drink his blood, you have no life in you. Whoever eats my flesh and drinks my blood has eternal life, and I will raise him up at the last day" (John 6:53–54).

We, as Christians, eat bread symbolizing the body of Christ, and we drink wine (or grape juice) symbolizing His blood — a ritual known to most of us as communion. For Protestant Christians, communion is an outward expression of our internal faith in Jesus, our Lord and Savior, and is done to emulate the Last Supper.[1] It was also the Biblical practice of the early church.[2] So, if Jesus was not Lord and Savior, He should have been institutionalized for saying the words we just read, and we should be institutionalized for participating in communion today. In fact, many people did turn away from Jesus because of teachings like these, and Jesus wondered if His own disciples would as well (Revelation 6:66). It was crazy for Him to say such things unless He was who He claimed — the Savior of the world whose body and blood were the necessary sacrifices to satisfy God's justice. It is all about the blood, since blood represents life.

Blood

I mentioned earlier that you and I are made up of about 100 trillion cells. All of these cells require a steady supply of fuel and oxygen. We get our oxygen by breathing and we get our fuel by eating. Our digestive system breaks down the food we ingest into microscopic size. Blood is the carrier of fuel and oxygen, and the heart is the engine that pumps blood through the 60,000 miles of our circulatory system into our cells. Take away the blood, or muck it up by poor nutrition (or air quality), and we suffer the consequences. First, we "run out of gas," metaphorically speaking. That is what happened to Julie Moss in 1982 at the Kona Ironman Championships. She was in first place of that race when she collapsed just yards from the finish line because of fatigue and dehydration. Many of us may recall the images of her famous crawl (barely able to move any of her muscles), which actually popularized the Ironman, since it had not been televised until that episode.[3] That is what happens when we run out of gas. Often, it is a result of a misunderstanding of nutrition, digestion, and, therefore, blood. She did not have enough food in her body to continue racing. Her blood was depleted. While we all may understand the need for blood, we might overlook its importance. Blood represents life:

> *For the life of a creature is in the blood, and I have given it to you to make atonement for yourselves on the altar; it is the blood that makes atonement for one's life (Leviticus 17:11).*

Throughout the ages, blood has been shed in order to make a payment for our sin or shortcomings. It is symbolic of atonement. Since God owns everything, the only way to pay Him back for our sin, is for our own blood to be shed. But, because of His grace and mercy, He shed His own blood rather than requiring each of us to do it ourselves. Take away the blood of Jesus, and all of humanity is left to deal with sin without any way of justice being served to God for our faults:

> *For God was pleased to have all his fullness dwell in [Jesus], and through him to reconcile to himself all things, whether things on earth or things in heaven, by making peace through his blood, shed on the cross (Colossians 1:19–20).*

Jesus' resurrection

Jesus was crucified, then raised to life on the third day, and He ascended into heaven to sit at the right hand of the Father. These words are from the apostle Paul:

> *For what I received I passed on to you as of first importance: that Christ died for our sins according to the Scriptures, that he was buried, that he was raised on the third day according to the Scriptures, and that he appeared to Peter, and then to the Twelve (1 Corinthians 15:3–5).*

God defeated death by putting all of our sins on His sinless Son:

- allowing Jesus to be killed with those sins,
- raising Jesus from the dead,
- returning Him to Heaven.

Mysteriously, for those who believe in this amazing act of grace, we receive that resurrected Spirit, which is our ticket to Heaven. Without the resurrection of Jesus Christ, we would not have access to His Spirit. We would still have to account for our sins on our own. Since God cannot be in the presence of our sin, we would remain separated from God forever. We could live life as we pleased:

> If the dead are not raised, "Let us eat and drink, for tomorrow we die" (1 Corinthians 15:32).

But the Bible makes it clear that those who trust in Jesus will live forever with Him:

> Listen, I tell you a mystery: We will not all sleep, but we will all be changed — in a flash, in the twinkling of an eye, at the last trumpet.

> Then the saying that is written will come true: "Death has been swallowed up in victory."

> "Where, O death, is your victory?" …But thanks be to God! He gives us the victory through our Lord Jesus Christ. (1 Corinthians 15:51–52, 54–55, 57).

It is the Spirit of Jesus, inside of us as believers, that gets us to Heaven. Not our good deeds.

Footnotes

1   [19]"And he took bread, gave thanks and broke it, and gave it to them, saying, 'This is my body given for you; do this in remembrance of me.' [20]In the same way, after the supper he took the cup, saying, 'This cup is the new covenant in my blood, which is poured out for you'" (Luke 22:19-20).

2   1 Corinthians 11:23-29.

3   The Most Famous Finish in Ironman History: Julie Moss Takes You Through Her Race, Iron man, February 26, 2003, Julie Moss.

— CHAPTER 22 —

THE HOLY SPIRIT

Since I had just taken a needy man to lunch, I felt I had already done my good deed for the day. Furthermore, I wasn't in the mood to hear another perfectly convincing fairy tale from the street. On the other hand, I am always reluctant to miss someone who has a legitimate need, so I stopped — again. Now, having heard the man's story, and upon my refusal to help, I watched the man sit down on the ledge of the sidewalk outside the courthouse, in a huff, shaking his head, then put his head in his hands as I was walking away. I could see his genuine frustration. I felt prompted to stop and turn around. So, I did. I grabbed the sheet of paper he held in his hand and asked him a couple questions to verify his original story. It checked out; he needed money for a bus ticket. Since all I had was a twenty dollar bill, I needed change. So I began asking folks, on the crowded street, for help. To both of our surprise, I was completely ignored — by everyone! Nobody even made eye contact with me, as if I were invisible. Now, this frustrated black man looked at me with this lit-up look on his face and said, "Man, they are ignoring you like they ignored me! And I thought it was a black thing!" I gave the guy the entire twenty and told him that people can and will be cold and judgmental to anyone. I also reminded him that God is not. He is our Rescuer and Redeemer. We just need to keep the faith. My new friend hugged and kissed me, while running off to catch his bus. I was glad I hadn't passed this man by. I was glad the Holy Spirit prompted me to stop. *(Author's journal entry, September 2, 2010)*

*This is how we know that we live in him and he in us: He
has given us of his Spirit (1 John 4:13).*

The Trinity

One of Christianity's most important tenets is God the Father, God the
Son, and God the Holy Spirit, comprising the Trinity:

*Therefore go and make disciples of all nations, baptizing
them in the name of the Father and of the Son and of the
Holy Spirit (Matthew 28:19).*

The Trinity is another one of those unexplainable mysteries that we
can describe, but not fully understand on this side of eternity. There is a
way, however, of looking at it that might give you some perspective as
to what it means. Consider water. In one form, water is liquid, in another,
it is ice, and in yet another, it is moisture. We know that our weather
consists of all forms — rain, snow (a form of ice), and mist or clouds
(moisture that is not yet rain or snow but still water). So, while it is
always water, it takes different forms. This is not the greatest explanation
of the Trinity, but it helped me to at least get a grasp of the concept.
Perhaps it will help you, too. So, God remains the CEO of the universe,
Jesus is His Son, who was redeemed for our sin, and the Holy Spirit
is the part of God that we receive when we believe in Jesus. It is what
gets us into Heaven. The fictional book *The Shack* identifies the three
persons of the Trinity: "Papa" is God the Father, Jesus, God the Son,
and "Sarayu" is the Holy Spirit.

The Shack

The Shack, by William Paul Young,[1] is the fictitious story about
Mackenzie Phillips (Mack), whose daughter Missy was abducted and
brutally murdered while Mack was rescuing his son from a canoeing
accident during a family vacation. After years of grieving, he receives
a note inviting him back to the same shack where his daughter was
murdered. Someone signs the message with the name "Papa."
Reluctantly, after much internal struggle and suspicion, Mack accepts
the invitation and returns to the shack. There, he meets an African-
American woman named Elouisa, whose nickname is "Papa" and who

is said to be God. He also meets Jesus and "Sarayu," the Holy Spirit. They are three supernaturally gracious and hospitably distinct persons, equally submitted to one another and interacting perfectly. Over his time at the shack, Mack develops personal relationships with all three, understanding Papa to represent a father figure. Jesus is more like a brother, and Sarayu represents a Spirit.

Though this story is fictional, you will see its similarities with the Bible. You will see that God is, in fact, a personal God. You will see that Jesus *is* His Son. You will see that the Holy Spirit *is* the Spirit of Jesus. That is what the Bible describes, a triune God.

But the Holy Spirit is the one who speaks to us.

The Spirit of Jesus

Many Christians talk about the Holy Spirit, but overlook His personhood and importance in our Christian lives. The following scriptures support this important component of Christianity, starting with Jesus' own words before His death and resurrection:

> But the Counselor, the Holy Spirit, whom the Father will send in my name, will teach you all things and will remind you of everything I have said to you (John 14:26).

> "When he comes, he will convict the world of guilt in regard to sin and righteousness and judgment" (John 16:8).

> [The Holy Spirit] will guide you into all truth (John 16:12).

The Holy Spirit is referred to as the Counselor who teaches us what Jesus taught and convicts us of sin. It's Jesus living in us. We receive the Holy Spirit (John 20:22) upon accepting Jesus:

> Christ lives in you. This gives you the assurance of sharing his glory (Colossians 1:27, NLT).

It is His Spirit that transforms us from the inside out. God does His work through us, by way of His Spirit. Although there are many intellectual defenses of Christianity, the Holy Spirit is the central issue and distinction.[2]

Be filled!

Furthermore, it appears we need to be "filled" with the Holy Spirit daily through our obedience to the Spirit's guidance and through our surrender of our own ways and life to God (Ephesians 5:18).[3] It is not a one-time act that transforms us into perfect saints.

Just like an athlete needs to continuously stay in shape physically, we need to stay in shape spiritually.

Just like we all need to eat for our physical being, we need to stay connected to Jesus for our spiritual filling.

Jesus says:

> I am the vine; you are the branches. If you remain in me and I in you, you will bear much fruit; apart from me you can do nothing (John 15:5).

The apostle Paul confirms this need to stay connected to the Spirit as he talks about his own struggle:

> I do not understand what I do. For what I want to do I do not do, but what I hate I do (Romans 7:15).

When Paul tried to live a saintly life on his own, he fell short — just like you and me. He could not withstand the temptations of sin in his own strength. But Paul clarifies what he means later when he tells believers that we have an obligation to live by the Spirit of Jesus rather than by our own flesh:

> Therefore, brothers and sisters, we have an obligation — but it is not to the flesh, to live according to it. For if you live according to the sinful nature, you will die; but if by the Spirit you put to death the misdeeds of the body, you will live (Romans 8:12–13).

When we follow the Spirit of Jesus living inside of us, He gives us the ability to withstand the temptations of the world, our flesh, and the devil. Jesus was without sin, and those of us who believe in Him have His Spirit inside of us. We deny ourselves ungodly things that we might desire, we love people we might not feel like loving, we believe in a second wind for ourselves and others. Things like that happen, as we depend on the Holy Spirit who resides in believers.

Let's be real about this, too. Many of us continue to profess the Holy Spirit intellectually, while we continue to live in the flesh. I do that far more often than I should. That is why I get stressed out by life. I worry. Maybe you know what I mean. We must continually surrender to the Spirit inside of us as believers.

The Holy Spirit is a Biblical truth that changes our stories.

It is a Biblical truth that can change the stories of those around us.

God's Spirit. Within us. Around us. Teaching us. Guiding us. Empowering us.

Join me in asking God to fill us with His Spirit — every day. Stay connected to the vine.

It makes a second wind possible for each of us.

Footnotes

1 The Shack (2007, William Paul Young, Windblown Media).

2 Here are more scriptures that reference the Holy Spirit. Acts 2:38: "Peter replied, 'Repent and be baptized, every one of you, in the name of Jesus Christ for the forgiveness of your sins. And you will receive the gift of the Holy Spirit.'" Acts 5:3: "Then Peter said, 'Ananias, how is it that Satan has so filled your heart that you have lied to the Holy Spirit and have kept for yourself some of the money you received for the land?'" Acts 8:15: "When they arrived, they prayed for them that they might receive the Holy Spirit." Acts 8:17: "Then Peter and John placed their hands on them, and they received the Holy Spirit."

3 Don't get drunk with wine, which leads to reckless actions, but be filled with the Spirit.

— CHAPTER 23 —

GOD IS OUR HEAVENLY FATHER

"God?" I asked. "I know You get frustrated with people for not having faith in You or our prayers, but sometimes we do ask for things and have faith and then nothing happens. I think that is why some doubt You. At least, that is true for me." I went on while I accompanied my mom and dad on a trip to the Bahamas aboard their boat. "So, I have this video camera here in my hand, and I pray that You would bring this ocean to life while I am filming, for the sake of my mom and dad, who think my belief in You as my heavenly Father, who is listening and answering prayer, is misguided. I pray this in Jesus' name. Amen." I turned on the video camera, believing God would answer that prayer. The next few moments seemed like forever as we cruised over the deep blue Atlantic swells in the heat of the afternoon sun with nothing moving from us to the horizon. Then, like a coordinated sea world show, five dolphin shot straight up out of the water in unison, right where my camera was pointing! I screamed down from the flying bridge to my mom and dad, hoping they might have seen the show or at least gotten a glimpse. All they saw were the remaining suds and ripples from the splash of God's creatures. But, it was caught on tape! My dad printed a picture of it and put it on the wall. Another answered prayer. My Dad heard me.

Because of the crime, regular gunshots, and the freedom our residents have at Hoskins Park, I was often looking out of my bedroom window in the middle of the night, wondering what I might see. And I saw a lot. One night, when I looked out the window, someone was urinating in my front lawn. On another night, two men (not our residents) were smoking crack out in the street. On yet another night, I saw a U-Haul trailer drive in at about 2 a.m. Unusual. The police agreed, when they found it abandoned. That's about the time when Buddy showed up. Buddy was a large, male, black-and-white husky — a street dog who just showed up at our property, out of the blue. Buddy was intimidating just by his size and stature. Now, looking out the window at night, I saw Buddy sitting in the middle of what became our "quad," night after night.

Sitting.

Watching.

Protecting.

I rarely saw any other activity, until Luci showed up. Luci is a female mutt who looks like a combination between a hyena and Australian dingo (pointed ears that are oversized for her head). While Luci is a sweet and humble dog if she likes you, she is intimidating to those who want to do harm. Buddy and Luci became an item. Now when I look out the window at 2 a.m., I see them running around playing in the same quad, all night. My heavenly Father brought me two more friends so I can rest easier. (Author's journal entry, November 3, 2003)

> *Our Father in heaven, may your name be kept holy (Matthew 6:9, NLT).*

Our Father

Most of us know that the Lord's Prayer begins with, "Our Father, who art in heaven." It is a remarkable truth Christianity proclaims: God is our Father. It is also why Jesus was crucified; He would often publically say that God was His Father:[1]

> *For this reason the Jews tried all the harder to kill him; not only was he breaking the Sabbath, but he was even calling God his own Father, making himself equal with God (John 5:18).*

The Bible also testifies that God *said* that Jesus was His Son. At Jesus' baptism and at the Transfiguration, the Father spoke from

Heaven saying, "This is my beloved Son, in whom I am well pleased."[2] When Peter confessed Jesus to be the Christ, the Son of the Living God, Jesus also said that the Father Himself had revealed this to Peter.[3]

Jesus' Father

It was considered blasphemy, to the religious leaders of Jesus' day, to say that God was your Father and you were His Son. But Jesus spoke of God as His Father like we would of our earthly dad. When He was in agony, knowing He was to be crucified, He cried out to His Dad just like we would if we knew we had a loving dad:

> "Abba, Father," he said, "everything is possible for you. Take this cup from me. Yet not what I will, but what you will" (Mark 14:36).

People often miss the fact that God left Heaven to live as a man, in order to make the sacrifice necessary to save humanity. As a man Jesus had human characteristics — He was tired (John 4:4), angry (Mark 3:5), hungry (Matthew 4:2), growing in wisdom and stature (Luke 2:52), He wept (John 11:35), and He was tempted like us:

> For we do not have a high priest who is unable to sympathize with our weaknesses, but we have one who has been tempted in every way, just as we are — yet was without sin (Hebrews 4:15).

Jesus depended on His Father to get Him through each trial. Since God is our Father too, He will take us through all of our trials, just like Jesus.

Furthermore, while we might not like our trials, oftentimes, they are necessary to get our attention. Perhaps, that is why we are to consider them with joy rather than sorrow:

> Consider it pure joy, my brothers, whenever you face trials of many kinds, because you know that the testing of your faith develops perseverance. Perseverance must finish its work so that you may be mature and complete, not lacking anything (James 1:2–4).

What's our part? Surrendering to His will. Living empowered by His Spirit. It becomes a matter of faith.

The perfect Dad

The Bible tells us to ask our Father for what we need as if we were children asking a perfect dad what we wanted:

> *"Ask and it will be given to you; seek and you will find; knock and the door will be opened to you. For everyone who asks receives; he who seeks finds; and to him who knocks, the door will be opened. Which of you, if his son asks for bread, will give him a stone? Or if he asks for a fish, will give him a snake? If you, then, though you are evil, know how to give good gifts to your children, how much more will your Father in heaven give good gifts to those who ask him!" (Matthew 7:7–11)*

We may have preconceived notions about God as a Father, perhaps because we typically compare God to our earthly fathers. But, He is the perfect Father. He is the essence of love itself. He does not represent the same characteristics of our earthly fathers, despite how great or flawed our own fathers may have been. God is perfect. He loves us perfectly.

He speaks

As our Father, God speaks to us — all of us. He is not some distant being waiting until we say the perfect prayer or behave perfectly. He is our Dad. He hears us. God primarily speaks to us via the Holy Spirit, as we read and study the Bible, and through prayer.[4] When Jesus asks, "What is it you want?" in the Bible (Matthew 20:21), He is speaking to us. The words spoken by Jesus in the New Testament are the actual words of God Himself. That is why we can answer that question. That is also why we refer to the Bible as the "living" Word:

> *In the beginning was the Word, and the Word was with God, and the Word was God. He was with God in the beginning. Through him all things were made; without him nothing was made that has been made. In him was life, and that life was the light of men. The light shines in the darkness, but the darkness has not understood it (John 1:1–5).*

> *The Word became flesh and made his dwelling among us. We have seen his glory, the glory of the One and Only, who*

came from the Father, full of grace and truth (John 1:14).

The Word becoming flesh is referring to God's words as spoken by and through Jesus Christ:

> *All Scripture is God-breathed and is useful for teaching, rebuking, correcting and training in righteousness (2 Timothy 3:16).*

> *For the word of God is alive and active. Sharper than any double-edged sword, it penetrates even to dividing soul and spirit, joints and marrow; it judges the thoughts and attitudes of the heart. Nothing in all creation is hidden from God's sight. Everything is uncovered and laid bare before the eyes of him to whom we must give account (Hebrews 4:12–13).*

Do you want to "hear from God"? Read the Bible. For this reason, nobody should have to be forced to read the Bible; every person on the planet should long to do so.

Speaks in English

God speaks to us in the silent voice heard in our minds, reflecting from our hearts. He speaks often in the form of Scripture. But God also speaks to us in English — more like conversing with another person. While this might sound crazy, it is Biblical:

> *"Whether you turn to the right or to the left, your ears will hear a voice behind you, saying, 'This is the way; walk in it'" (Isaiah 30:21).*

> *"I would not have told the people of Israel to seek me if I could not be found. I, the Lord, speak only what is true and declare only what is right" (Isaiah 45:19, NLT).*

> *"So I also will choose harsh treatment for them and will bring on them what they dread. For when I called, no one answered, when I spoke, no one listened" (Isaiah 66:4).*

> *"When I called, they did not listen; so when they called, I would not listen," says the Lord Almighty (Zechariah 7:13).*

Here is a personal example of what I mean. I swam in a 5-mile swim race in St. Croix. The race started two miles off shore at pristine Buck Island. The water was deep blue and crystal clear. The strong current was hardly noticeable until I began to swim. We were told to keep our eyes on some on-shore condos that helped us to stay on course, which I did. I also used them to gauge my progress (or lack thereof). After swimming for about an hour, I didn't seem to be making any progress. That concerned me — I had to be able to swim faster than the current in order to finish the race. That is when I had what I consider another conversation with God. It went something like this:

"OK God, what is going on? I trained for this swim. I prayed for Your help to get me through it. I felt You give me the OK to swim. And here I am swimming as hard as I can, and I appear to be going nowhere!"

I followed that complaint with a question, "God, what exactly is Your role in this race, and what is mine?"

This was the instantaneous reply I heard in my head, "Thomas, your role is to keep those arms and legs moving."

"And Yours?" I asked.

"Mine is to get you to the end."

With a deep breath, I put my head down and continued to swim. That is exactly what happened — despite a fairly severe cramp in my right arm, I did not quit. God got me to the end. While many might question whether that dialogue was between God and me, I truly believe it was. God speaks and we should be able to hear Him. Jesus says:

> *My sheep listen to my voice; I know them, and they follow me (John 10:27).*

We are the sheep, and Jesus is our Shepherd. He is saying that we can hear His voice. That is the consistent message of the entire Bible and the entire purpose of the Bible.

This story is similar to mine, but of much greater depth and importance. In the book of Exodus, God responds to Moses as they were running from the pursuing Egyptians:

> *Then the LORD said to Moses, "Why are you crying out to me? Tell the people to get moving!" (Exodus 14:15, NLT)*

God speaks.

Let's be ready and able to hear Him.

Careful ...

Having said that, we must be careful to discern what we hear in our minds before we attribute it to God. Very careful. I heard someone ask a friend I know if he heard from God directly, and if so, when. He paused before recalling a time when he felt absolutely sure that God had spoken to him. I still believe my friend talks to God on a regular basis, as I do. But, he felt more confident talking about being led by an inner compass, rather than an actual voice. Paul confirmed this approach, as he felt compelled by the Spirit to go to Jerusalem rather than being told to go:

> *And now, compelled by the Spirit, I am going to Jerusalem, not knowing what will happen to me there (Acts 20:22).*

This is important to understand. Some people who say God told them to do this or that may be wrong — including me. We may later admit that we were wrong about what we thought God was saying. But whatever potential damage could have been done was done. Mother Teresa described God speaking to her in the silence of her heart.[5] So, while God speaks, the Bible clearly warns us about uttering too quickly to or about God:

> *Do not be quick with your mouth, do not be hasty in your heart to utter anything before God. God is in heaven and you are on earth, so let your words be few. A dream comes when there are many cares, and many words mark the speech of a fool (Ecclesiastes 5:2–3).*

We must all be careful what we attribute to God:

> *Dear friends, do not believe every spirit, but test the spirits to see whether they are from God, because many false prophets have gone out into the world (1 John 4:1).*

Henry Blackaby, co-author of *Experiencing God*, believes God communicates the clearest through His Word — the Bible, prayer, our circumstances, and the church (or other godly Christians). I believe his approach is sound. I use those other elements to decipher what

I attribute to God, along with certain dreams I have, which are often incredibly vivid and poignant.[6] All of these sources should be in sync. The point remains — God speaks and we should be able to hear Him:

> *Why can't you understand what I am saying? It's because you can't even hear me! (John 8:43)*

A Father's love

God is also a good Father. That is not the same as saying God is love.

Love comes with similar attributes, certainly, but when we say someone is a good man, we typically think of him as virtuous, thoughtful, moral, competent, proper, honorable, and likeable. It is someone we enjoy being around or someone we just want around. The word *love,* in this instance, might actually be an adjective that supports someone we consider good. Not only does the Bible say God is good Himself, it says God is good to us.[7] So, while many might misunderstand God's goodness, He is a good God, a gentleman in that respect. As part of God's goodness, the Bible says that God is just.[8] That means He treats us all fairly, despite our own misunderstandings about the suffering we see in the world. Yes, He will discipline us, just like a Father. But He does so perfectly.

It is the kind of discipline we all need.

It is the kind of discipline that comes from someone who cares enough about us to stick with us.

It is the kind of discipline that will teach us:

> *My son, do not despise the Lord's <u>discipline</u> and do not resent his rebuke, because the Lord disciplines those he loves, as a father the son he delights in (Proverbs 3:11–12, emphasis added).*

We are to "endure hardship as discipline" remembering God is treating us as sons. "For what son is not disciplined by his father?"[9]

Dad

Many people did not have a loving earthly dad.

Many people did not have a dad who was around.

Many people had fathers who have passed away.

God wants to be our Father, and He is overly qualified for that responsibility. Unlike earthly dads, we can trust Him to love us perfectly. In order to trust His love, to obey Him, and to know Him personally, we need to read the Bible. That is primarily how our Dad speaks.

My Dad loves me.

Your Dad loves you.

Our Dad loves us.

That is a fact. That is why He created us. God is our heart's desire:

> Whom have I in heaven but you? I desire you more than anything on earth (Psalm 73:25, NLT).

And we are His:

> Delight yourself in the LORD and he will give you the desires of your heart (Psalm 37:4).

What a story! Shouldn't that change our thoughts? Shouldn't that give us a second wind, whatever we are experiencing?

Footnotes

1 Jesus said, "I praise you, Father, Lord of heaven and earth, because you have hidden these things from the wise and learned, and revealed them to little children. Yes, Father, for this was your good pleasure. "All things have been committed to me by my Father. No one knows the Son except the Father, and no one knows the Father except the Son and those to whom the Son chooses to reveal him (Matthew 11:25-27).

2 Matthew 3:17 & Mark 9:7, American Standard Version (ASV).

3 Matthew 16:13-17.

4 2 Timothy 3:16-17.

5 Her words. http://www.ewtn.com/motherteresa/words.htm

6 Experiencing God, Henry Blackaby and Claude V. King, pg. 87.

7 "Give thanks to the LORD Almighty, for the LORD is good; his love endures forever" (Jeremiah 33:11). "The LORD is good to those whose hope is in him, to the one who seeks him" (Lamentations 3:25).

8 John 5:30 - my judgment is just. See also Romans 3:22-26. Christ paid for our sin.

9 Hebrews 12:7.

— CHAPTER 24 —

GOD IS FORGIVING

Randy first came to Hoskins Park Ministries in 2003, struggling with alcohol and crack cocaine. He was first dismissed because he was not *struggling* against his addictions — one of our few requirements for our residents. But, we never gave up on Randy. He is a fantastic mason, so I would personally hire Randy to do things I wanted done, but didn't really need. I did that to keep in touch with him and to help him out. I kept hiring him and paying him despite many who would tell me I should ignore him until he repented. But, I believe people need time to surrender to God on their own, rather than be cut off, although at some point, I may have stopped my support. I say that from my own personal experience. *God never cut me off.* I have wasted far more money than most on things that I wanted, but certainly didn't need, and as I have already mentioned, I have had my own share of egregious sins against my Lord and Savior. God was gracious to me while I figured out my way didn't work. Many may have another view of God as a Father, but Biblically, and from my experiences, as a loving Dad, He is a forgiving one. Eventually, Randy came to the same conclusion and returned to Hoskins Park to get his life in order. He became a regular leader of Bible study. He finally let go of the sin that so easily entangled him (Hebrews 12:1).

> He has removed our sins from us as the east is from the west (Psalm 103:12, NLT).

God forgives

Perhaps implied, but important to reiterate, God is also a forgiving Father. I don't mean to be presumptuous, but if you have not found yourself in the desert needing a second wind, you still may not understand the importance of God's forgiveness. Recently, I had someone ask me to do a criminal background check on one of our participants at the ministry. The fellow wanted to make sure he was not supporting someone with a criminal background, since the man in question said he didn't have one. Sounds like a reasonable request. We cannot share that information — regardless of our findings — but an important lesson I had to learn in my experience with God is that we all have criminal backgrounds before Him. Some of us get put in jail because our offense was against others, and we got caught. So, we need to constantly remember:

God is holy.

We are not.

Jesus and the immoral woman

It brings to mind the Biblical story of the immoral woman (Luke 7:36–50). The Pharisees invited Jesus to dinner. While there, a known sinner came in with an alabaster jar of perfume. As she wept, she wiped Jesus' feet with her tears, kissed them, and poured expensive perfume on them. You can imagine the sorrow in her heart over her sin. She appeared to know exactly who Jesus was, while the Pharisees still wondered. In fact, the self-righteous, religious leaders were appalled to see Jesus associate with such a sinner. Jesus made the point that those who are "on the bottom" often understand their offense against a holy God, more so than those who teach that truth.

Everybody who calls on the Lord is forgiven

Anyone who has accepted Jesus Christ as their Lord and Savior is forgiven of sins because of what God did on the cross. To the chagrin of many, everyone is forgiven, regardless of what crime they committed. More than that, the Bible says God forgets our past sin:

The LORD is compassionate and gracious, slow to anger, abounding in love. He will not always accuse, nor will he

harbor his anger forever; he does not treat us as our sins
deserve or repay us according to our iniquities. For as high
as the heavens are above the earth, so great is his love
for those who fear him; as far as the east is from the west,
so far has he removed our transgressions from us (Psalm
103:8–12).

It goes to reason that if a murderer or child abuser cannot be saved by God's grace, then we cannot either. Until we finally understand that God condemns all of mankind for being disobedient, we will stand in judgment of God and of God's people as a "holier than thou" person.

I am not perfect.

You are not perfect.

We are not perfect.

We all need God's forgiveness. We get that through the cross. Through Jesus.

The forgotten

That means all criminals, whatever their crime, are the same as, say, Mother Teresa, when they accept Jesus. They get the same Spirit of Jesus Christ, which is their ticket to Heaven. Their own fleshly spirit, the fuel to murder, rape, abuse, or other such misdeeds, is replaced, once they have confessed their sin and repented of it:

Therefore confess your sins to each other and pray for each
other so that you may be healed. The prayer of a righteous
person is powerful and effective (James 5:16).

All of their sins are, therefore, forgiven and forgotten:

"Oh what joy for those whose disobedience is forgiven,
whose sins are put out of sight. Yes, what joy for those whose
record the Lord has cleared of sin" (Romans 4:7–8, NLT).

That doesn't mean they receive a get-out-of-jail-free card either. We do reap what we sow (Galatians 6:7). It just means God forgives them of everything. And we, too, must forgive others.

Forgiving others

Because God has forgiven us of all of our sins, we do not have the right to accept God's forgiveness while we hold grudges against others:

> *For if you forgive other people when they sin against you, your heavenly Father will also forgive you. But if you do not forgive others their sins, your Father will not forgive your sins (Matthew 6:14–15).*

Although this appears to discount our feelings, if God was led by His feelings, none of us would be headed to Heaven because of our sin and His holiness. Jesus would never have gone to the cross, if feelings were His priority. Therefore, we must continually remember that we are not to pretend to be God; we are simply called to obey Him.

There is a rather harsh parable about this point for those who resist its teaching. It is the Parable of the Unmerciful Servant. In this story, a king ordered one of his servants to pay him what he was owed — which was a lot. The servant didn't have the money and pleaded for mercy from his master. In his compassion, the master forgave the servant's debt, all of it. The servant, now freed from the debt to his master, went to those who owed him money and demanded payment. When his debtors asked for mercy from him, he refused to give it — he was unmerciful. When the king found out what his servant had done, he rescinded his mercy and demanded all of his money to be repaid:

> *'You wicked servant,' he said, 'I canceled all that debt of yours because you begged me to. Shouldn't you have had mercy on your fellow servant just as I had on you?' In anger his master handed him over to the jailers to be tortured, until he should pay back all he owed. "This is how my heavenly Father will treat each of you unless you forgive your brother or sister from your heart" (Matthew 18:32-35).*

The reason we can forgive others for their wrongs against us is because we understand that our sin hurts God the same way others hurt us. That is why the recognition of our own sin is so important to Christianity. If we think we are better than others, we are going to have trouble forgiving those who hurt us. But, that is an inaccurate understanding of our sin nature. One conclusion I came to by living among the homeless is that had I walked in their shoes and experienced what they have experienced, I would likely have done whatever they did. Despite the despicable things they might be doing, had I experienced their life, I would likely be doing the same thing. Who am I to think I can understand what someone else has been through when I have not walked in his or her shoes? I cannot. But, I didn't always think this way.

Cultural stigma

For most of my adult life, I noticed homeless people on the street corner, but did not help them. I thought if I gave them money, they would use it to get drunk or high. I had heard that a good alternative to giving them money was to take them to a restaurant and buy them a meal, but since they were considered criminals who may be dangerous, that was not a viable option. The final reason to ignore them was because most of them were just lazy bums who deserved to be homeless.

When I worked at Apple, a homeless man approached one of my clients. I was verbally confrontational with the man for those same reasons. He was interfering with my life and I wasn't comfortable with that — at all.

But, when I became a Christian, things changed. I changed. I could no longer ignore them.

Whether they made me uncomfortable or not.

Whether they were to blame for their situations or not.

Whether they were lazy or not.

I just could not ignore them.

I felt compelled to help, even though I didn't know how. What could I do? What should I do?

So, I checked myself into the local shelter for a long weekend.

Homeless and in the shelter

In October of 2001, I checked myself into the Uptown Men's Shelter in Charlotte, North Carolina. It was perfect timing. I was fed up with my excuses not to help the poor, while the Bible clearly admonished me to do so. I had also become tired of hearing the homeless tell me what an awful place the shelter was to stay, when I directed them there for help. It was time to find out for myself. As soon as I walked through the door at the shelter with just the clothes on my back, I became part of the community of the homeless. So I thought. Determined, but a bit nervous, I got busy becoming acquainted with the rules and regulations of the shelter. I also helped the on-duty supervisor, when volunteers were requested. I have a natural tendency to help when needed. Meanwhile, the supervisor would ask others to help without success. This acted as a trigger for me. *No wonder they are homeless! My suspicions are confirmed, they are just plain lazy!* I thought to myself. Incredibly, in just a few hours living in the shelter disguised as a homeless person, I already had them pegged! Quickly finding my confidence as a "doer," I began challenging some of the men sitting around. I felt like a homeless, airborne ranger ready to put my platoon to work!

One fellow caught my eye. I approached him with a bit of Christian arrogance and challenged his sloth attitude, "Why are you still sitting there when the supervisor continues to ask for help?" I asked. He gazed at me with a distasteful expression — ignoring my critical tone. "The Supervisor needs help, so why don't you help?" I exclaimed as he walked away shaking his head in disgust. *"Lazy. No wonder all these guys are homeless,"* I uttered under my breath.

Judgment

If I had been in a court of law, I would have charged and convicted that man of laziness. I would have sentenced him to several months in a homeless shelter — despite the fact I did not know one thing about him and despite the fact he was already in one! They call that a Pharisee in Christian lingo, better known to most as a hypocrite. Later that evening I found my bed amongst the crowd of 200. In God-like humor, it was right next to the fellow I had asked to help clean up.

And, guess what else? He was lying in his bed reading his Bible! That was the icing on the cake! My judgment was complete. This man was a lazy homeless person using the Bible and Christianity to keep him from doing a thing. As the saying goes, he was so heavenly focused that he was no earthly good! As a good Christian man, I was not going to ignore him, though. I would be kind, even though my thoughts had already convicted him. I walked by his bed and could tell he was upset. That is when he looked up at me and began to speak. With his voice crackling from emotions, he explained to me his life story:

- He was crippled and showed me his right arm, which was shriveled up and half the size of his other.

- His father had thrown him into the street when he was three years old, abandoning him for good.

- He was run over by a passing car, which deformed his right arm.

- While he would like to work, he was unable to do so.

With my eyes swelling up, I apologized to him and walked away a humbled man. I got it — at least with that one potential exception to the laziness label cast on this group of strangers.

Another lesson

The next day, humbled by my stupidity, I decided not to judge anyone before I looked him over first. I saw a fairly big man who looked physically all right, and who was not helping out at all. I repeated yesterday's attack on a more obviously lazy man. "Why aren't you helping the supervisor when he is asking for help and you are standing right here?" I asked in that same critical tone. This man did not gaze at me, nor did he turn away from me. He looked right at me, anger all over his face, and began shouting at me, "I have a heart condition and am not allowed to volunteer!" he said at the top of his lungs. "Had you taken the time to ask me, perhaps you would have found that out before opening your big mouth! Who do you think you are anyway?" Lesson two, complete! Later, I talked to the supervisor and sure enough, these stories were accurate. Although it took many more experiences like those, I have learned an invaluable and Biblical lesson — don't judge!

Many know the story of Michael Oher from the movie *Blindside*. At one time, he was homeless and considered stupid. He later became an NFL offensive tackle.

He was never stupid.

He was alone — without a home.

He needed help.

He needed what we all need — to be loved — as we are.

Not judged as a stranger.

That is why I have concluded that had I walked in their shoes, I would be just like them. We all fall short of God's glory. We all need a Savior. We need to do more loving and less judging. And because Jesus forgives us, we must forgive others. Remember what Jesus said to His accusers while on the cross:

> *Father, forgive them, for they do not know what they are doing (Luke 23:34).*

If Jesus can forgive those who killed Him, we should forgive those who hurt us. Only through the Spirit of God who lives in us, do I think it possible:

> *'Not by might nor by power, but by my Spirit,' says the LORD Almighty (Zechariah 4:6).*

Forgive people who have hurt you — because your Heavenly Father forgave you.

Can you? Will you?

How great is our God!

What do we glean from these attributes of God?

- He is the God who created everything we know to be true, including us as His own critics (Genesis 1:1, 1:27).

- He saves us from the ultimate schemes of the devil, as long as we resist Satan and submit our lives to Him (James 4:7–8).

- He is the one Satan must request permission from before doing anything to anyone (Job 1:6–12).

- He is the one from whom we get hope when everything appears hopeless.

- We will "soar on wings like eagles," "run and not grow weary," and "walk and not be faint" with Him (Isaiah 40:31).

- He is also the God we all long to be with forever, because this God is love itself (1 John 4:16).

- None of us can love apart from God, however hard we try or think we love on our own.

- He is "faithful to all his promises and loving toward all he has made" (Psalm 145:13).

- He is the God who has a plan for our lives and is faithful to complete that plan (Jeremiah 29:11, Philippians 1:6, Psalm 138:8).

- He is the one who goes before us and fights our battles (1 Samuel 17:47).

- He is the one who also demands our allegiance (Deuteronomy 11:26–28).

- He is the same God who forgives us of all our sins, our faults, and our shortcomings (Psalm 103:8-14).

- He is the God we can delight in all the days of our lives, despite our circumstances, because He is with us, and He is good.

- He is our heavenly Father (Romans 8:15, Galatians 4:6).

- He is Jesus — the visible image of the invisible God (Colossians 1:15).

This is our God.

This God is great.

All the time.

So, the issue isn't really about how great God is. The real issue is about receiving His forgiveness — the forgiveness of a Dad who loves us.

> *So be strong and courageous! Do not be afraid and do not panic before them. For the LORD your God will personally go ahead of you. He will neither fail you nor abandon you (Deuteronomy 31:6, NLT).*

Receive His forgiveness and pass it on. It will change the world. One person at a time.

— PART FOUR —

TIME FOR THAT SECOND WIND

"However, when the Son of Man comes, will he find faith on the earth?" (Luke 18:8)

— CHAPTER 25 —

BELIEVING IN THE UNSEEN

"Hypothetically speaking, what do you think I would do if the city showed up to plow down one of our houses?" I asked the Tuesday night Bible study I teach at Hoskins Park, attempting to make a point about faith.

To my chagrin the immediate and overwhelming response was: "You wouldn't let them!"

Chuckling, I asked, "OK, how about if it had happened to Mother Teresa?" Same answer — she probably wouldn't let them. I went on to tell the true story about how Mother Teresa had faced such a situation and how she had relied on prayer to save her building rather than her own might. Within two weeks of that Bible study, the City of Charlotte condemned our newest house at Hoskins Park. It was scheduled to be bulldozed, at our expense, in the next 30 days. I immediately contacted the city and asked for an extension, but was denied. We all prayed. While we did not agree with the city's timing of the condemnation during Christmas or think it was fair that they condemned the house as soon as we owned it, we chose to rely on faith rather than our wisdom or strength, following the example of Mother Teresa. We certainly did not believe this was coincidental. Ultimately, we were granted time to bring the house into compliance with the city ordinances, and the city reversed its decision. The house was never plowed down. Today we call that house "Kurt's House," named after the late Kurt Wiltsey, a faithful Christian whose heart was burdened for the least and lost.

Doug called me at 1 a.m. to let me know Wayne had likely overdosed on his meds (he was on fourteen different medications) and was barely conscious. I rushed over while Doug called 911. They called about 4 a.m. to let me know he was OK and at University CMC. He was discharged around 7 a.m. Doug and I went to the hospital to see him. We told Wayne that we were trying to get him admitted to the shelter, first because he lied to us about his medication, second because he lied about his addiction to prescription drugs, and third because he needed more help than we could give him at this time. He threatened suicide and got extremely angry. We ended up taking him to mental health. I got home about 3 p.m. having been up all night. Long day. No church. Missed everything. But, another red flag about taking guys on lots of medication. I am tired and feel a bit stressed. We have a lot of work to do. We need funding to do it. Not sure I have the experience. God does, though, so I trust He will help me and find a way. It's just a bit overwhelming when a lot of people start going down the wrong path, which seems to be happening right now at Hoskins Park. Thankfully, we are called to be faithful to our call rather than successful. That is emotionally draining and intellectually challenging because circumstances are like fingerprints: never the same, but everyone has them! Who, but God, can truly know what is going on inside the head of another person? (Author's journal, April 24, 2005)

"According to your faith will it be done for you" (Matthew 9:29).

Sea faith or land faith

Although many say we are what we eat or what we are genetically, we really are what we believe, since our behavior is rooted in our minds. What each of us believes to be true about this life comes out in the various ways we live each day, particularly in our choices. This is despite what we might say about our faith. Most of us are old enough to know that talk is cheap:

Talk is cheap, like daydreams and other useless activities (Ecclesiastes 5:7, NLT).

I have a funny story that illustrates this point. It's a story about an African pastor who was always preaching for his congregation to have faith. They would come to counseling sessions, and the pastor's answers were always the same: "Just have faith. God will help you through your trouble." As the story goes, he and some of his congregants went off on a boating outing to preach to another church during the rainy season. The rivers were raging, and they hit a fairly bad storm in their little boat. The congregants began to pray as the pastor sat silently on the boat sweating in fear. It was that bad! They asked the pastor to pray too, and he replied, "Shut up, shut up, we need to see what is going on and not pray!" To which they replied, "But pastor, you said we were supposed to have faith and to pray! We are just exercising our faith!" The pastor replied: "Shut up! Where were we when I told you to have faith?" They responded, "In the church." "Where is the church?" he asked. "It's on the land," they replied. "And where are we now?" The pastor asked. "On the sea," they replied. "Yes, that's right, on the sea," replied the pastor, "and sea faith is different from land faith!" We might preach to someone else who is at sea that they just need to have faith while we are comfortable on land. But when we are in a storm, see if our faith remains unshaken.

Faith — not just a religious term

While many people define faith religiously, faith is really not a religious term. Even the Bible defines faith as "being sure of what we hope for and certain of what we cannot see" (Hebrews 11:1). Webster defines faith as "belief and trust," "firm belief in something for which there is no proof." Despite many who define faith religiously, faith is really what we put our trust in before an event has happened, whether or not there is proof that it will ever happen. Translated, faith is belief in things without seeing or knowing the result. Take my dad, for instance. He was a VFR (visual flight rules) pilot and small boat captain. As such, he trusted in his instruments and proved it all the time. One morning, I was with my dad in fog so dense we could barely see the entrance to the marina where we were docked. Because it was so thick, I was thinking we would wait until the fog cleared before leaving port on our journey to Rhode Island. Surely, my dad would not leave in this weather. Wrong! My dad turned over his twin diesel engines, told me to grab the lines, and we headed out despite the fact we could not see much of anything. The boat is equipped with radar that allows users to continue on despite poor visibility. As most captains and pilots do, my dad trusted those instruments to guide us safely through the fog even as our visibility fell to thirty feet once we were off shore. My dad proved that he had faith in those instruments as he cruised at our speed of eighteen knots, watching the blinking dots on the screen representing other boats running parallel, within feet of our boat. That might sound normal for a captain or a pilot to trust in their instruments in the fog — which it is for those experienced with instruments — but put yourself in the pilot's seat in dense fog like that and see how much faith you have that you really will arrive alive, like me that day.

In the name of Jesus!

It was scary traveling at eighteen knots in thirty feet of visibility, seeing only fog. I didn't trust those instruments as much as my dad did, but my dad had me steering the boat! So, there I was up on the flying bridge (the upper deck), steering with these supposed boats to my left and right, unable to see a thing. My faith was more the "land" or "see" kind in that situation — similar to the great swimmer Florence Chadwick. But, I do trust in prayer and God. While we were underway in the dense fog, I reached down into the cabin, grabbed my mother's hand, pulled (probably yanked!) her up to the flying bridge, and — without asking — said, "Let's pray!" We prayed, "God, please take this fog away immediately, and let us see the boats alongside of us now, in the name of Jesus!" I let go of my mom's hand, and she went below in the cabin with my dad, who was still keenly watching the radar screen. Within sixty seconds, the fog had cleared. My mom came back up on the flying bridge and said, "We just witnessed a miracle!" And we had. Many might chalk that one up to another coincidence. For me, that would take more faith than believing God answered that prayer!

Typical faith

Many of us put our faith in lots of things — until our world is shaken or shattered. Then we find out if that was our "land" faith or our real faith. When we get sick, we typically put our faith in a doctor, surgeon, or medication. That sounds fairly obvious. We want to get well, and they have the most knowledge about our medical situation. Some people now understand the value of good nutrition with regards to disease, and are putting their faith in what they eat. If we are in a predicament with the law, we will hire the best lawyer to get us off the hook. Financially, we often put our trust into our financial advisor, the past performance of the stock market, or our own predictions for the economic future. Most put trust in the government for provision, particularly when we feel insecure. I am sure you can see where this is going. Our faith then is in us, our choices, in a bit of luck or good fortune, which is really faith in the world.

Worldly faith

Worldly faith could be defined as faith in almost anything. The most illusive place we put our worldly faith is in the uncatchable carrot, whatever that might be for any one person. It's probably the one thing you think you need right now in order to be happy. You should also know it moves from one thing or person or event to another, changing as we catch the thing on our list, only to discover that "it" wasn't really "it." Chasing the uncatchable carrot might be the main distraction from having faith in God. It is what keeps us spinning on the wheel of life.

According to Ted Turner's biography, his dad gave him two powerful life instructions. First, he taught Ted never to quit, an important lesson for all of us. Second, he taught him to have more to do than he could ever accomplish. Translated, have a carrot that is uncatchable. This is from Ted's book:

> Son, you be sure to set your goals so high that you can't possibly accomplish them in one lifetime. That way you'll always have something ahead of you. I made the mistake of setting my goals too low and now I'm having a hard time coming up with new ones.[1]

Sadly, Ted's father committed suicide. Yet, Ted Turner learned never to quit in the business world, and he has been incredibly successful pursuing incredibly large "carrots." However, his achievements came at the expense of his family — the price of his success.

So, what carrot are you chasing?

A promotion?

A spouse?

A child?

Revenge?

First place?

More money?

Being more in control?

Meeting or exceeding expectations?

At what expense? At whose expense?

Split second

I have learned that if we live for this world, as I have defined it, then it is only a matter of time before it lets us down. That change can occur in a second's notice. One second, things are fine, the next, an earthquake hits, causing a tsunami that decimates people and territory, all in the blink of an eye. Our worldly faith just doesn't help when things get out of control in that split second. Perhaps, that is why God says if we are friends with this world, trusting in it to save us, we are His enemies:

> You adulterous people, don't you know that friendship with the world means enmity against God? Therefore, anyone who chooses to be a friend of the world becomes an enemy of God (James 4:4).

That doesn't mean that using doctors, lawyers, or other professionals is wrong. It just means we should not put our ultimate faith in them. The Bible mentions one of the Kings of Israel, King Asa, as case in point. His confidence was in the physicians rather than God:

> Though his disease was severe, even in his illness he did not seek help from the LORD, but only from the physicians (2 Chronicles 16:12).

So, while we use people for help, our ultimate faith should be in God. I was thinking about the debate on nuclear energy after the nuclear threat at Japan's Fukushima power plant. Many people did not want us to continue to use nuclear energy due to the threat of a meltdown. It reminds me of the oil explosion in the Gulf of Mexico in 2010 — the Deepwater Horizon disaster. While the oil rig was burning, many prominent political figures were questioning whether we should drill for oil off the coasts of the United States. Most decided it was a bad idea in reaction to the tragedy. But then, gas prices shot up, fluctuating around $4 per gallon, and the debate subsided. In fact, most are now supporting drilling off of our coasts — again. That is what happens when you put faith in something other than God. One day, we solve an energy problem, the next day the energy problem that we solved causes environmental problems that need to be solved by reversing the solutions to the energy problem. It's the same with gun control; one day we want our freedom at any expense. The next we experience another mass murder shooting that kills our kids and many want the government to do something about it. It never ends — like a pendulum, it just swings back and forth depending on our circumstances. And it certainly cannot save us:

> *"When you cry out for help, let your collection of idols save you! The wind will carry all of them off, a mere breath will blow them away. But the man who makes me his refuge will inherit the land and possess my holy mountain" (Isaiah 57:13).*

Nobody, but God, can ultimately save us.

Faith in ourselves

We are all familiar with the importance of trusting both in ourselves and in our dreams. We hear stories of people like Oprah Winfrey, who overcame difficult circumstances in her own life to become one of the most popular television personalities ever. Rudy Ruettiger is another story many are familiar with because of the movie *Rudy*. Rudy's dream was to play football at Notre Dame even though he was not smart enough or big enough (five foot six) to play college football. Rudy persevered and prevailed, despite challenging obstacles. He got accepted into Notre Dame, ended up on the team, and actually played a couple of downs in a college game. Colonel Sanders (Kentucky Fried Chicken) spent two years driving across the United States looking for restaurants to buy his chicken recipe because of the faith he had in himself and in his idea. He was turned down over one thousand times before he made it. And it all began with a sixty-five-year-old man who used his $105 Social Security check to start a business.[2] Faith in ourselves can be the fuel we need to persevere despite obstacles. But, that faith won't bring back a loved one's health or life or restore our lives to the way they were. It just doesn't always work out the way we want it to. Consider Patrick Swayze, who wrote this upon his discovery of pancreatic cancer:

> *I had always felt like a lucky person, but that was being replaced by another feeling: that life wasn't ultimately going to work out the way I'd thought it would. It felt like this was what real life was — that I was finally growing up and facing the truth, and the truth was ugly.*[3]

The truth of life can be ugly, just as Patrick Swayze thought. But the truth of God and His purposes for life is beautiful. Faith in ourselves is important, but has its limitations. We must remember that God created us for a purpose and He has equipped us and gifted us to complete that purpose. It's not as much about what we do as what He has done:

> *He did all this so you would never say to yourself, 'I have achieved this wealth with my own strength and energy.' Remember the LORD your God. He is the one who gives you power to be successful (Deuteronomy 8:17–18, NLT).*

Faith in what people think about us

Many of us also put our faith in what people think about us as "people pleasers." I suppose that is because we all want to fit in and be accepted by the crowd. At least, that was true of me. My behavior followed that idea. That is why I once smoked cigarettes, why I drank, why I did drugs, and why I sought after sex — because that was what my peer group was doing and what I was taught was necessary to fit in, which is nothing new. It is part of the performance-based belief system we discussed earlier, rather than the Biblically based one. Many of the kids who join gangs do so just to be accepted and or to get attention. But following this path, endangers our identity. I was becoming something I was not just to fit in, until I became a Christian and discovered my true identity in Christ. My faith may not have appeared to be in pleasing people, but it was driving a lot of my behavior. I was a product of our culture as I unsuccessfully pursued it for my happiness. What is also interesting about people pleasing is that you are only as good or competent as the goodness or competency of the person or persons that you are trying to please. It has taken me many years to finally figure this out, but it's true.

Your competency

Think about it. If someone who lacks competency is judging yours, then that person is unable to do so accurately because of his or her incompetence. This could be your boss, your co-workers, your friends, family, your professional advisor, or your critics. That does not mean that those who do judge you are always wrong. It just means that often we take too seriously what other people think of us because sometimes they *are* wrong. As an example, take Job's friends, Eliphaz the Temanite, Bildad the Shuhite, and Zophar the Naamathite. When Satan reported back to God that he had been roaming the earth looking for someone to devour, God boasted about His faithful servant Job. Satan told God that the only reason Job didn't curse God was because God protected him. God gave Satan permission to intervene in Job's life to prove to Satan that Job would be faithful regardless of his circumstances. In the discourse of the book, Job's friends told him that it was Job's sin that was causing God to harm him. If he stopped sinning, the trouble would cease. That was not true. In the final chapters of the Book of Job, God sternly puts Job in his place, but then reprimands Job's friends for incorrect counsel. They were wrong and had Job listened to them, he would have been misled.

You're fired!

Another example of this issue of competency is with those who may have been fired from a job. What do we take from being fired? Of course, we probably don't like it very much, whether it is deserved or not. Perhaps it is an indicator of our own limitations as a person, or perhaps it is an indication of the limitations of the one doing the firing. Lee Iacocca, for example, was fired as president of Ford Motor in 1978 after a 30-year career with them. He started as an engineer, then moved into sales, then VP, executive VP, then president from 1970-1978. Interestingly enough, Ford posted a $2 billion profit under his leadership — the same year they fired him. According to sources, Henry Ford II just didn't like Iacocca's idea about the Mini-Max, a Ford version of the Toyota Mini-Van, which Toyota was successfully selling overseas. Later that year, a struggling Chrysler Corporation, on the verge of bankruptcy, hired Iacocca as their president and CEO in a desperate attempt to turn Chrysler around. Iacocca's first order of business was to ask the federal government for a bailout loan, which was as controversial then as now. He got it and ultimately brought in his mini-van idea to Chrysler, which became highly profitable. In fact, their mini-van led automobile industry sales for 25 years.[4] So Ford's fire was Chrysler's hire. As one of my friends often preaches, "People make lousy gods," and we do because we all have our limitations. That is why putting our faith in people is problematic.

Politicians

As controversial as it might be, I include politics because I believe a true god of our culture is politics, therefore, politicians. That implies faith in our government, since politicians are running the government. Politicians are flawed human beings, regardless of their political party — just like the rest of us. Often, we have no idea what is really behind the man or woman in office, regardless of what party or political platform they support, just like we don't really know what is going on with other people. I am always intrigued by how surprised most people are to hear shocking news about others when they get caught doing something unbecoming, politicians or otherwise. Congressman Weiner found himself in the hot seat for inappropriate behavior, then lying to cover it up. Sound familiar? Politicians are people just like you and I, fighting in the same war we are. They just have authority in the government — authority we have given them through the election process. And they are visible — newsworthy. That reminds me of another funny story:

> *A politician dies and upon his arrival at the pearly gates he is told he has the choice of going to heaven or hell, and that he will spend one day in each to help him decide. Upon his visit to hell, he is greeted by some of his fellow politicians who take him to a fancy golf club, where they spend their day golfing, drinking champagne and eating caviar. During his visit to heaven, he spends his day floating on clouds, playing harps and singing. When asked by St. Peter where he wants to spend eternity, he chooses hell. So, St. Peter escorts him down to the gates of hell, where he sees his fellow politicians now dressed in rags as they slave away for the devil. The*

212

politician is confused and asks the devil what happened, it all
was so wonderful yesterday. The devil responds: 'Yesterday
we were campaigning. Today you voted.'[5]

Or maybe it's not so funny.

Accountability to a higher standard

Republicans and democrats point fingers at one another over our deficit, for instance, while the facts are both parties are responsible. Under George W. Bush, the debt rose from roughly $5.7 trillion in January 2001 to $10.7 trillion by the end of his term in 2008. Under President Obama, the debt increased over $4 trillion by the end of his first term.[146] One moment the finger we have pointed at someone else is implicating us, but without us ever saying so or admitting it. That is what I mean by politics. The biggest difference between politicians is typically that one is a democrat while another is a republican. I know I am over-simplifying the matter, since there are serious ideological, moral, and social differences that separate candidates.

But like I have said, we are all diverse people. Without accountability to a higher authority, an authority we all stand under, not chosen independently by our opinions, we are going to come up short, democrat, republican, libertarian or independent. In that regard, we are missing the metaphorical boat. Based on this understanding, politics is like the movie *Groundhog Day*: same deal, different day, and different person. At least, it is the same until someone serious about God runs for office or is elected. Someone who calls our nation together for a day of prayer and fasting and who admits he or she cannot figure out how to deal with the mess we are in without Him despite the political ridicule created by such an honest admission. Then, the focus is correct and politics is not the prevailing theology. Furthermore, this political point I am making implicates a lot more people than the elected officials. It implicates all of their critics as well; those who think politicians are supposed to rescue us when God wants that role for Himself.

Hate crimes

We join in the politicization of matters such as our morality and safety, either explicitly or implicitly, as we neglect the Bible many of us say we believe even if we do so selectively. The hate crimes bill that was passed into law is an example.[6] The bill gives a harsher punishment to crimes that are considered inspired by "hate" rather than some other selfish motive, because hate crimes are on the rise. The sad incident of eighteen-year-old Tyler Clementi brought it to the forefront as prosecutors accused his Rutgers roommate of a hate crime by videotaping him having sex with a male, which then was the potential catalyst for Clementi taking his own life. The point I am making is not to debate the seriousness of the crime or the hate behind it (if hate played a role) — clearly it is serious. Nor is it to debate an effective penalty for committing such a crime. It is to understand why these crimes are escalating and why we continue to focus on our government to protect us rather than understanding why our kids are becoming so hateful and disoriented.

Getting to the root

The question should not be how we delegate enforcement of the law to government, it should first be, why did we — a supposed Christian culture — raise a young man like Tyler Clementi to understand sex before marriage is OK? Second, how did we come to accept homosexuality as moral?

Third, how did we train another young man, Dharun Ravi, to want to judge and thus spy on his roommate? Unless and until we focus on the root cause of what is driving our behavior, we are just buying time. Harsher punishment might help, but it gives more authority to the people in power — our politicians — while we relinquish more and more of our freedom. In fact, we are delegating what we consider right and wrong behavior, to our government. That will ultimately lead to a socialistic government or dictatorship — because of us! Without belief in the Bible, we have no authority higher than the one we make up ourselves, which is the law that is developed by our elected officials, our government. Believe me, most have no idea where this lack of faith in God and the Bible will ultimately take us — but it won't work out the way many think.

All of us voters need to consider what we ourselves believe and then vote for those whose faith is in the God of the Bible above those who we think can save us, when they cannot. People don't just make lousy gods — they aren't gods at all. And when we put our faith in them over

God, we are considered cursed:

> *This is what the LORD says: "Cursed is the one who trusts*
> *in man, who depends on flesh for his strength and whose*
> *heart turns away from the LORD. But blessed is the man*
> *who trusts in the LORD, whose confidence is in him"*
> *(Jeremiah 17:5, 7).*

We might continue to consider such words negotiable, but Biblically those who depend on man to save them, including dependence on our federal government, are cursed.

God puts people in office

Finally, according to the Bible, God puts folks in office and, therefore, we are putting way too much emphasis on "the man":

> *Let everyone be subject to the governing authorities,*
> *for there is no authority except that which God has*
> *established. God has established the authorities that exist.*
> *Consequently, whomever rebels against the authority is*
> *rebelling against what God has instituted, and those who*
> *do so will bring judgment on themselves (Romans 13:1–2).*

We might want to separate church and state, but when a person does this internally, they must follow one or the other — you cannot serve two masters at the same time:

> *No one can serve two masters. Either he will hate the one*
> *and love the other, or he will be devoted to the one and*
> *despise the other (Matthew 6:24).*

Christians are supposed to pray our way out of circumstances because our allegiance is to God. We are not supposed to fight with the typical weapons of man, despite how rarely we see this demonstrated in the United States:

> *The weapons we fight with are not the weapons of the*
> *world. On the contrary, they have divine power to demolish*
> *strongholds (2 Corinthians 10:4)*

Faith is more than rhetoric. Faith is reality for each of us. That should challenge us all, particularly today, since we are on a slippery slope as we leave our Christian faith behind as a nation. Many people will still consider this issue of faith negotiable, as they fight to hold on to their religion, but the Bible is clear, even to those who try to say otherwise.

Bill Maher

At the end of the day, we all need to understand where we have put our faith. And we should not continue to think that religious people are the only ones who have faith. I heard Bill Maher, star of the show *Politically Incorrect* and more recently star of the documentary called *Religulous*, ask people of faith on CNN to tell him why they have faith.[7] His admitted frustration is that religious people tend to avoid the question, in his opinion. While he might be right, another question he should consider is why he has faith in what he has faith in? Like Ellie in *Contact*, it really is easy to question someone else's religious faith, until someone pushes us about our own. So, again, a better question might be what does Bill Maher believe and why? Or who is his god?

And how about you?

What do you have faith in?

Or better yet, who is your god?

That leads to the next question: Where is the proof? Did you know that 60 percent of Americans believe in aliens? But where is the proof?

Biblical Christians just believe in the Bible. As crazy as that might sound, it might take less faith to believe the Bible than to believe something else.

> *Without faith it is impossible to please God, because anyone who comes to him must believe that he exists and that he rewards those who earnestly seek him. (Hebrews 11:6, NLT).*

Join with me, doubting Thomas, and stop (doubting)!

Footnotes

1   Call Me Ted (Grand Central Publishing, New York, 2008), pg. 56.

2   Wikipedia, Colonel Sanders.

3   Swayze, pg. 222.

4   Lee Iacocca, Wikipedia.

5   Canada Free Press, Yesterday, we were campaigning, Canadian Taxpayers Federation, August 11, 2008.

6   CNN Politics. Obama signs hate crimes bill into law. October 28, 2009.

7   October 8, 2010.

— CHAPTER 26 —

HIS STORY

" I don't believe the Bible is true," one of the participants told me.

"Have you ever read it?" I asked.

"Some of it." He replied. This is the standard answer for those who never have.

"I had a friend of mine say the same thing while criticizing the life I was leading, serving the poor. Finally, after I had had enough conversations suggesting I was wasting my life, I told him to just shut up and read the Bible for himself! So he did. Now, he is a Christian who supports our work here at Hoskins Park. Maybe you, too, ought to try reading it before judging it as untrue!" I said, thinking, "How is it that so many people believe their opinions over the Bible, when most of them have never read it?"

Your word is a lamp for my feet and a light for my path (Psalm 119:105).

Belief in the Bible

Because the foundation of the Christian faith is built upon the Bible, and because it is the source of my own beliefs as outlined in *Second Wind*, discussing details about the Bible is important. By the way, did you know that over ninty percent of Americans have Bibles in their homes? Not that many people believe it though. According to *The Washington Times* (and Gallup), thirty-one percent of respondents believe the Bible to be literally true, while forty-seven percent say it was inspired by God (and thus, much of it is true although nobody agrees on which parts are true and which are not, so this statistic might be useless), while just under twenty percent believe it to be more fiction (myth) than fact.[1] Belief in the Bible has always been mixed. But, as I pointed out earlier, we cannot fully understand how we are currently spinning at 1,000 mph as we live on earth, while it shoots through space at 67,000 mph in the sun's orbit.[2] Still, we have minds and should use them to understand the challenging aspects of the Bible.

The challenge

For instance, the Bible was written over a period of a couple thousand years. It was also written a few thousand years ago. It would be hard to believe that what was originally written is what we read today, especially knowing it has been translated from Hebrew, Greek, and Aramaic. The Bible mentions people, civilizations, and events without much evidence to support its claims. There are also some apparent contradictions and grammatical errors. Moreover, it was written by people who didn't have the benefit of science or technology, so while the authors may have meant well, they just may not have known any better. Finally, some of the stories are so far-fetched that believing them would be analogous to believing in Santa Claus. So, I don't deny that believing the Bible does take faith, particularly for intelligent human beings of the 21st century. But then, there is the other side. William Tyndale (1494-1536) translated the Bible into English, which is what got him burned at the stake in 1536. He graduated from Oxford and was known as a scholar and genius.[3] The authorities of his day, the Roman Catholic Church, found him to be a traitor and guilty of treason for his work in translating the Bible. There are others who died to give us the ability to read the Bible today. I suppose that begs the question: if the Bible is "just a book," then why all the fuss over allowing the masses to read it themselves?

Jesus: Liar, Lunatic, or Lord?

In fact, if it is "just a book" written by ordinary writers (uninspired by God), and we have chosen not to believe it, then how do we even discuss Jesus as a good person? Historically, He was a criminal, per other writings. Where do we get this generalized understanding of Him being a "good guy"? The Bible is the only book that tells us specifically who Jesus was — and it says He was God. Many say that Jesus never claimed to be the Son of God and will show some scriptures to back up their claim. I used to entertain that thought myself until I read the Bible. I have already mentioned some of the passages that show Jesus considered Himself to be the Messiah. In fact, He said so directly to a Samaritan woman:

Then Jesus told her, "I AM the Messiah!" (John 4:26, NLT).

While people might continue to use that as their defense, it is not accurate Biblically, nor is it accurate historically. The historical Jesus died for His claims. For those who doubt He really claimed to be God (even after the Bible repeatedly says so), then why did they kill Him? We know Jesus Christ was a real man known as a criminal by historical secular documents and who was executed for claiming to be the Son of God. Now, we can say He was just wrong, but Biblically we know that He was found guilty of blasphemy. There are other Biblical facts.

Biblical facts

First, the Bible is the most influential book in civilization. It was written over a 1,500-year period by more than forty authors, and it testifies to being the inspired word of God. Do you know of any other book near as popular that suggests God wrote it? The Qu'ran, Book of Mormon, and the Jehovah's Witnesses' Bible make similar claims about their own writings or interpretations, but their distribution is a fraction of the Holy Bible's. It has been estimated that over 7.5 billion Christian Bibles have been distributed throughout the world. No other book comes close to that number. The Bible testifies to revealing God's character, revealing the means to every human being's eternal salvation, and it acts as a guide for human life. Regarding the Bible's accuracy, no archeological evidence has been produced to refute the historical testimony of the Bible. It is historically accurate, according to the evidence we have on hand.

A matter of faith

Perhaps that is why many intelligent people have believed and do believe the Bible, like most of the founding fathers of the United States. Despite their lack of consensus of its authority, the founding fathers still founded the United States of America on the Bible.[4] Furthermore, C.S. Lewis, an Oxford professor and atheist who set out to prove the Bible wrong, ended up becoming one of the great Christian theologians of the 20th century.[5] Sir William Ramsay of Oxford University, regarded as one of the greatest archaeologists ever to have lived and who formerly was a Biblical skeptic, converted to Christianity because of the ancient archeological discoveries.[6] Presidents Ronald Reagan, Jimmy Carter, and George H.W. Bush are other respected people who appeared to trust the Bible, along with former NFL coaches Joe Gibbs, Tom Landry, and Tony Dungy. The list of believers goes on and on. Here are some quotes from former leaders of our country that many of us may recognize and respect:

> *We cannot read the history of our rise and development as a nation, without reckoning with the place the Bible has occupied in shaping the advances of the Republic. Where we have been the truest and most consistent in obeying its precepts, we have attained the greatest measure of contentment and prosperity. —Franklin Roosevelt[7]*

> *The fundamental basis of this nation's laws was given to Moses on the Mount. The fundamental basis of our Bill of Rights comes from the teachings we get from Exodus and Saint Matthew, from Isaiah and Saint Paul. I don't think we emphasize that enough these days. If we don't have a proper fundamental moral background, we will finally end up with a totalitarian government which does not believe in rights for anybody except the State! —Harry Truman[8]*

> *The spirit of man is more important than mere physical strength, and the spiritual fiber of a nation than its wealth. The Bible is endorsed by the ages. Our civilization is built upon its words. In no other book is there such a collection of inspired wisdom, reality, and hope. —Dwight Eisenhower[9]*

Are they all forsaking their minds for their faith? Or could it be that there is enough evidence to make it a matter of faith whether we believe the Bible or not?

Historical documents

There are other ancient documents that have been discovered

attesting to the historical accuracy of the Bible. Examples are ancient letters from Bithynia. In one of these letters, Pliny, the appointed governor for the providence of Bithynia circa 110 AD, had sought the emperor's advice on how to handle a troublesome group referred to as "Christians." Pliny also asked specifically if renunciation of Jesus would earn pardon to the offenders. Certainly, this historical letter attests to the life of Jesus, and it suggests He was considered to be more than a mortal man (why would they have to renounce Jesus if not?). Moreover, about the same time Pliny was appointed, Tacitus was made governor of the province of Asia. This famed historian is noted as a historical source for the Roman world of New Testament times (55 AD). In one quote from a passage found in a letter by Tacitus, he confirms that Tiberius was the emperor of Jesus' day, Pontius Pilate was the Roman governor, that Christ was known as a criminal, and that Christianity was spreading from Jerusalem to Rome.[10] For those of us who know the testimony found in the New Testament, this is consistent with what we read today.[11] Evidence like this has lead historian Dr. W.F. Albright[12] to say that the historical evidence of the Bible is confirmed beyond a doubt by archeology. Renowned Jewish Archaeologist Nelson Glueck agrees. He said in a *New York Times* article:

> ...*no archaeological discovery has ever been made that contradicts or controverts historical statements in Scripture.*[13]

Many of us say Christians are Christians by faith alone — that we are not using our minds. Please, use your minds for a moment, and look at the evidence as if you were on a jury. Are Christians really that ignorant?

The Old Testament

Furthermore, since we don't have the original manuscripts, historians must determine the integrity of all ancient documents by the number of existing documented manuscripts or fragments. The Old Testament, the first half of the Christian Bible written before the life of Jesus, is divided into hundreds of chapters and is said to have been completed circa 400 BC. The oldest existing copy of the Old Testament was dated circa 900 AD, until the discovery of the Dead Sea Scrolls. However, in 1947 two Ta'amireh tribesman in the Wadi Qumran area found pieces of leather scrolls that have allowed historians to reconstruct all of the books of the Old Testament, except for one.[14] These findings are dated by paleographers (those who study ancient writings) to around 125 BC. These scrolls are essentially identical to the copy written in 900 AD.[15] That means for one thousand years, the Bible was hand copied with only minor grammatical errors.[16] This alone should eliminate any doubt that what we read in the Old Testament is what the authors originally wrote. Now, once again, we can dismiss this evidence but that is exactly what we are doing, dismissing real and solid evidence. The Old Testament was written before Jesus was born. That is a fact.

The New Testament

The New Testament is also supported by a plethora of evidence. It is the second half of the Christian Bible, and it relates the life and death of Jesus. There are twenty-four thousand manuscript copies or portions of the New Testament in existence today.[17] Many were written within twenty-five to fifty years of the originals, which were written approximately thirty years after Jesus died. In volume, the next closest document to the New Testament is the epic *Iliad* by Homer. The *Iliad* is a historical poem set during the Trojan War and considered historically sound, but there are only 643 copies in existence. Furthermore, when the text of the *Iliad* and New Testament were critically studied, the New Testament was said to contain one half of 1 percent discrepancies, while the *Iliad* had a 5 percent textual corruption.[18] In other words, the New Testament is 99.5 percent reliable. Because of findings similar to this one, historian F.F. Bruce has said, "There is no body of ancient literature in the world which enjoys such a wealth of good textual attestation as the New Testament."[19]

Biblical predictions

Thus far, we have discussed the accuracy of the Bible, but not its authority. One area that attests to its authority is Biblical prophecy. Any document that accurately predicts the future is considered authoritative, and the Bible has made numerous predictions that have come true. If you read through the prophets of the Old Testament, like Jeremiah or Isaiah, you will find many prophecies and their fulfillments. For instance, we have evidence that the Old Testament writers predicted details about the Messiah at least one hundred years in advance of the life of Jesus.

We have proof, historical and scientific proof. There are three- hundred-thirty-two predictions of the Messiah in the Old Testament Bible. The Old Testament says that the Messiah would be born of a virgin (Isaiah 7:14), in Bethlehem (Micah 5:1–2), that he would be a descendant of David (2 Samuel 7:12-16), that he would be betrayed for thirty pieces of silver (Zechariah 11:12-13), that he would have his hands and feet pierced (Psalm 22:16, Zechariah 12:10), that his bones would remain unbroken (Psalm 34:20 — which is, by the way, in contradiction with the ancient process of crucifixion, which did break bones),[20] that the soldiers would cast lots for his clothing (Psalm 22:18), that he would die with transgressors (Isaiah 53:9–12), and that his death would atone for the sins of mankind (Isaiah 53:5–7). For those who are familiar with the life of Jesus, we know this testimony is confirmed in the New Testament.

New Testament scripture

The New Testament says that the Messiah was born of a virgin (Matthew 1:18–2:1), in Bethlehem (Matthew 2:1, 2:6), that he was a descendant of David (Matthew 1:1), that he was betrayed for thirty pieces of silver (Matthew 26:15), that he did have his hands and feet pierced (Luke 24:39), that his bones were not broken (John 19:31–37), that the soldiers did cast lots for his clothing (Matthew 27:35, John 19:24), that he died with transgressors (Matthew 27:38), and that his death did atone for the sins of mankind, (John 1:29, Acts 8:30–35). What is incredible are the odds of this happening coincidentally. According to scientist and mathematician Dr. Peter Stone, the chances of just four of these prophecies being fulfilled by Jesus have been calculated to be one in four hundred million. Furthermore, the calculation for all of the Biblical prophecies to be fulfilled in the life of Jesus is a number in the trillions and trillions of billions.[21] Now, I realize that some will still contest that the New Testament half of the Bible was written after some of these Old Testament predictions occurred. Once again, you are not following the scientific evidence as you make that conclusion. As Ronald Reagan used to say (typically to Jimmy Carter), "There you go again!" As historians have vouched, these books were all written before the time the historical events happened. There is no mistaking that the prophecies in the Bible are prophecies recorded by the Bible. You might be able to disregard them, but as an intelligent person who has studied the evidence, I cannot.

Jesus endorsed the Bible

It should also be noted that Jesus Himself testified to Scripture's authority. Besides saying that the Scriptures could not be broken, He said that every word of the Old Testament law would be fulfilled (Matthew 5:18). He also used scripture to fend off Satan, quoting the Old Testament several times when tempted by him (Matthew 4:1–11). And He said that God was speaking through David in the Old Testament (Mark 12:36). Jesus even rebuked the religious leaders for not knowing the Scriptures when He said:

> *"You are in error because you do not know the Scriptures or the power of God" (Matthew 22:29).*

In fact, He appeared to become intolerant about their lack of understanding of the Scriptures when the Pharisees would not believe Jesus or listen to Him. Jesus said:

> *And the Father who sent me has himself testified concerning me. You have never heard his voice nor seen his form, nor does his word dwell in you, for you do not believe the one he sent. You study the Scriptures diligently because you think that in them you have eternal life. These are the very Scriptures that testify about me, yet you refuse to come to me to have life (John 5:37–40).*

This is another one of those areas in the Bible that clearly identifies Jesus as the Messiah, but one that is often overlooked as He is simply considered a good guy or just a prophet. According to these passages, Jesus trusted the Scriptures to be the Word of God. It is hard to deny otherwise.

Far-fetched stories

Finally, there are also some stories in the Old Testament that many of us find difficult to believe. The Genesis account of creation, the tree in the Garden of Eden, and Jonah's experience with the whale are some examples. But compared to what, do we find these stories hard to believe? Many believe in the theory of evolution, believing we evolved from a microscopic amoeba. Do we find these stories harder to believe than that theory? Just consider how you got to be a person for a moment and you might understand my point. Is it really harder to believe that God created you than to believe you evolved into the complex person you are from a cell you cannot see with your eyes? Stephen Hawking, a respected British theoretical physicist, has written a book called *The Grand Design*, where he argues there is no need to consider God in creation because of his theories. He believes that we (people) could have evolved out of nothing, just like the universe. I know he is an intelligent man, but his views appear to be in contrast with great scientists like Albert Einstein (1879-1955), Isaac Newton (1642-1727), Galileo Galilei (1564-1642), and Nicholas Copernicus (1473–1543), who all believed God was involved in creation.[22] Like I said earlier, nothing happens in our own lives without us "doing" something, particularly the more complicated things. So, while some of these stories might be difficult to believe, everything has a bit of a mystery to it, so there is no reason to render them fiction:

> *As you do not know the path of the wind, or how the body is formed in a mother's womb, so you cannot understand the work of God, the Maker of all things (Ecclesiastes 11:5).*

So — is the Bible true?

So, despite any skepticism, many of us might now agree that there is enough archaeological evidence to persuade us that the Bible is historically accurate. Although we don't have all the evidence, the evidence we do have seems to verify, rather than contradict the Bible. Many of us might now conclude from the evidence, such as the Dead Sea Scrolls, that what we read in the Bible today is what the authors originally wrote. Any document hand-copied for one thousand years with only minor grammatical errors is likely to be accurate. With the abundance of copies of the New Testament that exist, it too is likely to be what was originally written. Moreover, many of us might conclude that the Bible is authoritative because it made hundreds of predictions that eventually came true. It is hard to deny the Old Testament predictions about the Messiah are not fulfilled through the Jesus we read about in the New Testament. Furthermore, although we all admit some of the stories in the Bible are rather hard to understand, perhaps they are believable. If God can create the universe and life as we know it, far be it for us to say He could not have made those stories happen just as they are written. We are all miracles living in a world far more complex than our finite minds can fathom or that science can prove. As we have already discussed, we all have faith in something. Some of us simply have faith in the Bible that says God did all this. But regardless of what you believe about the evidence, the real testimony of the Bible is found in the words written on its pages. Words that say it was God breathed, that it is a guide to an abundant life on earth and the key to eternal life with God in heaven or an eternity separated from God in hell. In order to understand this evidence, however, you must read the Bible yourself while seeking its truth with an open mind and heart.

So, what do you think?

Is the Bible true?

Footnotes

1 http://www.gallup.com/poll/27682/onethird-americans-believe-bible-literally-true.
  aspx.

2 Goddard Space Flight Center, Ask an Astrophysicist, April 1, 1997, http://imagine.
  gsfc.nasa.gov/docs/ask_astro/answers/970401c.html.

3 Wikipedia, William Tyndale.

4 I do not have the space to add all the footnotes that attest to this as fact, but I did
  study the facts about our founding father's faith before drawing this conclusion.
  If you disagree, please make sure you study the facts. Of course, our founding
  fathers disagreed on the authority of the Bible, but they founded the country on it
  nonetheless. Read the prayers, quotes, comments, and then look at how we are
  governed. This is not up for debate for those who trust the evidence.

5 Wikipedia, C.S. Lewis.

6 http://www.faithbasedonfacts.org/main/?q=node/84.

7 Conservapedia, Franklin Roosevelt.

8 Thinkexist.com, Quotes of Harry S. Truman.

9 US Presidents & The Bible, http://www.bebaptized.org/u.htm.

10 Paul Barnett, Is the New Testament Reliable? (Downers Grove, Ill.: InterVarsity Press,
   1986), pg. 21. See Luke 3:1, Matthew 27:2, Luke 23:2, Acts 1:4 and 28:14.

11 R.K. Harrison, Introduction To The Old Testament, (Grand Rapids: William B.
   Eerdmans Publishing Company), pg. 94. White, pg. 70.

12 Late professor emeritus at Johns Hopkins University.

13 Harrison, pg. 94. James Emery White, A Search for the Spiritual (Baker Books,
   Grand Rapids, 1998), pg. 70.

14 Harrison, pg. 134. The condition of the so-called large Isaiah manuscript (IQIsaa) is
   testimony to the care taken in preserving the manuscript against time. See also pg.
   137.

15 Harrison, pg. 92. Radiocarbon dating has become the reputable dating technique of
   modern history using a carbon-14 system of dating artifacts. This process is based
   upon the recognition of the fact that every living organism contains a proportion of
   radioactive carbon. Paleographers are specialists in ancient writings.

16 Josh McDowell, A Ready Defense (Nashville: Thomas Nelson Publishers, 1993), pg.
   53.

17 White, pg. 73. Barnett, pg. 44. One example is Codex Sinaiticus, a complete
   edition of the New Testament from the fourth century that can be found in the
   British Museum. It was discovered by Count Tischendorf in 1844 at St. Catherine's

monastery, Mt. Sinai and was believed to have survived due to the security of the monastery and dry climate.

18 McDowell, pg. 43. Old Testament Isaiah scrolls have similar variation. For more information on the Old Testament see Archer, Gleason L.A. A Survey of the Old Testament, (Chicago: Moody Press, 1964), pg. 25.

19 Bruce, F.F. The New Testament Documents; Are They Reliable? 6th ed. (Grand Rapids: Erdmans, 1984), pgs.16-17. Also McDowell, pg. 53.

20 U.S. News & World Report, October 25, 1999, "Is The Bible True?," page 58. In 1968, the skeletal remains of a crucified man were found by explorers. The shin bones were broken which corroborated Biblical testimony. In John 19:32-33 it says that the bones of the others being crucified with Jesus, were broken.

21 White, pg. 74.

22 Evidence for God, Famous Scientists Who Believed in God, http://www. godandscience.org/apologetics/sciencefaith.html.

— CHAPTER 27 —

WHAT SHALL WE DO?

Dave would not open his door for Doug, but he did for Johnny. He had just used crack in the house and was now sitting on his bed. Incredibly, he goes to prison for a couple years if he gets caught using drugs. Knowing that he used anyway. Dave is bi-polar and a little slower than some. We found out that Wayne, next-door at Johnny's, had been buying crack for Dave. Unbelievable. Still trying to figure out what to do about this situation. Have not heard back from Mike either. He just disappeared like he does after a few months. Chris is MIA. Have not heard from him since last weekend, another incredibly gifted carpenter ruining his life with alcohol. In summary, Jerome did crack, Dave did crack, Jon drank a fifth of liquor, Lewis stayed out again last night, and Chris is gone. Not sure what to say anymore. Something has to change around here, and I am really not sure what to do. I am raising drug addicts. Only God can change them, but can I really help? *(Author's journal entry, October 8, 2005)*

> *"The work of God is this, to believe in the one he has sent"* *(John 6:29).*

Accept Jesus

So now what? If you believe the Bible and realize you are in a war, you need to know what to do about it. Please consider these suggestions as how to live a victorious life, God's way. Or as Kelvin Smith, Sr. Pastor of Steele Creek Church preaches, how to live "on target."

The first step is to accept Jesus Christ as your Lord and Savior, if you have not already done so. I have already mentioned that, in order to be saved, you must confess Jesus with your mouth, and believe He was raised from the dead in your heart:

> If you declare with your mouth, "Jesus is Lord," and believe in your heart that God raised him from the dead, you will be saved (Romans 10:9).

When we confess Jesus as our Lord and believe He was raised from the dead, mysteriously, we are born again and get new spirits — Jesus' Holy Spirit:

> And I will ask the Father, and he will give you another advocate to help you and be with you forever — the Spirit of truth. The world cannot accept him, because it neither sees him nor knows him. But you know him, for he lives with you and will be in you (John 14:16–17).

That is our first step. If you believe Jesus is the Christ but have never put your faith in Him, please do that now. Just tell Jesus that you believe He is whom He claims to be — the Son of God — and that you believe He was raised from the dead as your Lord and Savior. It's a matter of sincere faith, rather than of intelligent words. You don't have to be in church either! Sit, stand, or kneel where you are, and pray a short prayer like this:

> Dear Jesus, I admit I fall short of Your glory and need You as my Savior. I believe in all my heart that You came to earth from heaven, lived a perfect life, took the sins of the world upon Your body, including mine, were crucified, died, and raised from the dead defeating death for all who believe and forgiving our sins because of Your shed blood. I am grateful to know that had I been the only person on the planet You would have died just for me, because You love me that much. Please now fill me with Your Spirit, use me as You see fit, live through me all the days of my life, and protect me from the evil one, as I have chosen to live for You. I pray this in Your name Jesus, amen.

If you prayed that prayer (or similar), either now or at any point in your life, you are a born-again Christian. The Spirit of God now lives inside of you, replacing the spirit you had when you were born. The veil has been lifted![1] Whether you feel any different or not, you are now a new person in Christ and saved by His grace![2] Congratulations! This is the most significant decision a human being can make.

Or are you still waiting, wondering?

Baptism

Next, after we have put our faith in Jesus Christ as our Lord and Savior, we need to be baptized. Baptism is the outward expression of that inward change; it shows we are serious and represents our new life. If you have accepted Jesus as your Lord and Savior, you should find a church with faithful Christian leaders who will baptize you:

> When the people heard this, they were cut to the heart and said to Peter and the other apostles, "Brothers, what shall we do?" Peter replied, "Repent and be baptized, every one of you, in the name of Jesus Christ for the forgiveness of your sins. And you will receive the gift of the Holy Spirit" (Acts 2:37–38).

Moreover, while the actual baptismal process is controversial amongst many churchgoers, it really shouldn't be. It is simply a meaningful ceremony that uses water as its primary ingredient and that is symbolic for cleansing us from sin. Jesus Himself was baptized:

> Then Jesus came from Galilee to the Jordan to be baptized by John. But John tried to deter him, saying, "I need to be baptized by you, and do you come to me?" Jesus replied, "Let it be so now; it is proper for us to do this to fulfill all righteousness." Then John consented (Matthew 3:13–16).

The amount of water might be determined by what is available rather than what is necessary, but water is necessary in the actual baptism.

Confess and repent (stop sinning)

As believers, we will also confess our known sins and then stop that behavior. The Bible is clear that we will not be able to live a life controlled by our sinful nature, while pleasing Him at the same time:

> Those who are still under the control of their sinful nature can never please God (Romans 8:8, NLT).

We may struggle against our sin for a while as we fight against our flesh (1 Peter 2:11) — but as born-again Christians, we now have the Spirit of God inside of us, and He doesn't want to participate in sin. Many people think Christians, like me, choose to be good for goodness' sake. But that is not true. I have the Spirit of Jesus in me (Colossians 1:27). I get convicted when I follow my flesh and choose not to live a Biblical life. I can no longer just drink, do drugs, smoke, eat poorly, watch pornography, have sex outside of marriage, flirt, hurt people intentionally, break the law, or even run over people in the name of productivity without being convicted by His Spirit. It's more than my choice — it is now God inside of me who is leading me to the truth. My part is to "walk" by His Spirit:

> So I say, walk by the Spirit, and you will not gratify the desires of the flesh (Galatians 5:16).

In fact, it is impossible to let go of our sin nature without turning to Jesus for His strength. That is what I had to learn through my work with the homeless and now what we teach. When we turn to Him we can do all things — even the impossible:

> I can do all things through Christ who strengthens me (Philippians 4:13, NKJV).

Only when we accept our sin as OK, do I believe we find ourselves in dangerous water. That is what appears to be happening today in the area of sexual purity, eating, and abortion,[3] to name a few of the issues. We are accepting sin as OK, politicizing it, defending it in fact, while it is contrary to God's Word. We must confess our sins to one another and struggle against them until we are freed from them (James 5:16).

Are you having sex outside of marriage? Stop it.

Are you addicted to a substance? Seek help.

Eating too much? Give it up.

Pride stopping you from asking for help? Ask anyway.

And remember, you are forfeiting God's best life for you every day you keep satisfying your flesh at His expense (Jonah 2:8).

Are those things really worth that price?

Remember our new identity

We all know many "Christians" do act hypocritical at times. That is because even with God's Holy Spirit in us, we have to constantly choose to surrender to God by remembering our new identity. Larry Crabb says it this way:

> It is clear that we are a strange mixture of good urges and bad urges, and that these urges seem to have a life of their own. With God's spirit, we can love as Jesus did, but we can also sin like the devil. Indwelling sin is a lifelong problem. Indwelling goodness is a lifelong reality awaiting release.[4]

Think of it like this: Just because you show up at the gym ready to work out doesn't mean your physical body gets in shape. It is a continuous choice to exercise, it is a continuous choice to eat well, and it is a continuous choice to allow the Spirit of God to rule your life. You must remember who you are in Christ, the new you. The Bible says you:

- are God's child (John 1:12),
- are Christ's friend (John 15:15),
- are justified as right by God (Romans 5:1),
- are united with Jesus and one spirit with Him (1 Corinthians 6:17),
- belong to God (1 Corinthians 6:19–20),
- are a saint (Ephesians 1:1),
- have been redeemed and forgiven of your sins (Colossians 1:14),
- are complete in Christ (Colossians 2:10).

As a Christian, all these verses apply to you! Still, we must remind ourselves daily of our new identity, lest we slip back into the old self — the one we have let go.

Remember your new identity.

Read His Word

The next step is getting to know God by reading the Bible. It is important to remember, too, that this step is primarily about getting to know God, rather than reading the Bible because it is the Christian thing to do. It should be considered a privilege rather than a check box on a to-do list. I once read the Bible because I thought I had to, but

I read it now because I am developing a relationship with the God of the universe, every day. I want to hear from God and I do, through His Word. That is what is offered to us by the Bible, as repetitive as this may be. That is also why it is so astounding how few people read it. Can you imagine dying for something that everyone needed, while only a few people valued your sacrifice? Remember, many people were burned at the stake for translating the Bible so we could read it. The Bible is a gift to mankind from the One who created us. We are privileged to be able to read it (if you know someone who cannot read, you can find it on CDs or other forms of media for them). I promise you this: If you read the Bible every day, you will be a different person, a better person, a changed person.

Read it and see.

And get a version you understand. For the most part, I have used the New International Version in *Second Wind.* Try that version if you are having difficulty understanding King James. You may have a preference for King James because of traditional or sentimental reasons, but that is not the point of the Bible. The point of the Bible is to read it so you understand what it says, what God is saying to you.

Perhaps, only prayer contends with such a gift.

Pray

"Devote yourselves to prayer."[5] Prayer is defined as our communication with God. Mother Teresa was known to have woken up every day at 4 a.m. and prayed for hours.[6] Perhaps, that is why she was successfully able to give up the world's transient pleasures that so many of us desire. Jesus was known to go away and pray as well, and He was God (Luke 22:41–44). The Bible says Jesus prayed so hard that His sweat became like blood. Now that is prayer! So, if He had to pray to endure His calling, how much more should we need to pray to fulfill ours?

Ask Dad

Furthermore, although many of us might claim to pray, we must consider what we mean by our definition of prayer. For instance, do we look at our conversation in prayer similarly to our relationships with other people in our lives, like our spouse (if we are married)? My wife and I spend a fairly good amount of time talking about our day, every day of our lives — we are in touch with each other, for the most part. And our conversations are typically two-way. Communication is essential to relationships. Prayer is having that conversation and relationship with God — the God of the universe — the One who created everything we know to be true, including each of us. Now, I know the big issue for some of us is whether we believe God hears our prayers or whether we can really hear from Him at all. But, can you imagine eliminating communication with your wife, kids, friends, employees, employers, or even people at the store where you are shopping (although maybe some of us have)? What would happen if you did (or what is happening if you have)? In most cases, the relationship would die (or is dead). You just cannot have a healthy relationship without communication — healthy communication. Thus, prayer and Bible reading are our ways of communicating with God. Without them, our relationship with God, however well intended we may be, is likely nonexistent. These are the two things Satan hates the most about Christians. I once read that "Satan laughs at our toil, mocks at our wisdom, but trembles when we pray."[7] Honest, sincere prayer, having faith that God hears us and is answering those same prayers, seems to be what God wants from us all (Matthew 6:9).

Pray, every day. You will be a different person. Will you make that commitment?

Worship

When we finally understand who God is, our natural response will be to worship Him. Worship is our expression of love toward and appreciation for God. We should ascribe Him His due, as the psalmist says:

> *Ascribe to the LORD the glory due his name; worship the LORD in the splendor of his holiness (Psalm 29:2).*

> *I will exalt you, my God and King, and praise your name forever and ever. I will praise you every day; yes, I will praise you forever. Great is the Lord! He is most worthy of praise! No one can measure His greatness (Psalm 145:1–2, NLT).*

Typically, worship is considered what we do in church while worship music is playing. But worship crosses our traditional boundaries. For instance, worship is also considered obedience to His Word, by keeping His commandments:

If you love me, keep my commands (John 14:15).

Loving God by doing what He says Biblically is worshiping Him. This is one more reason why we just cannot live any way we want to and think it is OK with God. We must do what God tells us to do, and that is found in His Word. Obedience is an act of worship:

Therefore, I urge you, brothers, in view of God's mercy, to offer your bodies as living sacrifices, holy and pleasing to God — this is your spiritual act of worship (Romans 12:1).

Our bodies

Besides using our bodies as living sacrifices, the various expressions of our bodies are used to show our adoration for Him. This is what many people do in church:

Ezra praised the LORD, the great God; and all the people lifted their hands and responded, "Amen! Amen!" Then they bowed down and worshiped the LORD with their faces to the ground (Nehemiah 8:6).

The outward expression of God is an important aspect of worship. But, worship is more genuinely shown on Monday through Saturday, rather than at church on Sunday. Lots of people can raise their hands to God in church, but it is really not worship if we are disobeying Him with our lives. We need to be real before our Father. Worship is about giving our entire lives back to God, dying to self, in response to who He is and what He has done for us.

Worship the God who created you.

He is worthy.

Giving of our resources

Giving is part of the Christian life and should be our response to God because of all He has given us. God actually asks us to test Him in the giving of our money. It is the only time God asks us to do this:

> *"Bring the whole tithe into the storehouse, that there may be food in my house. Test me in this," says the LORD Almighty, "and see if I will not throw open the floodgates of heaven and pour out so much blessing that there will not be room enough to store it" (Malachi 3:10).*

Biblically, the tithe was a portion of money known as 10 percent of the gross of what someone earned. It is found in the book of Genesis as a promise from Jacob to God:

> *"Then the Lord will be my God and this stone that I have set up as a pillar will be God's house, and all that you give me I will give you a tenth" (Genesis 28:21–22).*

As Christians, under grace, we are not obligated to give 10 percent of what we make just because it is a "rule" or "practice." But understanding God as our provider, we should want to give back to God and His Kingdom's work, particularly when we know it is important to Him. Therefore, 10 percent should be our starting point. We are storing up treasures in heaven — by what we give on earth.

Find a cause that burdens your heart, and give.

Give our time

We hear countless stories of people who go to help those in need and whose lives are forever changed because of their service to them. After I checked myself into the Uptown Men's Shelter in Charlotte, North Carolina, as a homeless person and spent some time there, I was pleasantly surprised at the beauty of these men who are often considered criminals or addicts. Eventually, I moved into the inner city myself, and started my own ministry to help men off the street — Hoskins Park. I felt called to help them, which I finally figured out meant I had to live amongst them. I had to give up my selfish ways in obedience to the Scriptures:

> *Do nothing out of selfish ambition or vain conceit. Rather, in humility value others above yourselves, not looking to your own interests but each of you to the interests of the others. In your relationships with one another, have the same mindset as Christ Jesus: Who, being in very nature God, did not consider equality with God something to be used to his*

239

own advantage; rather, he made himself nothing by taking
the very nature of a servant, being made in human likeness.
And being found in appearance as a man, he humbled
himself by becoming obedient to death — even death on a
cross! (Philippians 2:3–8)

Although I do help lots of people by my efforts at Hoskins Park, God has used my service to His people to change me. The natural result of serving is God molds us into His image. Serving others is important to God and, when we have His Spirit inside of us, it is something we do in response to His nature and His goodness living through us.

Find a place worthy of your time — and serve.

Attend a church

Belonging to a local church is important. It's part of the community God planned for His people. Many people think church attendance is the single most important aspect that distinguishes Christians from non-Christians, while others don't think the church matters at all. However, Jesus said:

And I tell you that you are Peter, and on this rock I will
build my church, and the gates of [hell] will not overcome it
(Matthew 16:18).

The church is known as the bride of Christ, therefore part of Jesus Himself (Ephesians 5:25–27). So, we need to belong to a local church despite the fact that no church will be perfect.[8] It makes sense. My wife works at the YMCA, and she is always around people who want to stay in or get in good physical shape. The Y provides a community where people can come together under one roof with something in common: exercise and health. In essence, it is its own community. Most of us are familiar with the benefits of being around like-minded individuals — it can be affirming, inspiring, helpful for training, and good for our social life. Whereas the Y's main focus is physical (even though considered a Christian organization), the church is simply spiritual. It is a place to worship God, to bless Him for who He is, to hear His Word, and to get involved with like-minded people who truly do want to be used to change the world. It is also God's army, at least that is its intent.

Find a Bible-believing church that preaches the Word to both the lost and the saved, one that serves all, to even the least of God's people. And attend.

Seek your calling

We have already been over the fact that God has a call on your life and on mine, either specifically, generically, or both:

> But each of you has your own gift from God; one has this gift, another has that (1 Corinthians 7:7).

> Therefore do not be foolish, but understand what the Lord's will is (Ephesians 5:17).

The latter verse appears to suggest we have a part in understanding our calling. Think of it this way: In order to join a football team, you have to have some inkling of your desire to do so, as with any other sport or career. Something has to set you in motion towards a sport, career, or calling. Then you have to try out for a specific team. Another example is your education. At some point, you need to decide if you want to attend college or not. If so, then you have to decide which one you would like to attend and apply. If not, you go through a decision-making process about a potential job or trade. I believe it is a similar process with our calling. Something in us has been wired for a certain calling, and we have a part in discovering what it is. Pray for God to reveal the calling He has on your life. When He does, go for it! You will find yourself much more focused than most, too. The more focused, the more effective.

Do you know what God has called you to do, specifically?

Seek it.

Know it.

Follow it.

Join a small group

It is also important to be involved with a small group of people who share life together. If we don't hang around like-minded people, we are likely going to fall back to old habits. So remember:

> Do not be misled: "Bad company corrupts good character" (1 Corinthians 15:33)

A friend of mine preaches it this way: "Friends are like an elevator shaft — they either take you up or down!" When I became a Christian, my relationships changed. My old friends are still some of the finest, most talented, hard-working, and most beautiful people I know. I still love them, but when God took over my life, my loyalty was to Him first, even at the expense of old friends.

Join or start a small group.

We must surrender

Most of us realize the choices we have to make on a daily basis. They vary from person to person, but we all have to make them. If we are trying to eat well, for instance, it is a choice to do so — all day long. It is the same with an addict. Addicts cannot wake up in the morning adamantly opposed to participating in their addictions and then give in to the temptations of the flesh later in the day, if they want to be freed from the addiction. It is a moment-to-moment, day-by-day struggle to stay clean. That is the fight and accompanying surrender I am talking about for all of us. Henri Nouwen said it this way:

> The spiritual life requires a constant claiming of our true identity.[9]

We must constantly fight against a tactical enemy who wants us to believe his lies rather than follow God's truth, as we have been over. As Christians we have been crucified with Christ, so it is no longer us who live, but Christ in us:

> I have been crucified with Christ and I no longer live, but Christ lives in me. The life I now live in the body, I live by faith in the Son of God, who loved me and gave himself for me (Galatians 2:20).

And when we do follow God's truths rather than Satan's lies, God develops our faith (Romans 10:17). That in turn develops our testimony.

Surrender your will to God.

He will develop your testimony.

Faith and our testimony

The changes God makes in our own lives become our own personal testimony — our undisputed testimony. Christians do not naively believe the Bible on faith alone. We, too, must "get on the scale," metaphorically speaking. The scale should show someone that we actually lost weight on the diet we said we were on! The scale shows proof. Who can refute the obvious changes in our lives upon conversion? As Christians, our testimony is developed as God changes our lives, which deepens our faith, and allows us to overcome Satan and our accompanying vices:

> *They overcame him … by the word of their testimony (Revelation 12:11).*

Consider what I have written in this book as part of my testimony — my admission that I am a sinner, my repentance of my former ways, my choice to follow Jesus, and the result: my change. I am not the same person, and everyone who knew me before my conversion understands this. It's that obvious. Before I understood this message, my faith was in the world, in my circumstances, and in my strength. Now, it is in Jesus Christ, my Lord and Savior. Tell people how God has changed your life — it is difficult to challenge visible change. On the other hand, someone whose life does not reflect such a change might be hard to believe. Using the metaphor of a diet, until we have lost some weight, we will likely be considered a talking head. Our testimony is proof of our faith.

Do you have a testimony?

Share it.

Spiritual armor

We also need to put on the armor of God every day. The apostle Paul talks about this armor, using the armor of a Roman soldier as a figurative example of spiritual armor:

> *Finally, be strong in the Lord and in his mighty power. Put on the full armor of God, so that you can take your stand against the devil's schemes. For our struggle is not against flesh and blood, but against the rulers, against the authorities, against the powers of this dark world and against the spiritual forces of evil in the heavenly realms. Therefore put on the full armor of God, so that when the day of evil comes, you may be able to stand your ground, and after you have done everything, to stand. Stand firm*

then, with the belt of truth buckled around your waist, with the breastplate of righteousness in place, and with your feet fitted with the readiness that comes from the gospel of peace. In addition to all this, take up the shield of faith, with which you can extinguish all the flaming arrows of the evil one. Take the helmet of salvation and the sword of the Spirit, which is the word of God (Ephesians 6:10–17).

The belt of truth refers to the Biblical truth spoken by Jesus. We must wear His truth, which is the foundation for battle. The breastplate of righteousness appears to be associated with our righteousness found through Christ, and not in our own efforts. We must keep our eyes on Jesus and live according to His righteousness. We must live holy lives. The feet fitted with readiness appears to be speaking of our ability to stand firm in the peace of God, despite our circumstances and despite the frontal attack that comes when we proclaim the gospel. The shield of faith maintains our faith in Jesus, knowing the darts of doubt will constantly be hurled against us. The helmet of salvation references the protection of our minds. We have to ignore thoughts that creep into our minds that try to undermine our faith or tempt us to follow another god:

We take captive every thought to make it obedient to Christ (2 Corinthians 10:5).

All of our behavior starts in our minds, so the helmet of salvation protects our minds and keeps us focused on Heaven and our strength: Jesus. Finally, the sword of the Spirit is the Word of God, our only offensive weapon against the enemy.[10] We recall when tempted by Satan that Jesus used the Word of God to defend Himself, as we are meant to emulate (Matthew 4:1–10). So, while God still allows Satan to come against us, all that should do is turn us to the Bible. We then fall to our knees, and draw closer to God, thus distancing ourselves from Satan:

Submit yourselves, then, to God. Resist the devil, and he will flee from you. Come near to God and he will come near to you (James 4:7–8).

As Christians, new or old, we are committed to the God of the Holy Bible. We fight against Satan and for God, no matter the cost, despite the perceived odds.

Now that you know what your armor is ... Wear it!

That is what we should all do to live a victorious life.

Will you?

Will I?

Will we?

Eternity is right around the corner.

What we do in this life echoes there.

Footnotes

1   2 Corinthians 3:16.

2   2 Corinthians 5:17.

3   When do you think an accident is an accident? When it happens or after everyone has understood its impact? Of course, we know an accident is an accident the nanosecond it happens. A child is a child the nanosecond it is conceived.

4   Connecting, Larry Crabb, (Nashville, Word Publishing, 1997) pg. 74.

5   Colossians 4:2.

6   http://www.catholic.org/featured/headline.php?ID=417.

7   Fresh Encounter, Henry& Richard Blackaby (LifeWay Press, Nashville, TN, 2009), pg.122.

8   Don't stop meeting together with other believers, which some people have gotten into the habit of doing. Instead, encourage each other, especially as you see the day drawing near (Hebrews 10:25). Keep watch over yourselves and all the flock of which the Holy Spirit has made you overseers. Be shepherds of the church of God, which he bought with his own blood (Acts 20:28).

9   Nouwen, pg. 53.

10   Real Armor of God, http://www.realarmorofgod.com/armor-of-god.html.

— CHAPTER 28 —

WE MUST BE REINVENTED

"I'm on dialysis, Tom, three times a week," Johnny B. said. He's a former resident and employee of Hoskins Park Ministries. "I need a new kidney. But I'm good with it Tom, whether I get a kidney or not, I'm good with it. If I get a kidney, I get to stick around a little longer. If not, I get to go home (heaven). Either way, it's OK. I am still thankful to be here."

He went on, "But, I did have to change my diet. I used to be able to eat whatever I wanted. Not anymore. I have to be concerned about my iron level. I have to be concerned about potassium. I have to be concerned about my phosphorus levels. I am so sick of nurses, doctors, needles, dialysis machines, and people telling me I can or can't have this or that. If I wasn't mindful of who is in control of this (God), I'd go crazy, Tom. I'm serious, Tom."

I acknowledged with an occasional "Uhuh," thinking he just needed to talk.

"I found something at Hoskins Park that was better than anything I had ever found, a relationship with Jesus Christ," Johnny B. continued. "People talk about Him, but He is much more than that — He is real. I was able to get away from all my past mess. My relationship with Jesus has gotten me through drug usage, hypertension, alcohol abuse, all that added up to my kidney failure. There is a whole lot more I would like to do in life, and some days, it hurts thinking about it to be honest. But, every day I wake up is a blessing and I know it. I just wanted to call and say thank you, Tom. If it weren't for you and Johnny, I don't think I would be alive today, Tom." Johnny B. is a changed man.

> *"I tell you the truth, unless you are born again, you cannot see the Kingdom of God" (John 3:3, NLT).*

Born again

The concept of being born again confounds many people. Even in Biblical times, Nicodemus didn't fully comprehend what Jesus meant when he was told he must be born again:

> *In reply Jesus declared, "I tell you the truth, no one can see the kingdom of God unless he is born again." "How can a man be born when he is old?" Nicodemus asked. "Surely he cannot enter a second time into his mother's womb to be born!" Jesus answered, "I tell you the truth, no one can enter the kingdom of God unless he is born of water and the Spirit. Flesh gives birth to flesh, but the Spirit gives birth to spirit. You should not be surprised at my saying, 'You must be born again.' The wind blows wherever it pleases. You hear its sound, but you cannot tell where it comes from or where it is going. So it is with everyone born of the Spirit." "How can this be?" Nicodemus asked (John 3:3–9).*

It can be a difficult concept to understand or even take seriously, so I would like to try to explain it through the concept of being reinvented. Of course, this is not identical to being born again, because when we accept Jesus into our hearts, we mysteriously get a new spirit, His Spirit. This Spirit gives us the ability to change into our new identity or our new self. Knowing that, perhaps you will understand the idea of what happens upon conversion, when you accept Jesus Christ as your Lord and Savior. Your life will change, *because* you accepted Jesus. It is not because you have to change *in order* to accept Jesus. Did you catch that? Your life will change because of your decision. You cannot get your life right before making such a decision. It doesn't work that way. God's Spirit allows us to change. He reinvents us.

He gives us new breath.

He gives us a new chance.

Our lives should no longer be like *Groundhog Day*.

Groundhog Day

In the movie *Groundhog Day,*[1] the main character, Phil (Bill Murray), wakes up on successive mornings to discover it is Groundhog Day every day. Every 24-hour period, for Phil, is relived. At first, after figuring out what was going on and coming to terms with it, he selfishly indulges in anything he wanted to: going on eating binges, robbing banks, breaking the law in various other forms, driving his car off a cliff, having sex with women he thought were attractive, etc. — but without any satisfaction or consequences. Every day, he wakes up as if the day before never happened. Although he was a selfish, arrogant, condescending weatherman before all this happened, this perpetual cycle just made him worse. The Bible says:

> *So, as the Holy Spirit says: "Today, if you hear his voice, do not harden your hearts" (Hebrews 3:7).*
>
> *So I also will choose harsh treatment for them and will bring on them what they dread. For when I called, no one answered, when I spoke, no one listened" (Isaiah 66:4).*

God is asking us *not to harden our hearts,* and refuse to hear and obey Him as if we were Phil reliving Groundhog Day. Rather, He wants us to change course and follow Him. As the movie goes, that is similar to what happened to Phil: He was reinvented by seeing how ridiculous his life was before Groundhog Day, and he decided to become a better man, using every day to improve himself, rather than indulge in decadent behavior. He learned poetry, learned how to play the piano, began to treat people nicely, and even started helping a homeless man. He changed his focus from doing things for his own personal and selfish gain to using his life to enhance the lives of others. Guess what else changed? The day.

Many of us are still living Groundhog Day, doing the same thing over and over, but without ever going anywhere as we try to make ourselves happy. It doesn't work. God wants to reinvent us by His Spirit (not through our efforts or reasoning). That is what the concept of born again appears to mean, Biblically. But, it comes at the cost of our old life. As Henry Blackaby says in the study *Experiencing God*, "You cannot stay where you are and follow God."[2] In fact, your old self must die (John 12:24). While many of us might think this is hard teaching, which it is, alcoholics and drug addicts know they must die to their desires every day. It is the battle we all fight on a daily basis. After I had my own health scare, I stopped drinking sodas. I haven't had one in years. Yet, I want one every day! If we truly want to live the dreams deep in our hearts, we must deny ourselves daily, as the Scriptures indicate, and follow Jesus. That is the only way to live the plan God has for your life, which is better than any plan we might choose on our own. The only way we can do this is by choosing our new identity, the one born of God's Spirit. And when we do, it will be obvious that we are "different":

> At that time the Spirit of the Lord will come powerfully upon you... You will be changed into a different person (1 Samuel 10:6 – NLT).

But still that leaves an unanswered question for Christians: How will we be different?

Where's the beef?

"Tom," Bobby said, "I am through with drugs. I've done gotten as low as I can. Lost everything, again. I'm sicka livin' like this." Bobby is a very talented electrician and former Hoskins Park Ministries resident who had just lost his truck and tools to drugs. "Bobby," I responded, "You have been telling me this for many years."

"No, Tom, this is different." Bobby interrupted. "I ain't never been in the shape I'm in now. I've lost everything this time."

"OK, Bobby. But this time, let your life speak louder than your words."

Change requires resistance to the things that harm us. It is far easier to talk about change than to actually do so. When we accept Jesus as Lord and Savior, we will be different.

I have mentioned many stories about Hoskins Park Ministries, but never any statistics. Most of the men enter our ministry involved in a life threatening addiction, typically crack cocaine, the drug of choice on the street. As with most organizations serving those struggling with addictions, we give random drug tests. When we do, the majority of our men test negative for drugs. They surrender them to God. That was the change that happened in me — I finally got out of God's way and let Him control the ministry rather than me. Once I did that, everything changed for the good. I discovered that I can't change people, but God can, and He wants to use me as His hands.

> *Therefore, if anyone is in Christ, he is a new creation; the old has gone, the new has come! (2 Corinthians 5:17)*

New creations

As Christians, therefore, we are new creations; the old is gone and the new has come. That is the good, but challenging, news. That reminds me of an old Wendy's ad (recently brought back to life) mocking other competitor's hamburgers, implying little beef inside of their burgers. Wendy's came up with a television ad that featured an elderly woman looking at a competitor's hamburger, asking the question that helped make Wendy's famous: "Where's the beef?" It's another way of asking for proof. When we talk about being born again or reinvented, we should see some proof of that change other than what comes out of our mouths, particularly since we have God's Holy Spirit living inside of us. And I mean results that are Biblical, not based upon our competitive and performance-oriented culture that focuses more on numbers than crucial personal changes.

The Bible calls it fruit.

Your fruit

Fruit is a Biblical term that is about the measurement of a Christian, in a personal transformation type of manner rather than a works oriented one. The Bible says our fruits are fruits of His Spirit. They are love, peace, patience, kindness, goodness, faithfulness, gentleness, and self-control (Galatians 5:22). While we are drawn to numbers or performance in a worldly sense, the Bible is clearly not about those physical things. The Bible says we will all get those things that we need for that kind of success, but we must put God first:

> *But seek first his kingdom and his righteousness, and all these things will be given to you as well (Matthew 6:33).*

Let's start with the fruit of the Spirit, love.

The fruits of the Spirit — love

By now you likely understand the Biblical definition of love is a bit different than our culture's definition. In that regard, we are not talking about the feelings kind of love, which has more to do with romance; rather we speak of the deeper definition of love that puts others ahead of ourselves. That is the kind of love the Bible is talking about when it says people will know us because of our love for one another:

"By this everyone will know that you are my disciples, if you love one another" (John 13:35).

We can give away all of our money, be prophetic, and have all kinds of gifts, but if we do not love one another, the Bible says we are like a clanging cymbal (1 Corinthians 13:1–3). Love is at the root and heart of Christianity, the kind of love that dies to itself for the sake of someone else. The kind Jesus showed us on the cross when He took our sins onto Himself, allowing Himself to be tortured and killed for us. That is the right kind of love. Not the kind where we get what we want at someone else's expense. It is worth mentioning that if we are typically getting our way on a daily basis, people doing things the way we want, choosing our own schedule, etc., we are likely being loved more than we are loving, even if we are in charge.

Joy

Joy is another fruit of the Spirit. Years ago, I remember hearing Joni Erickson Tada speak about her own struggles to have joy in the midst of her decades of paralysis. Every day, she said she had to let Jesus give her His joy and peace, since she could not find it in the physical aspects of the world. Every day. That gave me hope and still does. We need to accept the joy from God by remaining attached to Him, our vine, rather than muster it up ourselves. Henri Nouwen says it this way:

Joy does not simply happen to us. We have to choose joy and keep choosing it every day.[3]

While struggling is normal, in the midst of our struggle, we must choose to believe in God, and must continue to do so on a moment-to-moment basis. Chuck Colson, former Special Counsel for President Nixon, then a converted Christian leader, once wrote:

We are called to embrace suffering and the cross as followers of Christ. We are to expect it. It will bring dark nights of the soul. In fact, it should give us cause for concern if we claim to follow Christ and never experience any suffering.[4]

In the midst of our struggle, we must ultimately choose to have faith in God and persevere — just like Joni Erickson Tada and so many others who understood that while life is hard, we can still get a second wind and experience the joy of God.

Our moments

I must add, however, that does not at all mean that we will go around joking and laughing with a big smile on our face as many suggest. Jesus was clearly frustrated with His disciples at times and angry with His people when they were unfaithful. Look at what Jesus said to His disciples when they could not heal a boy suffering from seizures:

"O unbelieving and perverse generation," Jesus replied, "how long shall I stay with you? How long shall I put up with you? Bring the boy here to me" (Matthew 17:17).

Jesus then healed the boy Himself. I don't know about you, but that sounds like a frustrated Jesus! How about this verse:

So he made a whip out of cords, and drove all from the temple area, both sheep and cattle; he scattered the coins of the money changers and overturned their tables (John 2:15).

So, while we should often experience joy, having our "moments" appears normal too, for followers of Jesus. We just need to remember that even in our anger, we must not sin (Ephesians 4:26).

Gentleness, faithfulness, and peace

In our cold, harsh, distrustful, and impatient world, a disposition of gentleness tends to have been replaced by arrogance and rudeness. But it maintains its status as a fruit of the Spirit of God. The Bible says:

Rejoice in the Lord always. I will say it again: Rejoice! Let your gentleness be evident to all (Philippians 4:4–5)

Christians ought to exude a kind and amiable disposition in the midst of the grind of daily life. That doesn't mean there won't be times when we don't feel like being so gentle. I get accused of being pushy at times, sometimes arrogant even, as I challenge folks who often say they want to help the poor or change their ways and then aren't able to help us where we most need it. Maybe I am. But, I never mean to be disrespectful. Many might disagree with me, but sometimes we need people around us who will challenge us out of our comfort zone to actually *do* something different, rather than talk about it. As they say, even an eagle needs to be pushed. Having said that, having the Spirit of God living inside of us will overcome our own impatience as we battle the performance-driven world that is constantly pushing us to conform to its image. The Bible says:

> *The Lord is near. Do not be anxious about anything, but in every situation, by prayer and petition, with thanksgiving, present your requests to God. And the peace of God, which transcends all understanding, will guard your hearts and your minds in Christ Jesus (Philippians 4:5–7).*

We can remain gentle and maintain our sense of peace, despite our circumstances, by our trust and faithfulness to God. We just need to believe.

Self-control

Self-control is the part of a controlling personality that is actually a good thing. Furthermore, self-control is a lot harder than controlling others, because it means we have to ignore our feelings. So, we stop eating when we should, we stop spending when we should, we stop working when we should, we stop resting when we should, we stop talking when we should. Then on the other hand, we keep (or start) working when we don't feel like it, we keep exercising when we would rather rest, and we do what God asks us to do. A synonym for self-control then, is discipline. I will not go over the issue of feelings again, since I mentioned it as a tactic of Satan to keep us from following God, but do you see why self-control is so much harder than controlling others? It means we have to do the hard work ourselves, rather than pushing others to do that which we won't. We must all keep our eyes focused on God by continuing to read the Word of God, continuing to pray, continuing to study, listening to those who preach the Word, and staying the course despite daily distractions. We must stay in control of ourselves through surrender to God's Holy Spirit living inside of us.

Live holy lives

As for our past sin, we stop it because the Bible tells us it is wrong and because the Holy Spirit convicts us of it. We are meant to live holy lives (Colossians 3:5, 8–10). And our main objective is to please a holy God:

> So we make it our goal to please him, whether we are at home in the body or away from it (2 Corinthians 5:9).

The only way to please God is to do what He says — Biblically.

Acts 2:42–47

I want to mention some other fruit that was prevalent in the early church. It is often considered the Biblical mandate for the church, and it teaches how Christians should act in community with one another:

> They devoted themselves to the apostles' teaching and to fellowship, to the breaking of bread and to prayer. Everyone was filled with awe at the many wonders and signs performed by the apostles. All the believers were together and had everything in common. They sold property and possessions to give to anyone who had need. Every day they continued to meet together in the temple courts. They broke bread in their homes and ate together with glad and sincere hearts, praising God and enjoying the favor of all the people. And the Lord added to their number daily those who were being saved (Acts 2:42–47).

These early followers taught what Jesus taught, ate together, prayed together, watched miracles performed amongst themselves, saw the lost saved, and gave God all the credit. They also shared their possessions. When Christians truly model the early church, this should be true of our flock.

Humility

Finally, one of the most important aspects of a Christian is humility. We should be humble in our approach to others as Jesus was for us (Philippians 2:3–8).

However, our humility should not be at the expense of our boldness in proclaiming Jesus to the world. Many Christians forget that Jesus was considered arrogant to the Pharisees of His day, who were too closed-minded to actually listen to Him (Matthew 23:27–28). So, now we can all get on the scale:

> *Examine yourselves to see if your faith is genuine (2 Corinthians 13:5, NLT).*

Is there enough evidence to convict you of being a follower of Jesus Christ?

Is there enough reason for you to desire a second wind?

Footnotes

1   Murray, Bill, perf. Groundhog Day. Dir. Harold Ramis, Columbia Pictures, 1993.

2   Blackaby, Experiencing God, page 235.

3   Nouwen, Henri, The Heart of Henri Nouwen (Crossroad Publishing Co., New York, NY, 2003), pg. 45.

4   Mother Teresa, Chuck Colson, and Faith, September 1, 2007. http://www.mrdawntreader.com/the_dawn_treader/2007/09/mother-teresa-c.html.

— CONCLUSION —

LIFE IS BUT A DREAM

" I 'm scared, Tom," Paul, my long-time friend and resident of Hoskins Park, said. "I don't think I am going to be around much longer." Paul struggled with drugs for years and now is diabetic.

"Why?" I asked.

"I just have this feeling I am going to be dead soon. And that scares me," He continued, as he inhaled another cigarette.

"Have you truly accepted Jesus Christ as your Lord and Savior?" I asked.

"Yes, I have," He answered confidently. The tears he had shed at church recently appeared to confirm his conversion, as well as the fact we knew he had finally given up drugs.

"Well then we can pray — but like me, you just have to trust Him with your life and with your death," I said. "And make sure you are eating well, Paul. Your body needs all the nutrients it can get and those cigarettes are not helping your cause."

"I know. But I've cut back a lot since I had my heart attack," Paul retorted, as he kept smoking. Paul died peacefully about two weeks later in his bed at Hoskins Park Ministries. He was forty-eight, and he was a new man — in Christ. He lives on today, in heaven.

"Tom?" Paige asked on my cell phone.

"Yeah," I replied.

"We just found out Junot died in Afghanistan," she said, voice cracking. "The vehicle he was in was hit by a roadside car bomb." I was silent, too saddened and shocked to reply. "He just came back three weeks ago to say good-bye to us. All that work to become a US citizen so he could join the Army, and now he is dead. The local news station is looking for Bill. They want to interview him since he was instrumental in helping Junot get US citizenship," she said. Junot was at Hoskins Park Ministries for about a year. He came from Haiti. A new creation, he too is now with his Lord and Savior.

> *Everyone is but a breath, even those who seem secure (Psalm 39:5).*

Physical verses spiritual being

Most of us consider ourselves to be physical bodies that have a spirit of some sort living inside of us. But, we are really the reverse. Our souls have been created to live forever, while our physical bodies have not. The Bible says, "God is spirit" (John 4:24), and the flesh (human effort) counts for nothing (John 6:63). C.S. Lewis puts it this way:

> *"You don't have a soul, you are a soul. You have a body."*[1]

I know, I have said it before. It is a huge leap of faith to believe this, at least if you are a new believer or someone considering the truth of the Bible, but it is true nonetheless.

You and I will never die.

But, where we end up is a matter of our choice regarding Jesus Christ. That is why we need to stop feeding our flesh, and start feeding God's Spirit, because it is His Spirit that lives forever and allows us to get to heaven.

Earthly body

The Bible actually describes our earthly body as a "tent" with all its aches and pains, while implying that we are all longing to have our eternal bodies, since they will be so much better than our earthly ones:

> *For we know that if the earthly tent we live in is destroyed, we have a building from God, an eternal house in heaven, not built by human hands. Meanwhile we groan, longing*

to be clothed instead with our heavenly dwelling, because when we are clothed, we will not be found naked (2 Corinthians 5:1–3).

Our destiny is heaven, and it is far greater than life on earth, despite those who doubt. That is why the apostle Paul said:

For to me, to live is Christ and to die is gain (Philippians 1:21).

This is not our home.

A day

We should also remember how short we live in our physical bodies. According to statistical averages, about 2.4 million of us are going to die in the United States of America this year, 150,000 world-wide today.[2] You and I are not going to be living very long, despite whether we live another year or another 100 years. Life is short, and when we all think about it, we know it's true. Those of us who have lived a few years know all too well that our bodies aren't what they used to be and are fading away, quickly, even for those who treat their bodies well. Furthermore, the time we are physically dead lasts a lot longer than life on earth. This got me to consider a "day." I am speculating here, but perhaps a day is more than just a 24-hour period of time because of the rotation of the earth and our need for sleep. Perhaps, God designed it this way to give each of us as many chances to change course and accept Jesus, so that we will end up in heaven with Him. Each day has a start and finish, giving us new chances each day to see things His way. So, when we pass from this side of eternity to the next, if we have heard and rejected the Holy Bible and the Jesus it speaks of and about, and if it *is* true, we will be without excuse — all of us. We won't have a bunch of questions for God, as many people suggest they will have when they die and meet Him; rather, He will likely have a lot of questions for us:

Yes, each of us will give a personal account to God (Romans 14:12).

But our choice will clearly and firmly have been made about Him before we get to that day. Furthermore, since life does go by so fast, this life will be like a dream, but in this dream when we wake up, we will wake up living in eternity. The Bible says:

*Why, you do not even know what will happen tomorrow.
What is your life? You are a mist that appears for a little
while and then vanishes (James 4:14).*

This life will soon be gone for you and me, just like the estimated 100 billion who have gone before us.

Let's remember that: *Life is short. It will soon be over.*

Then what?

Heaven

For those who choose Jesus, God's method for salvation, Heaven is our prize and our destiny. That is why the apostle Paul wrote:

*I press on toward the goal to win the prize for which God
has called me heavenward in Christ Jesus (Philippians
3:14).*

*But we are citizens of heaven, where the Lord Jesus Christ
lives (Philippians 3:20, NLT).*

Heaven is the place where we find the essence of God. When we accept the Bible's message of salvation, we choose to be with Him forever there. Believers look forward to spending eternity with the essence of love, God. Moreover, Heaven is far better than we can ever imagine. That is why the Bible says:

*No eye has seen, no ear has heard, no mind has conceived
what God has prepared for those who love him (1
Corinthians 2:9, Isaiah 64:4).* [3]

*"He will wipe every tear from their eyes. There will be no
more death' or mourning or crying or pain, for the old order
of things has passed away." He who was seated on the
throne said, "I am making everything new!" (Revelation
21:4–5).*

Heaven is the true paradise that we all long for at the deepest place in our hearts. While we mourn the loss of our loved ones, who have gone before us, if they accepted the life, death, and resurrection of Jesus in their minds and hearts, then they are in Heaven and would never want to come back to earth again. The earth, as we know it, is not our intended home — Heaven is. But that is not what Satan wants us to believe. Randy Alcorn, in his book *Heaven,* makes this statement about Christians' eternal dwelling and Satan:

> *Satan need not convince us that Heaven doesn't exist. He need only convince us that Heaven is a place of boring, unearthly existence. If we believe that lie, we'll be robbed of our joy and anticipation, we'll set our minds on this life and not the next, and we won't be motivated to share our faith.*[4]

Until we understand this, individually, we will:

live for earth,

hope for heaven,

while potentially finding ourselves in hell.

> *Enter through the narrow gate. For wide is the gate and broad is the road that leads to destruction, and many enter through it. But small is the gate and narrow the road that leads to life, and only a few find it (Matthew 7:13–14).*

Get on the right road. The one that leads you home. The one that requires a second wind.

Hell

Despite how unfair someone might think it is (at least on this side of eternity), when people deny Jesus, they inadvertently choose to be in a place where God is absent, a place known as hell. It is our default eternal location, to the surprise of many. Hell (Hades) is a place devoid of love, which is the "blackest darkness."[5] The Bible typically refers to it as a lake of fire, where there will be gnashing of teeth:

> *If anyone's name was not found written in the book of life, he was thrown into the lake of fire (Revelation 20:15).*

Randy Alcorn says, "Hell will be agonizingly dull, small, and insignificant, without company, purpose, or accomplishment."[6] He continues:

> *The best of life on Earth is a glimpse of Heaven; the worst of life is a glimpse of Hell. For Christians, this present life is the closest they will come to Hell. For unbelievers, it is the*

closest they will come to Heaven.[7]

While none of us might like the consequences for disobeying God, the consequences come. They always do. Why would we be so surprised to find out our decision regarding Jesus also has its repercussions? Without Jesus, we are condemned. Furthermore, while I know how sensitive many are to hearing Jesus is the only way to God, the Bible says it is true and it explains why. And even if you still doubt, what if it is true? Wouldn't you want to hear the truth *if it were true*? Or …

> *Have I now become your enemy by telling you the truth? (Galatians 4:16)*

We should all long to know the truth. You may not like or believe this message, but what if you died and found out you were wrong and this message was accurate? You cannot come back to tell your family.

Make an informed decision for your sake and for the sake of those you love by reading the Bible and praying for God to reveal its truth to you — personally.

He will.

Don't be afraid of the truth either. It won't change it — but it will save you and your loved ones.

Eternal rewards

There is another area that the Bible talks about but that remains a mystery. It's the issue of eternal rewards for obeying Jesus in everyday life. Mother Teresa may have had a deprived life on earth, but according to the interpretation of some verses of Scripture, she may be fairly high up on God's hierarchical chain of command now as her deeds followed her to Heaven:

> *"Yes," says the Spirit, "they will rest from their labor for their deeds will follow them" (Revelation 14:13).*

Anyone who has left houses or brothers or sisters or father or mother or fields for the sake of the gospel will receive a hundred times as much and will inherit eternal life (Mark 10:29–31). Those who overcome and remain faithful to the end will have authority over the nations (Revelation 2:26). We should take this message seriously and not concentrate on what we accumulate in this lifetime. This should also provide understanding to those who wonder about folks who accept Jesus later in life. God is "just" in His treatment of each of us. The amount of time we were faithful might just matter in our heavenly duties.

Eternal perspective

If we don't believe in this spiritual war, but simply look at circumstances as "life," we aren't going to believe this message. We are forfeiting the best life we can live — the one God purposed for our lives before we were born — the one that lasts forever. There's no hope for the world, if we walk away from Jesus as both our Lord and Savior. A domino effect takes place as we get farther away from God, the source of our lives. People will become even more violent, angry, short-tempered, hardened, self-serving, everything ultimately spiraling out of control:

> But mark this: There will be terrible times in the last days. People will be lovers of themselves, lovers of money, boastful, proud, abusive, disobedient to their parents, ungrateful, unholy, without love, unforgiving, slanderous, without self-control, brutal, not lovers of the good, treacherous, rash, conceited, lovers of pleasure rather than lovers of God — having a form of godliness but denying its power (2 Timothy 3:1–5).

There has to be an ultimate authority holding us all equally accountable, not a random one we can choose to follow at will, and it has to be above human reasoning and standards — it has to come from God.

What will it take?

What will it take before you read the Bible and believe in Jesus with all your heart, soul, and strength?

The loss of your income? Your title? Your reputation?

The loss of a loved one?

The loss of your health?

How that must break God's heart. Can you imagine your own son or daughter not recognizing who you are or that you even exist? You give and give and give and give, but they continue to give the credit to luck, good fortune, their own efforts, the daily horoscope, or the psychic hotline. And the only thing that wakes them up is hardship – hitting bottom. Wouldn't that break your heart? Well, that may be many of us; those who often live as know-it-alls until we are put in a position where clearly, we don't.

Jesus said:

> *"When the Son of Man comes, will he find faith on the earth?" (Luke 18:8)*

Will He?

I know – it's hard to trust anyone these days, but that is why we must trust in the Bible and the God of the Bible. There has to be an authority greater than us and that authority cannot be based upon our opinions. So, please don't go through life fighting the Bible only to discover it is true and your feelings were misleading. I beg you: Read and study the Bible yourself before you find out its truth too late:

> *Seek the LORD while he may be found; call on him while he is near (Isaiah 55:6).*

> *Come near to God and he will come near to you (James 4:8).*

Jesus was and is God, our Lord and our Savior. Trust in the Bible's words spoken to us throughout the ages.

There is no tomorrow

God made you.

God loves you.

God has a plan for your life.

That is the truth of the Holy Bible. One day you are going to die just like everyone else. And you will face the truth — the absolute truth of this message.

It's still your choice whether to believe it or not. Don't waste any more time doing things the world's way — haven't you had enough? Surrender to your Lord and Savior, Jesus Christ. I promise you, He won't let you down:

> *Taste and see that the LORD is good. Oh, the joys of those who take refuge in him! (Psalm 34:8, NLT).*

In fact, He will lift you up and give you new life, fresh air, a second wind.

Will you?

Will you taste?

Will you see?

Will you take a breath?

Now is the time for a second wind.

Footnotes

1   Mere Christianity, CS Lewis (HarperSanFrancisco, Harper Collins edition, 2001).

2   Centers for Disease Control and Prevention (CDC), Deaths and Mortality, FastStats.

3   Also, "The kingdom of heaven is like treasure hidden in a field. When a man found it, he hid it again, and then in his joy went and sold all he had and bought that field" (Matthew 13:44). 45"Again, the kingdom of heaven is like a merchant looking for fine pearls. 46When he found one of great value, he went away and sold everything he had and bought it" (Matthew 13:45-46).

4   Alcorn, pg. 11.

5   2 Peter 2:17.

6   Alcorn., pg. 27.

7   Ibid., pg. 28.

HELP ME HELP THE POOR! WILL YOU?

If you buy another copy of second wind for just $10 - you will!

THEURBANOUTREACH.ORG

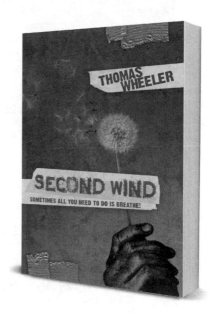

You've heard it said:

Give a man a fish and you feed him for a day; teach a man to fish and you feed him for a lifetime.

Many of us want to help others, but we want to do the most good, not just give the most, hoping it does some good.

Second Wind teaches people how to fish – particularly when our circumstances are dire, like the homeless.

That is why I want to get a copy of Second Wind into the hands of all the homeless in the United States. To help them get off the street!

But I need your help.

However you got your copy of Second Wind, will you buy one more from my website and give it away to at least one homeless person who crosses your path?

Here's how!

Go to my website and order extra copies. (Why not order a whole case so you have plenty to give away.) Keep your heart and eyes open for who the Lord may direct you to give a copy of the book. After you have their attention, ask if they like to read. If they say yes, give them the book. Tell them it was written to help them understand the spiritual battle they are in. Put a dollar in it too. They don't all waste money like so many think. Then remind them God made them in His image, God loves them, and God has a plan for their lives. But they have a choice – just like we do – to choose God or to walk away from Him. Remind them it's that simple. If they don't want the book, for whatever reason, tell them not to give up and then find someone else who might like it.

That's it.

If you'd prefer me to donate books on your behalf, just donate to the cause – any amount will help.

Either way, go to:

THEURBANOUTREACH.ORG

Together, we can make a lot of difference by providing fishing poles to the poor and needy.

God bless you and thank you your support! -Tom

Contact the author: tom@thomasawheeler.com

READ IT FORWARD

If you liked this book, feel it worthy of someone else's attention, and don't want to keep it for yourself, could you read it forward! Just sign it yourself and then pass it on. Keep it if you would like, no matter how many have read it before you, but otherwise, sign and pass it on to someone else! Thank you for reading *Second Wind*. May God continue to use it as He desires!

1. _____

2. _____

3. _____

4. _____

5. _____